PLEASURES AND SPECULATIONS

BY THE SAME AUTHOR

★

Animal Stories
Behold, This Dreamer!
This Year: Next Year
The Wind Blows Over
Early One Morning
The Lord Fish
Desert Islands
Seven Short Stories
Stories from the Bible
The Three Royal Monkeys
Memoirs of a Midget
On the Edge
The Riddle and other Stories
Lewis Carroll

PLEASURES AND SPECULATIONS

by

WALTER DE LA MARE

FABER AND FABER LIMITED
24 Russell Square
London

First published in June Mcmxl
by Faber and Faber Limited
24 Russell Square London W.C. 1
Printed in Great Britain by
R. MacLehose and Company Limited
The University Press Glasgow

To

BRUCE RICHMOND

Introduction

The contents of this volume come from many sources. 'Flowers and Poetry' is from a delightful anthology entitled, *Here's Flowers*, made by Miss Joan Rutter and published some years ago by the Golden Cockerel Press. 'Poetry in Prose', the Wharton Poetry Lecture of 1935, was delivered before the British Academy in that year. 'The *Dream*' is from the Scholar's Library Edition of *A Midsummer Night's Dream* of 1935. 'Rupert Brooke and the Intellectual Imagination', a lecture read before the School at Rugby on 28 March 1909, was published as a booklet in the same year. It is now out of print. 'Some Women Novelists', a lecture read before the Royal Society of Literature, was included in a collection of Essays entitled *The Eighteen Seventies*. 'Hans Christian Andersen', 'The Thousand and One', 'Tennyson', 'A Book of Words', 'The Great Adventurers', 'Naturalists' and 'Maps: Actual and Imaginary', were originally contributed to *The Times Literary Supplement*.

But everything here has been recently revised and to some degree—moderate or excessive—expanded, and in a few cases titles have been slightly changed. A version of the introductory lines entitled 'Books' appeared many years ago in *The Bookman*, an old friend now incorporated with *Art and Letters*. It is merely an attempt to express—and with an atrocious inadequacy—what books have meant to me since I learned to read: before that indeed, since then I was read to —the way out, the way in, the refuge, the enrichment and enchantment; the country shoes, the Seven League Boots, the Cap, the wings, the packed knapsack.

How was it possible, I ask myself now, to offer even the briefest tribute to these supreme blessings, and yet say nothing of the *company* one meets in books—mind, spirit, and even body. I remember Thomas Hardy, master of this physical 'three-dimensional' achievement, referring to a young woman in a novel, and not a pleasant young woman either, with the comment, 'She is so real you could touch her with your hand.' In all books, of course, we are in close communion with their writers. And neither love nor even liking, the best things we have to give, is indispensable to our enjoyment. In good fiction we are also made inmates and intimates, as it were, of human phantasms who have an effect on the imagination and the heart not far removed, not very different from that of the fellow creatures whom we encounter in our actual experience. They live within us. We can distinguish between the real and the imagined, but our insight and mastery of the one may frequently transcend our profoundest knowledge of the other. Unless indeed intuition, interpenetration come richly to our service in our association with our fellow creatures in the flesh, they remain little better than animated waxworks.

Of criticism, worthy of the name, there can, alas, be little, if any, in the pages that follow. A large number of them are the outcome of the activities of a reviewer, and there is only one secure retreat for the reviewer, modesty. The distinctions between this afflicted and maligned soul and the literary *critic* have been recently explored by Mrs. Virginia Woolf, Mr. Leonard Woolf and Mr. Frank Swinnerton. In the former office I must have been responsible for well over half a million words; Christian also had a prodigious bundle on his back. This reminds me of a remark made to me once by a furniture remover. 'Lor, sir, there must be three ton of books in this house.' The reader may blanch at any such confession, but it gives me the welcome opportunity of expressing my gratitude to the Editors for whom I have had the privilege and happiness of working. I am thinking chiefly of the Editors in the old days of *The Times Literary Supplement* and of *The Saturday Westminster Gazette*—alas, no longer in flower. Thc fact that to the former in my greenhorn days I once returned a belated proof revised in soft pencil, and that the latter had at last to convey to me an ultimatum from the printer regarding my monstrous treatment of his flawless copy (although, in retaliation perhaps, he once, in deciphering my copy, amended Herrick's line, 'And virgins with their wicker arks Bear all the flowers away' into 'And virgins with their wicked arts . . .') is only one minute indication of their patience and magnanimity. For years—not always without symptoms of dyspepsia but never unmindful of this good fortune—I continued to feed out of those gentle hands.

William Cory declared that literature, as compared with the feast of life, is only a side dish. Taken with a grain of salt, the statement may be irrefutable. Whether or not, for a long lifetime I have haunted thc sideboard. It displays in unflagging abundance bread, milk, meat and manna, not to mention the potable. And one has merely to help one's self. Anatole France, on the other hand, described the literary critic's activities as the adventures of a soul among masterpieces. The critic himself may accept this figure of speech with severe reservations; certainly his pondered response is at times less psychic than intellectual. Whether the mere reviewer possesses a soul may be left to those who unhappily have grave doubts concerning even that of Woman.

No reviewer, no common reader, no lover of books, however, is likely to spend his days solely in the consumption of masterpieces. They are in the nature of touchstones, and talismans, and the miraculous; and a diet restricted to them may be the supreme ideal. Yet there is much to be said for what falls short of this elevated standard, and even far short. The 'hundred best books'—when there may be only ninety and nine! Perfection may prove a sort of stubborn mental pemmican for otherwise admirable digestions; and an extreme fastidiousness an ivory tower, with needlessly limited accommodation. With Mr. Justice Asquith, I would even put in a plea for a not intolerable deal of bad books—and especially, when one is young, and when Nature is generous with her antiseptics. Augustine Birrell, he tells us, confessed that he loathed every word that Plato put on paper. 'Wasn't Mr. Chesterton perhaps right when he said, "In literature, next to authentic excellence, give me a rich badness." ' Our own best is the best for us.

However that may be, these pages are concerned chiefly with the 'pleasures' to be found in books whatever their intrinsic value; from the supreme heights of poetry itself down to—almost anywhere. As a bibliophagist, too, gifted from birth with an inexhaustible and insurmountable ignorance, I have never succeeded in keeping 'life' out. Hence the 'speculations'. To succeed in any degree in sharing one's pleasure in anything is by no means an easy feat; to speculate soundly and wisely—well, I can only hope that my title will be accepted with a spoonful of honey.

For reasons now obvious I am diffident in expressing my gratitude to Professor Oliver Elton for his kindness and counsel in connection with the lecture, as it was originally printed, on Poetry in Prose; and to Dr. Dover Wilson for reading and commenting on 'The *Dream*'. When a mere novice steals in upon a sacred territory where even an archangel might fear to tread, he goes with his life in his hand, let alone any shred of a reputation. My warmest thanks are due also to Dr. D. S. MacColl for permission to quote from his essay on Prose Numbers; to Mr. Robert Frost for a poem; to Jason Hill for an extract from *The Cur-*

ious Gardener; to Professor John Livingstone Lowes for an extract from *Convention and Revolt in Poetry*; to Mrs. Robert Bridges for three stanzas from Robert Bridges' poem, 'Idle Flowers'; to Mrs. Edward Thomas for an extract from Edward Thomas's poem, 'Words'; and to my son-in-law, Mr. Rupert Thompson, for sovereign advice concerning what printers call 'prelims'.

If, by inadvertence, copyright material has been here included for the use of which permission has not been granted, or if I have failed to return thanks where thanks are due, I hope my apologies will be accepted. Finally, my old friend Mr. Forrest Reid has read through my revised page-proofs. They alone could reveal my debt to him. This is the latest (but I hope, not even yet, the last) of many similar kindnesses. Again and again, so to speak, we have shared the same inkpot. Needless to add, the responsibility for what is now beyond recall is solely my own.

Books

Books!—
            for the heart to brood on; books for peace;
From the dull droning of the world release;
A music snared, a spring distilled of Spring;
At one spare board to feast on Everything!—
Plain, wholesome, racy, various and rare;
And yet—like Bird of Paradise—on air.

Books!—whose sweet witchery retrieves again
All that the heart of childhood may retain;
Its wonder, ecstasy; grief, terror, woes—
Salved by the leechcraft age alone bestows;
All youthful braveries, too, Time plucked away,
When Hope's clear taper could out-dazzle day.
Books—to intoxicate, to storm, to press
The soul insatiate to unearthliness;
To summon heaven where an attic high
Gleams in communion with a starless sky;
To entice pure Eros from his realm above,
To kneel, palm arched o'er lute, and sing of love;
To make men smell of laurel, and to be
Of wild romance the rue and rosemary;
And, with a truth by art alone divined,
To bare the close-kept secrets of the mind.

Books—laced with humour, and shot through with wit,
Pungent in irony, by wisdom lit,
Life to reveal, and purge, and quicken it,

Probe and explore, dissect and scrutinise,
Mirror its real, unmask its sophistries,
And leave it, fearless, where seraphic Death
Sits with his sickle, and none answereth.

Thought, fleet as errant fancy, comes and goes
As transient as the light upon a rose;
The visioned eye for but a moment sees
All heart hath craved for, in life's long unease;
Imagination, on its earth-bound quest,
Seeks in the infinite its finite rest;
Wrapt close in dark cocoon the Ego weaves
What of philosophy the mind conceives;
And night-long slumber, deep as Lethe's stream,
Rears evanescently the walls of dream:
And—like a dial by the sun forsook—
Their one enduring refuge is a book.

Eden the radiant, Crete, Athens, Rome
Shared have with Babylon the self-same doom,
All have to little more than paper come.
The age-long story of how men plan, act, think—
To be at last dependent upon ink!
Monarch and conqueror, Caesar, Napoleon—
Stilled are their trumpets; here they echo on:
Ay, Tyrant! ink alone, thy spectre gone,
Will blacken thy infamy—else, oblivion.
What, though long years the peaceful poet dote,
How thin a trickle keeps his name afloat!—
One line, of myriads—for Dull to quote.
Still, *one*—when most men from life's wheat-tare crop
Win no more record than a mute full-stop.

Stones fall, brass cankers, mummy thins to dust,
The voiceless grave stills frenzy, pride and lust;

BOOKS

The very gods that mete out shame and fame,
Save for the written word, were but a name.
All the bright blood by fevered passion spilt
Finds reflex only in unfading gilt;
And noble selfless friendship—nought again
But the pure vellum which that gold doth stain.
Helen's long centuries of peerless praise
Else had the wonder been of nine brief days;
An empty rumour, Sappho, Socrates,
Wind-spoil of nights foregone—O leafless trees!
Shakespeare a crumbling clot of wisdom left
In old men's cranies, of all else bereft.
The Star, Gethsemane, the stock of wood,
The garbled rune of an immortal good;
Saints, martyrs, mystics—Oh, what dust would lie
On their lean bones, sole-shrined in memory!
Nay, earth's strange Universe—that hive of suns—
Books gone, the enigma were of brute and dunce;
And Man—scarce witting of his grace and power,
Gone like a sunbeam in a winter hour;
Since mind unaided, though it knowledge breeds,
And blooms in splendour, yet can leave few seeds;
And memory, like wasting waterbrooks,
Needs reservoirs to rest in. These are books.

Abiding joy is theirs; rich solitude,
Where mortal cares a while no more intrude;
Here, by the day's sweet light, or candle-beam,
The waking sense finds solace in a dream;
And self flits out, like wild bird from a cage,
To preen its wings in a lost hermitage—
Gardens of bliss, whose well-springs never stay,
Where founts Elysian leap and fall and play;
And lo, a nimbus, from a further sun
Colours them with enchantments not their own.

Yet every word is void of life and light
Until the soul within transfigures it—
Then sighs, for rapture, wildly pines to see
Who wakes this music, under what strange tree—
And pines in vain; for it is Poetry.

Contents

The Great Adventurers	page 1
Hans Christian Andersen	14
Tennyson	24
Naturalists	47
The Thousand and One	66
Poetry in Prose	80
Rupert Brooke and the Intellectual Imagination	172
Flowers and Poetry	200
Some Women Novelists	233
The 'Dream'	270
A Book of Words	306
Maps Actual and Imaginary	335

The Great Adventurers

It is not merely because the Elizabethan era is reflected or focused in the great plays that our conception of it, however inadequate, is like that of a magnificent pageant. In imaginative retrospect it seems charged beyond parallel with the dramatic. As if to justify this illusion, we incline to isolate it. We contract its many years into a narrow compass, remove its famous men from beneath the dwarfing canopy of our daily sky, and erect for them a stage worthy of actors who seem to have been moved instinctively to accept mortal existence as 'a part', and to have played it, in dress and gesture, speech and art, to the best of their skill and craft and genius and with a whole-hearted abandonment. Not only that, they appear to have been conscious, as vaguely but certainly we may ourselves be to-day, of an absorbed audience worthy of their best, and mutely appreciative. The stage of that sumptuous half-century was a southern garden of opportunities. It must have been easy at least to 'walk on', without execrably disgracing a fitting disguise. Just to be alive was to be bubbling with life's arrogance. The final exit was of little account, so only it was effected with an air, a grace, a sally, or a wide glare of defiance. The gods, though silent, would mark us, even if, huddled among an inglorious mob of supers, we died with no word uttered.

It is for a very good reason, then, that Richard Hakluyt is a conspicuous as well as an exceedingly attractive figure. He is conspicuous because in the very midst of the vast panorama of Elizabethan life and literature he held on his own privy and quiet way, little noticed, not easily noticeable, and was yet one of the busiest moles that burrowed beneath those infloriated lawns. By contrast with the statesmen, admirals, and gentlemen adventurers with whom he 'held converse', he is for us only the quiet shadow of a man, but yet a man who, as we read on in his great wandering book of wanderers, becomes more and more friendly, approachable, and real. In a century of the creative, of such diverse men of genius and character and pungent individuality as Marlowe and Nash, Sidney and Raleigh, Drake and Bacon and Donne, he steadfastly fulfilled the office of an editor, second to none in the rare and modest virtues which should adorn it, yet confident of the loftiness of his ideal and the significance of his self-imposed duty. No toil was too arduous, no object too trivial, that could help to win for him that simple satisfaction which a man feels in accomplishing to the best of his ability his predestined task.

Amid contemporaries for the most part too active, too much engrossed in the supreme enthralment of the present, to dwell in imagination on the future, he steadily looked ahead. He was a patriot in the rarest and finest of senses, in that he foresaw England's true greatness while it was yet only in part achieved; and laboured all his life long to inspire and expedite her progress towards it. The best days of his sixty odd years of life were spent conning over dusty records of bygone travel and discovery and in the company of men, whether among his acquaintance at Court or at Ratcliffe, who were continually adding to them. He himself, in spite of two bold projects, traversed no more salt water than washes through the English Channel. Though his name wears a travelled look, it is only sound old English—Hacklewit. But his midnight oil illumined the Antipodes and dwelt on scenes of wonder, strangeness, extremity and beauty beyond the dreams of the Opium Eater or the fantasies of a Scheherazade.

Ariel of 'travelling mind and pen' though he was, the navigable, habitable globe his only hobby, he indulged his studious eye in no fine frenzy. Yet in his rectory at Wetheringsett, when he closed his study door on Suffolk he flung open his window to Cathay, and not only to Cathay, but to where dwell the Cyclopedes, where slumbers the three-headed serpent above 'the best diamonds in the world', where yells Slata Baba, lurks the deaf-delighting Cassacam, and where lifts towards a far-travelling moon that hill 'called the Pike, because it is piked'—wheresoever, indeed, wind, water, and darkness cry on the forlorn mariner, '*Avanchythocke!*'—get thee hence!

In spite of this variegated view, which might have turned even the soberest head towards poetry, Hakluyt's one desire was to ascertain naked facts, to ensure the salvation of the useful, to pursue and to capture the practical and practicable. Let it once be accepted of his countrymen, stirred out of that 'sluggish security' which was the scorn and astonishment of their rivals, that the 'yle of Thule' was no longer the uttermost limit of the earth, what trade might be theirs, what plantations to disport their great-grandchildren in, how grievously hipped would the proud Spaniard be, how the true Gospel might spread forth its branches! Last, and not least, how ardently would they one and all, having found their business in great waters, bring back, after experience 'of hunger and thirst, colde and wearinesse . . . no end', and despite 'the inconvenience of continual mortality', gems even more gracious than 'the greene stone called Emeraud', fruits even more rare than the potato and the pine—narratives, catalogues, curios, charts and maps, all for the instruction, the delectation of this, at last, venerable archdeacon, Richard Hakluyt, 'Preacher, and sometime student of Christ Church in Oxford'!

Gradually, by intermittent glimpses, we make the

acquaintance of this urbane and eager scholar. We see him coursing the country to retrieve his priceless treasure, intent only on harvesting and garnering up any conceivable fragment of recordable adventure or discovery that could incite the rivalry, enrich the science, or redound to the credit of English seamanship and in futurity tend to found this Empire. Such a glimpse is ours when in his own words he instructs Master Morgan Hubblethorne, Dier, in what manner he shall demean and busy himself in Persia—'to the end that the arte of dying may be brought into the realme in greatest excellency'. There, he informs him, he will find 'carpets of course thrummed wooll, the best in the world and excellently coloured—dyes neither raine, wine, nor yet vinegar can staine'. (Had he, one gasps, like Bacon with his frozen chicken, perilously put these dyes to the actual test while biding his moment 'in the Queen's privy gallery at Westminster'?) He bids Hubblethorne, again, keep some little pot in his lodging, for daily trials in his art, and beseeches him to set down in writing all that he may learn, 'lest you should forget, or lest God should call you to his mercy . . . that come death or life your countrye may enjoy the thing you goe for.' Advice is cheap enough; but how seldom is it so practical and so magnificent!

Such was Hakluyt's constant inspiration. Whenever he himself is present in his book we find him gravely intent on 'the good reputation of our country', with eyes fixed on far horizons beyond 'the watery walls of this our Island'. He realized from the first his appointed place, and how best he could fill it, and in his preface of 1589 he explains to the favourable reader what it was. From the earliest times, he tells him, he has sought out the records of stirrers abroad, and searchers of the remote parts of the world. He presents their testimony, either 'stranger or natural', word for word, appending particular name or page of book where it is extant. Consistently he keeps himself in the background.

His work is all; he himself but the favoured doer of it. One clear and most endearing view we win of him, and that of a kind very rare with his contemporaries. It is a famous passage, but irresistible. In the opening sentences of his first epistle dedicatory to Sir Francis Walsingham he records how in his childhood, when he was a scholar at Westminster, he happened to visit his cousin, an elder Richard Hakluyt, in the Temple, and found lying 'open upon his boord certaine books of Cosmographie, with an universal Mappe'. His imagination leapt to the occasion. It was tinder, and his cousin rapped out the spark from the flint. He opened up his future life to him, set shining his pilgrim star. With wand and map and Bible for illustration and emphasis, he discoursed on 'things of high and rare delight to my yong nature', and when he bade farewell to the boy he bade farewell to the Hakluyt of the travels. No old master, not Dürer himself, has painted a tenderer portrait of youth than is depicted in this delightful fragment of autobiography.

One cannot doubt that Hakluyt was held in esteem by the great men of his own time who had like aspirations at heart and could appreciate his zeal in his work. His own writing bubbles with indefatigable interest in the voyagers from whom at first hand he extorted its contents. But what, we wonder in vain, did these sea-worn mariners, home-returned from the ends of the world, think of this curious and earnest inquirer and scholar? There have been many private and personal literary scenes and occasions whereon one would gladly have played eavesdropper, 'the little bird': when for instance Sir Thomas Browne was knighted; when Goldsmith threw down his hat; when (if ever) Defoe met Selkirk at Mistress Damaris Daniel's in Bristol; when Dr. Donne sat for his shrouded effigy; when Emily Brontë cauterized her hand with her gophering iron; when Samuel Coleridge turned wistfully away from Dorothy and Charles and William and limped off into his lime-tree bower—any such little crucialities as these, according to taste. But few are more seductive to the fancy than that interview to which Hakluyt refers, when, after riding 200 miles solely to learn 'the whole trueth' of Master Hore's expedition to Newfoundland from the mouth of its one survivor, he visited Master Thomas Buts. A moving story was Buts's to tell. He had returned from his voyage so changed by shipwreck and famine and an awful escape, perhaps, from the very pot —since only the captain's oration regarding the penalties which await the anthropophagite in hell had saved the company from habitual cannibalism—that had it not been for a secret mark, a wart upon one of his knees, neither his father nor mother would have recognized their hapless son. But there is not one word extant, alas, of Buts's impression of Hakluyt.

As Hakluyt lived, moreover—hovering in the wings, lurking beneath the trap-door, intently peering out from behind the backcloth of the thronging, lustrous, resplendent Elizabethan stage—so he died. It was a kind of courtesy in happy keeping with his character that he who had done so much so modestly for his age and country, who had laid up an imperishable store of raw nectar for the imagination of the man of action as well as of dreams to feed upon, should have slipped out of the world on a voyage all his own in the misty November that followed the very April of the death of Shakespeare.

What the epic of *The Principal Navigations* represents in solid substance, how wide and profound was its influence on the English spirit in life and literature of its own day, and what gratitude we now owe to its compiler, many tributes have testified. None more comprehensively or vividly than Sir Walter Raleigh's *English Voyages of the Sixteenth Century*. But the only sure method of 'discovering' this prodigious work—and Hakluyt's unpublished manuscripts riotously overflowed into the shapeless and gossiping quartos of Purchas's *Pilgrims*—is to read in it. Next best to being a circumnavigator of the world is to be—a far less perilous but no facile adventure—a circumnavigator of Hakluyt. He is vastly instructive, and, although he never forces sermons upon us, he is edifying. So too is the *Encyclopaedia Britannica*, and thereby earns our respect. But respect is cold commons; and beyond any other collective, as distinguished from creative, author—beyond, perhaps, even the explorer of Melancholy—Hakluyt enkindles, vivifies, and enchants. His 'traffiques' are with the wares of the imagination, with poetry itself. He stirs the innate curiosity, the instinctive venturesomeness, whets all the fantastic appetites, of the mind. An eccentric here and there may still regret that our oblate spheroid is not only by reason of its very shape exhaustible, but bids fair, so far as any novelty is concerned, to be soon exhausted. According to Marco Polo, it was a conceit of the ancient Chinese that it is the heavens which are round and the earth square, their empire being seated in the midst thereof; and Christopher Columbus himself entertained the fleeting notion that our orb was pear-shaped.

Hakluyt indulges no such charming illusions. But though, while immensely enlarging the habitable globe for his contemporaries, he was intent on definition, on steadily and completely contracting the vague and unknown into the known and clear, yet the reward of reading him is the sense of a full and sparkling freedom. His world is not only endlessly spacious, measurable only by whole moontides of storm and travail, but it is also imaginatively manageable, whereas that of most of our own geographers and cosmographers, though it is vaster yet, seems desperately restricted for the wanderings of an immortal spirit. Flight, and wireless telegraphy, and the rest of our triumphs are robbing our fancies of the very notion of the humanly remote? Our mental yardstick is desperately capricious, our sense of space is as circumscribed as our sense of time. Yet one can perish of exhaustion on an English moor, be marooned like Lucy Gray in an English snowstorm, be 'lost' in an English wood. And doubtless there are still enormous wastes of sea and ice and sand that have been no more than occasionally traversed by the foot of man—Sven Hedin tells of discovering the footprints of his own dog in a stagnant sandy desert which he had last trodden, I think, no fewer than seven years before. There are islands no more than visited; vast forests that as yet have defied investigation; immense stretches of mountain, wilderness and plain that are as little busied or pestered with mankind as a Dutch cheese is with mites or the other side of the moon with the pryings of the telescope. But having drawn so much so near and made it more or less familiar, we are apt to forget the perpetual, scarcely mentioned presence of the far and of the strange. The earth we temporarily inhabit, not always to its obvious advantage, seems to have shrunken. And baseless illusion though it may be, what *seems* in this life of ours, to most intents and purposes, positively *is*. The psychologists, in spite of their plunging us into the inscrutable pit of the unconscious, have even circumscribed what we had assumed to be man's infinite mind! Something, alas, of the glory and the glamour is departed. It is this glamour and this glory which the companionship of Hakluyt in part restores.

Under the will of his mariners we are again and again the first to burst into nameless and silent seas. We set foot with them in virgin or forgotten forests, meet and consort with strangers most strange, whether illustrious or simple—savages in the sense that fruits are wild. A pewter spoon, a handful of beads—and the hogshead of precious stones is ours. This is the effect whether Odoric or Anthony Jenkinson, Mandeville or Drake, be our guide. Or whether Juan Martinez—Juan Martinez who discovered the city of Manoa, shared in its seven-day orgy with the gold-powdered naked guests of the Emperor, and christened it by the name of El Dorado. In the strangeness, and the marvellous for its own sake, Hakluyt was no believer. 'Great errors grow on mariners' fabulous reports.' On the other hand, he had little respect for the incredulous, and in the long scale from the merely misinterpreted to the miraculous, from the monstrous to the queer and the grotesque, his Voyages are one long banquet of surprises. They are the richest and oddest curiosity shop in the world, and no one comes to ask our business or to keep watch on our surreptitious rummagings.

Sometimes the surprise is that of the child who for the first time sees a guy; sometimes that of a man who unforeseeingly opens a cupboard door upon the family skeleton. Romance and horror are often much of a piece. We meet them in company when Raleigh describes the obsequies of the commanders of the goodly Tivitivas:

'They use great lamentation, and when they thinke the flesh of their bodies is putrified, and fallen from the bones, then they take up the carcase againe, and hang it in the cacique's house that died, and decke his skull with feathers of all colours, and hang all his golde plates, about the bones of his armes, thighs, and legs. . . .'

Naïvety will touch that romantic horror with an odd pathos, as when it is told that the people of Tebet are 'wont to eat the carkases of their deceased parents; that for pities sake, they might make no other sepulchre for them, than their owne bowels'. Again and again it would seem as if it were some archaic quality of the mind that is the secret beguilement, as when Jacques Cartier tells how for landmark in the natural haven of Gaspay his captain erected a fair lofty cross, thirty foot high, and hung upon it a shield with three 'Floure de Luces' in it, and carved its top with an antique posy, 'Vive le Roy de France'; or when Raleigh, again, tells of the hauntingly beautiful lady he saw in Guiana, or of how the queens of the Amazons keep feast with the kings of the borderlands, and how they and their peoples cast lots for their Valentines, and the she-warriors, being returned home, send anon their boy babies to the borderers, reserving their daughters for themselves.

Whosoever the writer may be, it is the things that he tells of, no less than merely the vivid untarnished words he uses, which he charges with that precision and liveliness which is the unfailing reward of the author who keeps his eye—and that a comprehending eye—on his object. And what wide sharp vision of expectancy and wonder these seamen had! They indeed delight beyond measure in things. Flowers and fruits, beasts and men, furniture and attire, are described with that bare exactitude we look for in Swift and Defoe, yet with that something of enchantment in addition which is the magic of *The Ancient Mariner* and of *Kubla Khan*.

We read of mountains 'steep-upright', of tropical rains—'Water like whole rivers did flood in the air', of 'lizards, like Evats, and as common as Mise in great houses' (thus redeeming at a stroke the mouse from the familiar and the Evat from the unknown). If the poor negro is nought more human than marketable ebony, the word *Gold* is embedded in a sentence that confers on it an intrinsic and supernatural preciousness, as if it were manna, or Helen's hair, or Keats's MS., or a child asleep. In outlandish circumstances the most trivial phenomenon may be touched with the fateful and ominous. So it was with the monster, 'a very lion to our seeming', which did slide and roar and balefully glare, with 'ougly demonstration of long teeth' upon the ocean, on that Saturday in August, 1583, when Sir Humphrey Gilbert turned back from his ill-fated enterprise. The creature might have been the devil; but whether or not, the General himself, we are told, hailed it as *Bonum Omen*.

Nine days after, at midnight, as they watched in the *Golden Hind*, the lights of the frigate suddenly went out; she had sunk. Gilbert's last words to them, called across the water that same afternoon as he had sate reading abaft, had been full of generous cheer—'We are as neere to heaven by sea as by land.' It was the very expedition in which Hakluyt himself had planned to share. How must this marvellous account of it have taken his heart!

This courage and piety, the piety of men in danger and in the lap of the unknown, is manifest again and again in the Voyages, and a keen sagacity and good sense are bound up with it. 'Serve God daily,' Sir John Hawkins counselled his men, 'love one another, preserve your victuals, beware of fire, and keep good company.'

This speech and style—at times, it may be, tortuous and broken, by no means always easy reading—is not that of one man but of scores; and through it all runs a raciness, in a double sense, which marks it of that unique age. It is frank and direct, and yet it gleams occasionally with the euphuistic. It is a mine of the vernacular, yet often elaborate. It affords ample room for Master Anthony Parkhurst's jocosity, for Sir Robert Duddeley's glibness, for Hakluyt's ceremoniousness, and for the honest yarn of every English sailor who could spring one worthy of his calling, worthy of an engrossed listener and to the praise of Gloriana. It will, unwitting of it, sometimes break into a melody and beauty that all but bring tears to the eyes:

'Here we beheld plaines of twenty miles in length, the grasse short and greene, and in divers parts groves of trees by themselves, as if they had been by all the arte and labour in the world so made of purpose; and still as we rowed, the deere came downe feeding by the waters side, as if they had been used to a keeper's call.'

The tongues of children set free in Paradise could not sing with a more ingenuous and impetuous delight.

Through words thus uttered straight and direct by those who had seen and done we learn to know the men themselves. One after another they imprint themselves upon the memory—that nameless and marooned tailor, for instance, in St. Helena, whom Henry May and his messmates heard singing in a chapel and supposed to be some Portugal. Poor soul, he went clean out of his wits at sight of their English faces, for excessive sudden fear and joy. What, too, became of Thomas Nash, of whom all that we know is that he was ducked at the yard's arm for pickery, and discharged? They come and go, these salt-water ghosts, who dared the seas north and west and east and south in ships like cockleshells, kept body and soul in precarious consort on a diet of weevils and putrid water, and as often as not reaped only the wind and a watery grave for their reward.

Their world—its lustrous colours, its prodigies and portents, its dangers and disasters, its marvels and distances and riches—is gone with them, and neither we ourselves nor posterity shall ever win it back. Yet Hakluyt will refresh what cannot but sometimes seem a needlessly staled one for the tiredest imagination. In his flames the Phoenix will reanimate herself. In his company we are no longer one of myriads in the drab livery of a common consciousness. As peeped Tom on Godiva, as felt these travellers who pierced into that far eastern province where no man grows older than chance finds him on the day of his entry, so sit we absorbed in Hakluyt's book. Our bane is that half-digested, libraried omniscience—the conviction that there is nothing new under the sun when even our extinct and hoary old satellite manages the miracle every month—which dulls not only the tang and freshness of the world, but the capacity to realize that to each of us as individuals it is still infinitely discoverable, ineffably strange. How else could Joseph Conrad, could Hudson, could Cunninghame Graham consent to have been alive? Something, indeed, of the spirit of these old voyagers must have stirred Arnold Bennett to make romance of a drab Five Towns draper's shop, and Henry James, also—in those self-sacrificial explorations of souls subtle, fastidious and sophisticated. We are incessantly tempted to accept what is common to all men as a personal rendering of experience, whereas there is not a nightly dim-lit window that does not conceal a complete universe of virgin experience, not one fellow-creature's face that does not mask and bewray an unbroken solitude.

Hakluyt lived in a day when the brighter threads of national destiny had woven themselves into an astonishingly dazzling patch of colour. The plot had thickened. The fingers of the long arm of coincidence were unusually busy. Humbly and unswervingly he pursued his chosen, his deputed, task. If there is anything to be learnt from his great book, it is a lesson the present is teaching—that men may have faith beyond their reason; may be wiser even than they are prudent; that their strivings are guided not only by what experience and the past have assured them of, but by influences also, inscrutable in their working. Paradox though it may appear, they are inspired, in their free choice and will, by the very fate which that divine inspiration makes inevitable.

Hans Christian Andersen

On April 2, a hundred and thirty-five years ago, in one of the most ancient and richly traditioned cities of Denmark, a city that claimed no less a personage than Odin for its first burgomaster, Hans Christian Andersen began the best of all possible fairy tales—his own life. In a bed made out of a deceased nobleman's coffin-trestles he opened unusually small blue eyes on a little lattice-windowed room in a steeply gabled house. It contained pictures hung all over the walls, and others rudely painted on the panels of the door. There were glasses and knick-knacks, and pewter plates, a pot of mint on the window-sill, and a shelf of books and ballads. And on the roof of the house flourished his mother's garden of parsley and onions. In this room all day sat a cobbler at his tic-tac-to—a cobbler who believed in no devil but one of the kind who keep company in sevens and delight to entertain themselves in a house swept and garnished. He was never seen to smile as he sat reading his Baron Holberg, his La Fontaine, and the Thousand and One Nights. However heterodox this father might be, Hans Christian could not doubt that the good God had sent him into a world full of things (with a wrong side to them, of course) 'charming to hear and lovely to see'. And his life was to be a Jacob's ladder from a wilderness of stones to golden balconies of fame, with kings and queens smiling down on him from the upper storeys and heaven at its summit. At night he lay in a little sofa-bed screened with calico curtains, and was drowsed to sleep by the shadows and movements and voices of those in the room beyond, including the cheerful rasping of a cricket whose descendant eleven years afterwards was to chirp the night through while Hans watched with his mother beside the hapless cobbler's corpse, until she cried out on it, 'You need not call to him; he is dead.'

Meanwhile, 'a little cracked', as the neighbours thought him (for he had what one calls 'go' in his brain, genius, 'and was afterwards to enjoy what is almost of as much importance—luck'), Hans had been accumulating a whole universe of vivid experience. Life then seemed to him a play of phantasms, as it often does to a child of a solitary, moody or conscientious disposition, confronted with the amazingly real. But it was a play of phantasms with sinister shadows. A deft-fingered old gentleman lived in a madhouse close by. On the only occasion when they met he addressed his grandson as 'they'. Two prisoners waited on the child at table when he dined one day in the neighbouring gaol. He impressed and alarmed the old women in the workhouse with a fantastic depiction of their insides. He peeped in one morning on a sweet-voiced naked lunatic in her cell, who clawed at her visitor through a hole in the door. He weathered school without a whipping, read Shakespeare before he could spell, wore, with impious pride, his first pair of creaking boots at his Confirmation, and after his poor, shiftless mother had consoled her widowhood with a second cobbler, he set out, with thirty-seven shillings in his pocket, for Copenhagen and fame. His voice, he thought (as did the ass, the dog, the cat and the cockadoodle in the folk-tale), would be his fortune. But, although he failed, and failed again, was often threadbare and hungry and too sensitive to confess it, he never lost faith in himself, in the future or in Providence. And from one end of his life—in mere years, precisely three score and ten—to the other, friends and benefactors thronged about him.

Almost every dream of his youth came true. Kings were his nursing fathers, or, at any rate, lavished on their promising *protégé* pensions that slowly crept from £50 ('less $12\frac{1}{3}$ per cent. for the widow's fund and the prison tax') to a clear £116 3s. 4d. And the bare circumstances of his early years had so sharply instilled thrift into him that for sixteen months he travelled, through France, Italy, the Tyrol and Germany, on well under this latter sum. Fairy-tale traveller he was. He found Cherubini sitting at a piano, with his cat upon his shoulder. Victor Hugo gave him his autograph (high up in the right-hand corner of the paper). He burnt his shoes on the slopes of Vesuvius. A good Lutheran, though a foe to the clergy, he refused to bow the knee to the Pope of Rome. At thirty, in spite of parody and lampoon, he was already a literary prince in Denmark. Easily dejected, timid, and awkward, he yet knew how to shoulder his way, how to make use of merely decorative nonentities, and prudently to dedicate one book to no fewer than nine distinguished patrons. And he worked. He wrote obstinately and incessantly—charming travel-books, history, romances, novels, and 'dramatic works'—*The Mulatto*, that ran like wildfire for twenty-one nights, and *The Moorish Girl*, that glimmered out in two; and a religious romance on a philosophical thesis, 'To Be or Not to Be'. There was an epic poem also, *Ahasuerus*, on the Wandering Jew, whom, after exacerbating transmigrations, he left stranded with Christopher Columbus in America:

A better poet in a better way
Will tell us of the wanderings that follow.

Not many English readers can have exhausted this extensive repertory. He coveted not a niche in the fane of literature, but a complete façade. He fondly dreamed that these great works at last would represent his gift to the world, that by them those unwearying pests, the critics, who had consistently 'poured molten lead into a wounded heart', and 'spat' upon the lambent 'glow-worm' of his spirit, would finally be crushed and refuted. To the end he hoped against hope. His 'dear young friend', Edmund Gosse (of how many blessed memories!), who, in 1872, watched sunset kindle sky and sea with rose while he sat, with Andersen's amazingly long, brown, bony hand clutching his shoulder, and listened to the magician's slow, hoarse reading of 'The Cripple'—not even this eager and gallant English admirer could reassure him. ' "Don't you think," he said to me in a sort of coaxing whisper, "don't you think that people will really come back to *The Baronesses* when these *Smaating* have had their day?" ' But Mr. Gosse had not read that work. 'I could only bend my eyes politely.'

Hans Andersen was one of the Aladdins, the Dick Whittingtons, the Little Clauses among writers. It was these despised 'trifles', fountlike improvisations, feats of pure nature and intuition rather than of art, strange and lovely tributes (like the books of the wanderer in 'The Shadow') to whatever is true and good and beautiful, that were the sesame of this wizard's life, his 'go' and his luck. His enterprise, his indomitable faith and courage, his consummate vanity and self-confidence are traits which men of rare talent frequently share who have no 'bag of magic' to spill in a glittering heap at the feet of the children of men. When indignation against poor, carping, God-forsaken Denmark overpowered him, these fairy tales flung open the gates of every capital in Europe—Berlin, Paris with its (no longer cautious) Hugo and dangerous Heine, its mocking Balzac, and, 'dearest of them all', the jovial Dumas; buzzing London, with its affectionate Prince Consort, its Lady Blessington, its haughty and artless aristocracy, and its 'dear, noble Charles Dickens', with 'his beautiful long hair falling down on both sides' and a 'heart equal to his mind'. Spain horrified the pilgrim with the goriest of bullfights. Constantinople, in mosque and minaret, dreamed his dreams before his eyes. Sweden, Portugal, Holland, Norway—it was all the same story, and Andersen died only just in time to avoid a 'reception' fit for 'a monarch' in the United States of America. The fairies can turn beech leaves into gold. They made of their gaunt, lank-limbed, shambling son of a cobbler, with his prodigious feet and Roman nose and tiny sunken eyes, a lion—of the first magnitude—in every gilded and silken *salon*. For their sake beautiful young Danish ladies had long since hung paper cagefuls of cockchafers on his bed curtains and put peas between his sheets. Rank and fashion had wistfully whispered, as he paced the fashionable Ostergade, 'There goes the poet!' 'Ancient Sapphoes' continued to dazzle but never dazed him. Jenny Lind shared a cosy little Christmas-tree with the 'good old poet'. And all the world's little people, generation after generation, have blessed the name of Hans in the same breath with that of St. Nicholas.

Is it a shock, or is it even pleasing, to remember that Hans Christian Andersen was not, to the last sentimental tinge, what is called a lover of children, that he greeted with unmistakable grumpiness the design for a statue to be erected in his honour, representing him as an old man overwhelmed and over-gambolled by a clamorous throng of young Copenhageners? One reason for this may be that to the last of his seventy long years he was himself a child at heart. And children are not necessarily lovers of children. They do not gape at their own innocence, or marvel at imaginations as natural to them as spectacles on an elderly nose, or sit cherubically smiling at themselves amid their trailing clouds of glory. They dwell and flourish in their own natures, præternaturally practical and crafty pygmies in the world of dull tyrannical giants into which it has pleased God to call them. Andersen's looks and general shape, too, although he had a heart-enticing voice and a transfiguring smile, and could write delicious letters to his 'Dear little Marie', telling of strawberries that one can 'taste right down into one's stomach', might at first be the cause of a furtive alarm in a small juvenile circle. And although his stories reveal almost every conceivable gift and grace, oddity, absurdity, whimsy and sentimentality dear to a childish fancy—a fancy to which the world and all that is in it is so much delicious clay in the hands of a potter, nevertheless a large number of them, and some of these among the best, appeal more directly to the ruminating, memory-bewitched mind of the grown-up.

Whatever their origin—and he gleaned his ideas from life and experience, from books, and friends—their atmosphere, their minute observation and inconsequentiality are childlike—the childlike, that is, which is in part the invention of the mature. There is little distinction of things or of persons. Mouse and mother-snail, rose and needle, nightingale and spittoon, the flea in the blanket, the goblin in the church-tower, the angel in paradise share the same order of existence, the same 'rights'. They are in a lively intimacy with one another, are equal by virtue of their being completely and divinely themselves. Kings live in dressing-gowns and embroidered slippers as naturally as geraniums in pots and cats on the hearthrug. Tears and laughter are old playfellows. Pathos and humour share a sentence. And how perfectly homely and confidential it all is! It is 'I' and 'thou' from the first nod, the first impetuous plunge: 'Now you shall hear!' 'Where did we get this story from?' 'There was once a shilling;' 'It was in the month of May.' It is homely, yet cosmopolitan to the last degree: 'On one of the Danish Islands,' 'In the German land of Wurtemburg,' 'Let us visit Switzerland,' 'In China you must know...'

Sheer hard reading went to the making of such a story as

'The Marsh King's Daughter', but the form seems always to be a happy accident, if form there strictly be. Anything and everything goes in, absolutely everything goes on, and with a breathless rapidity. They are stories not written but told—in a series of happy-go-lucky hops and skips and jumps. However fantastic and extravagant the theme, no ingredient is mere padding. The phrases are as clear and concise as the eighth Commandment, and as final; especially when they give the keynote to a style in a story whose seed must obviously have been borrowed from the folk. 'There lay Big Claus in the river, and sank at once to the bottom. "I'm afraid he won't find the cattle!" said Little Claus. . . .' ' "No!" cried the witch. *So* the soldier cut off her head. There she lay!' 'All the flowers were tied up to human bones, and in the flower-pots skulls stood and grinned. That was certainly a garden for a princess.'

The pen races the thought, the heart beats time, the invention never falters, the fantasy romps on, but beneath and around all this is the atmosphere of a tender pity, a universal friendliness, of how mellow a wisdom, how golden a simplicity—even if it *is* a little sophisticated at times. From 'The Tinder Box' of 1835 to 'Auntie Toothache' of 1872 there is little sign of flagging. Only a more placid beauty, perhaps, a quieter, surer imagination distinguish the last stories from the first, albeit in 'A Picture Book without Pictures', of 1840, Andersen wrote perhaps the most exquisite of all his lyrics in prose. This 'Night' recalls Heine; another, Tolstoy; and a third paints a picture of a child which only Velasquez could rival. The magician frequently condescended, or aspired, to draw a moral, but for the most part his ethics, as Edmund Gosse has pointed out, are of the Parthian and nursery order—a code which may or may not be nearer to that of the heaven which is our home. And so, on the one hand, Big Claus returns to his sack and to his fratricidal intentions much comforted by a psalm, and, on the other, poor little Red Shoes, although, like the mediaeval birds of paradise massacred for trade, she was footless, stumped off at first in vain to church. Whatever their theme or their lesson, the stories are full of light and life, of songs and wings. They cover whole generations of time in a few pages. 'Years have rolled on,' Andersen writes wistfully again and again. His little tin soldier is at one moment as immortally youthful as Eros, and at the next as old as the Pyramids. It is a green, enclosed unchanging *little* world, bushed with lavender and rosemary, and gilded with perpetual sunshine. And yet—except when he himself frequents this source, and not always even then—his stories are curiously unlike those ancient literary crustaceans, the Household Tales, the Märchen.

The Märchen were part of the primitive furniture in daily use in the House of Life—even when, architecturally, that house consisted chiefly of four stone walls and a hole in the roof for a chimney. Andersen's is a doll's house, an entrancing plaything that he kept in an upper room. The folk tales are of a universal, human sediment. Andersen's are peculiarly personal; their nature, human and otherwise, has been distilled and etherealized. There is almost as curious a difference between the two as there is between a flint arrow-head and a Victorian sampler. The wild bird of the folk tales sings, in Andersen's, in an exquisite cage. And there is little doubt that until the mocking bird beloved of the pedagogical—who, like a dog with a dry biscuit, are intent on dates and syntax—takes its place, it will continue to win the best of all entranced listeners—children.

Every propitious Christmas sees the publication of at least two or three Andersens, at least one or two Grimms—and the association in itself is a sly little jest, for Jacob Grimm appears to have been the only man of letters in Europe who mortally shocked Andersen by professing that until he paid him a visit he had never even heard of him. The majority of these reprints are—reprints, lavishly illustrated. A 'Complete Edition of the Tales', published nearly thirty years ago, had a higher and a more comprehensive aim. Not only does it include many tales that were then new to English readers, but 'those pieces', it tells us, 'which have not been specially translated . . . have throughout been carefully collated with the Danish text, with the result that many errors and inaccuracies have been corrected, interpolations excised, and omissions restored.' The outcome none the less is open to criticism even from those who have no first-hand knowledge of that text. An ideal translation might result from the process (*a*) a severely literal rendering into English of the text; (*b*) the transmutation of this into a free, pure and idiomatic style; (*c*) the collation of (*b*) with the original by an expert in both tongues. Even this translation is not flawlessly happy. Such little mischances as, 'He was shot straight *into* the heart', 'And the spectacle was *the most* beautiful,' for instance, would hardly extract plaudits from the Society for Pure English. And although, in the words of Mr. Nisbet Bain, Andersen's biographer, such fragments as the following may be 'loyally literal', they are hardly 'fearlessly free': 'You see that was the dialogue they held.' 'At last [the rain] came down in a complete stream,' 'Christine's father and his assistant propelled the boat with staves.' Or take the italicized words and phrases in the famous finale of 'The Emperor's New Clothes':

' "But he has nothing on!" a little child *cried out* at last. "Just hear what *that* innocent says!" said *the* father; and *one* whispered *to another* what the child had said, "There is a *little* child that says he has nothing on." "But he has nothing on!" said the *whole* people *at length*. And the Emperor shivered, for *it seemed to him* that they were right.' *

* For comparison, here are two other versions, one by Alfred Wehnert and Caroline Peachey, and the other from Andrew Lang's *The Yellow Fairy Book:*

Faithful to its original this may be, but it is scarcely racy vernacular. Apart from its flat 'says's' and 'saids', something is amiss with the rhythm of the sentences. The *voice* of the style has little life in it. It is also disconcerting to find that for its 'shivered' another translator has 'that *struck* the Emperor', another has *writhed*, and a third has *vexed*. Danish must indeed be a chameleonic tongue. All this only goes, it seems, to prove that not even yet—sixty-five years after his death—has this old friend and master managed to win in England the full courtesy, and pains, and the tribute that his genius so long ago richly prepaid.

'But he has nothing on,' said at length a little child.

'Good heavens! Listen to the innocent thing's voice!' its father said.

And one whispered to the other what the child had uttered.

'But he has nothing on!' all the people cried at last. This perplexed the Emperor, for it appeared to him that they were right. . . .

'But he has nothing on!' said a little child at last.

'Just listen to the innocent child!' said the father, and each one whispered to his neighbour what the child had said.

'But he has nothing on!' the whole of the people called out at last.

This struck the Emperor, for it seemed to him as if they were right. . . .

Mr. Forrest Reid tells me that by far the best translation is by L. F. Brackstad, which, with delightful illustrations and an introduction by Edmund Gosse, was first published in 1900. Here is his rendering of the above passage:

'But he hasn't got anything on!' cried a little child.

'Dear me, just listen to what the little innocent says,' said the father; and the people whispered to each other what the child had said. 'He hasn't got anything on!' shouted all the people at last. This made the Emperor's flesh creep, because he thought that they were right. . . .

Tennyson

'The good die first,' says Wordsworth in *The Excursion*,

> '*And they whose hearts are dry as summer dust*
> *Burn to the socket.*'

> '*Whom the gods love die young was said of yore,*'

sings Byron in *Don Juan*; and he himself breathed his last at Missolonghi in his heroic thirty-sixth year. It was said of yore, not perhaps for the first time, by Menander, who was drowned while swimming in the harbour of Piraeus when he was fifty-two; and it was rationalised about a century afterwards by Plautus, who lived to be seventy: *Adolescens moritur, dum valet, sentit, sapit*. However it may be with the generality of men, the inference is that it is not poets in particular who are thus set apart by the favour of the gods. Chatterton, Keats, Marlowe, Shelley, Emily Brontë, Rupert Brooke, Wilfred Owen were exceptional. But although sound health seldom blesses an old body, perception, surely, need not be dulled by age, and time may establish, ripen and enrich a natural judgment. Rogers, Waller, Tennyson, Landor and Hardy are among the Elders of the English poets; their average age, when they left this world, was eighty-seven; and neither *On the Last Verses in this Book*, nor *Crossing the Bar*, nor *The Darkling Thrush* suggests a dusty heart, or any lack of perception and of a natural judgment. All three poems appear almost as regularly in every new anthology of English verse as comes the cuckoo to our English spring in the third week of April.

Tennyson (then the only outstanding Alfred among the poets apart from the theatrical manager who was affectionately known to his intimates as Poet Bunn) died in 1892. The moon that night was at the full, the Plays, open at *The Tempest*, lay beside him on his bed. It was an aptly romantic close to an unrivalled career. He had made poetry not merely an English but a British institution. The name of Charles Dickens became a household word; Tennyson's a drawing-room shibboleth. Gilt-edged albums by the thousand enshrined the effusions of his devotees. No other poet and artist so fastidious can have both merited and won a more abounding popularity. When however the drums and tramplings in Poets' Corner were stilled and the Phoenix was at rest amid her ashes, there followed a prolonged pause. Death lays an icy finger on poets as well as kings. The work of a long life was now complete; the passage of time put it in a new perspective; enthusiasm gave way to a considered judgment and a more exacting criticism.

This is the destiny of most poets of unusual repute in their own day; and on many of them oblivion by no means blindly scattereth her poppy. The records of the Public Libraries none the less suggest that the pundits are less faithful and more capricious in their affections than the common reader; and the fact that a writer is no longer written about—a heedlessness that has certainly not yet overtaken Tennyson—is not necessarily a proof that he is no longer read. Well before the close of the last century, however, his direct influence had begun to wane. A wildly bright but in certain respects a not too particular star, Rudyard Kipling, had risen above the eastern horizon; there came the Naughty Nineties; the Yellow Book and Aubrey Beardsley broke into exotic bloom. Their activities more closely resembled a local mutiny than a lasting revolt. But 'lousy' is the last word that Victoria's poet laureate would have applied even to the most disreputable of 'ulsters', and yellow and naughty are epithets entirely alien to the author of *The Princess* and *The Idylls of the King*.

A change of far greater moment and magnitude was soon to follow. *The Dawn in Britain*, *The Dynasts*, *The Rout of the Amazons*, *The Sale of St. Thomas*, *The Everlasting Mercy*—such works as these, two at least of them of a supreme originality, were in marked contrast to a poetry typically Victorian, if, that is, we forget for the moment that Beddoes shared Tennyson's birth-year, that Emily Brontë was born when he was nine, and that Robert Browning, Swinburne and Meredith were his contemporaries. To the Georgians in general, who have little more than this convenient tag in common, he might have consented to be kind and yet reluctant to agree that he was akin. His estimate of the 'moderns', on the other hand, who reveal strikingly little kindness or kinship in respect to himself, can only be surmised. As a poet he had already declared that 'the deep moans round with many voices'; as an artist, 'some one has blundered' might have been his private summary. It is curious indeed that, while poetry itself is catholic, most poets of much account 'commence' non-conformist.

Tennysonian to the last degree Tennyson's verse certainly is. But his Juvenilia once left behind him, he seldom found himself among the rebels, and it is he himself who still remains in some degree enticingly obscure, rather than his poems. There can be few lines among his many thousands which it is a sort of exciting and perilous Blind Man's Buff to attempt to understand. There are poets who more or less resemble the recluse of Juan Fernandez; access to their inmost recesses may not be attainable. Tennyson belonged to the mainland. It is perfectly clear that he hoped and intended to communicate his thoughts and feelings, his interest and delight—to share them, that is, with every susceptible reader. At how much sacrifice of what was so individual and involved in his own mind and spirit as to be incommunicable in human language one cannot tell. Complete apprehension of the *poetry* in his poems is of course another matter.

Like most poets he had to await full recognition; but his genius was instantly detected. He was the literary Dalai Lama of his age. Third in age of three poets, born between 1807 and 1809, in a fraternity of seven sons, he embarked on an epic in his childhood. And epics (which entail even greater pains and patience to write than to read) seem to be the outcome of sheer instinct in nursery poets. In his earlier 'teens Tennyson also wrote a play which he aptly entitled *The Devil and the Lady*, since the lady is put into the care of the Devil when old Mundus, her husband, departs on his travels. This 'might easily have been the work of some young intimate of Marlowe's and Jonson's' come into the world 'two centuries late'. It may be compared with *The Bride's Tragedy*, which was published by Beddoes when he was sixteen. In certain respects it promises what was never actually fulfilled. Even more remarkable, Alfred was acclaimed by his own father. 'If that boy dies, one of our greatest poets will have gone.' When he was twenty, that 'extraordinary young man', Arthur Hallam, who, we are told, seemed to tread the earth as a spirit from some better world, described him as 'promising fair to be the greatest poet . . . perhaps of our century'. At thirty-six, he was in Wordsworth's estimation 'decidedly the first of our living poets', and a few years afterwards he was accorded the laureateship.

Poets in the past have survived the garret, neglect and semi-starvation; others must have succumbed to these incentives to live laborious days.

On the other hand, to be born in the purple may also prove to be a difficult destiny. It may encourage caution and the conventional, tend to keep the square peg in the round hole, and hinder initiative. The heart too can be ill at ease and unhappy whatever the colour of the sleeve; and Tennyson frequently told us so. He moved, even in young manhood, like a queen bee dispensing her priceless benefactions on a charmed circle of diligent and scrupulous attendants. His son's biography, the testimony of innumerable friends, so many of whom succeeded in making their mark on his generation, present the various, many-sided and yet consistent image of a closely and lovingly observed personality, although, of course, one must accept with caution tributes which are invited and intended to be more appreciative than critical. The sincere regret—'I wish I had been A.T.'s Boswell'—is almost comment enough, coming as it does from so intent a critic of humanity and literature as Edward Fitzgerald, who 'saw life lazily but saw it plain'. 'He uttered by far the finest prose sayings of any man I have ever met' is a telling corroboration.

Even Thomas Carlyle, that self-indulgent expert in the acid summary, apart from a caustic jeer at the poetical dung-heap of his day, talked of Tennyson good-naturedly as 'the spoiled Lifeguardsman'. Impressive, rough-hewn, downright manliness was the outstanding feature of this humorous 'grumpy' poet, who left his hair to the chance barbering of his candle; who answered a flattering and formidable invitation to breakfast with contemporary demigods with a brusque, 'I should hate it, Duchess'; who, eager to shine his brightest, could think of nothing but beer to talk about to Robertson of Brighton; and who chanted or intoned his 'hollow oes and aes' with 'a voice like the sound of a far sea or of a pinewood' out of a cloud of tobacco smoke to any old crony that would listen to the poems scribbled down in his historical butcher's book.

There is abundant testimony to that 'magnificent voice' —like the wind in a pine forest, to those gusty bursts of Cyclopean laughter, to the simplicity and unaffectedness of this never-failing fountain of wisdom, learning, stories and chaff. No less humanising is the information that he found it the 'height of luxury to sit in a bath and read about little birds', and soaked his straight Dublin clays in coffee, that he was pleased to be hailed by Whitman as 'the Boss', that he discovered 'a sort of tenuity' in Shelley's poetry, that he regretted he could not pass on to 'old Fitz' Jem Stephen's commentary on Wordsworth's *Heaven lies about us in our infancy*—'That is no reason why we should lie about Heaven in our old age', that he flatly refused to say 'padjent', and vowed that in all his life's wonderful work he had done nothing 'most perfect', 'only fragments of things that he could think at all so'; 'Come down, O Maid,' for example, and 'Tears, idle tears'. If only that supreme delineator of humanity, John Aubrey, could have returned for but one evening from the Shades to spend a few quiet hours in talk with so rich a quarry!

Trivial much of this may be, but it helps Tennyson to escape from the mawkish legends so helpful in making poets acceptable to those who are not in the habit of wasting time on their works. He lived in the sunshine of the world's curiosity and esteem. Devotees far and near sent him gifts of flowers, and tobacco. They begged their 'dear angel' for autographs, even for scraps of a cast-off necktie. One little Yankee boy pleaded for a cheese wherewith to tempt his mother's appetite, and an adventurous artist with a taste for the rural, begged to be endowed, at the poet's expense, with a live cow for a permanent model.

Edmund Gosse—then one of these youthful fanatics—relates how in 1871 (the poet's fifty-second year), having been hastily summoned from a 'horrible underground cage', known as the Den, in which he worked in the British Museum, he first encountered in the flesh this august and idolized frequenter of his dreams:

'Proud young spirits of the present day, for whom life opens in adulation, will find it scarcely possible to realise what such a summons meant to me. . . . The feeling of excitement was almost overwhelming: . . . Tennyson was scarcely a human being to us, he was the God of the Golden Bow. . . .

'It must, I suppose, have been one of those days on which the public was then excluded, since we found Tennyson with a single companion, alone in what was then the long First Sculpture Gallery. . . . At that time he was still one of the darkest of men, as he is familiarly seen in all his earlier portraits. But those portraits do not give . . . the singular majesty of his figure . . . in repose. . . . Bareheaded among the Roman Emperors, every inch as imperial looking as the best of them, he stood there as we approached him, very still, with slightly drooping eyelids, and made no movement, no gesture of approach. When I had been presented, and had shaken his hand, he continued to consider me in a silence which would have been deeply disconcerting if it had not, somehow, seemed kindly, and even, absurd as it sounds, rather shy. . . .

'Then somebody suggested that we should examine the works of art, which, in that solitude, we could delightfully do. Tennyson led us, and we stopped at any sculpture which attracted his notice. But the only remark which my memory has retained was made before the famous black bust of Antinous. Tennyson bent forward a little, and said, in his deep, slow voice, "Ah! this is the inscrutable Bithynian!". There was a pause, and then he added, gazing into the eyes of the bust: "If we knew what he knew, we should understand the ancient world." If I live to be a hundred years old, I shall still hear his rich tones as he said this, without emphasis, without affectation, as though he were speaking to himself. And soon after, the gates of heaven were closed, and I went down three flights of stairs to my hell of rotten morocco.'

Those halcyon days are over—for the time being at least. Hero-worship is almost confined to the tabernacles of Hollywood; Apollo is now in mufti. The 'great' Victorian poets, having warmed their hands before the fire of life—excellent Wallsend, flaming and sparkling beneath the marble chimney-pieces in the very best parlour—have departed; their very rôle in the cast of human affairs is now obsolete. Tennyson (whatever little private reservations may have been his) not only filled that rôle for many years with conscious and ceremonious amplitude, he also triumphantly looked the part, and not merely dressed to it. Andrew Marvell, the young Milton and the never-elderly Byron are among his few English rivals in this respect; but he had one trifling advantage over them. He never shaved. Does this fact and the change in this particular fashion among his Georgian successors and their detractors suggest that a Delilah has insinuated herself into the company of these Muses? *Can* Jacques, when discoursing on the world that is no more than a transitory stage, have by but one consonant been misreported by the printers of the first Folio?—his soldier 'bearded like the *p*ard'. Like him of Avon himself, many of the famous Victorians, Browning, Longfellow, Ruskin, Carlyle, Rossetti, Morris, Swinburne as well as Tennyson (who, it is said—'lifeguardsman' apart—was no stranger to 'strange oaths') at least suggest that the poet in this respect should resemble the seer. What art owes to the hairdresser is not indeed a purely frivolous speculation, since Love owes even more; and no idolizer of any particular writer, painter or musician, is unlikely to welcome beauty in his countenance, grace in his every motion, and grandeur in his gaze. There is only one little pitfall and danger that we need have here in mind. No poet, not even a great poet, is necessarily at his sweetest and his best merely because he has donned his singing robes. It was not his mantle that conferred the gift of prophecy upon Elisha. Springs may befall when even 'an old man with a beard' may fail to attract so much as the monotonous *chink-chink* of a chaffinch to its hospitality.

In direct contrast to many of the traits and oddities characteristic of Tennyson which have been referred to, are others no less salient and more significant; his extreme sensitiveness, for example. 'I *am* thin-skinned,' he once owned frankly, drawing up his sleeve to exhibit the two-inch ravages of a flea-bite, as proof that it was more than a merely metaphorical confession. His intense hunger, again, for that solitude within solitude, introspective, brooding reverie—the temporary Nirvana induced by sighing over and over his own name, 'Alfred, Alfred, Alfred' (and any other would have served the same purpose); his chafing against the least show of hostility, including even the 'pen-punctures of those parasitic animalcules of the Press', the reviewers, from which, none the less, and unlike his rough-hewn rival, Robert Browning, he deigned to accept counsel; his 'moods of misery unutterable'. Some of the less valuable elements in such a temperament are observable in the poems. That foursquare but highly temperamental sage Samuel Johnson—another English character!—as he is depicted by Boswell is only partially concealed in *The Rambler*, in *Rasselas* and the *Dictionary*. He is in full eruption in *The Lives of the Poets*. Is the Tennyson, whom Edward Fitz-gerald would have portrayed, as detectable in anything like the same degree in *his* life-work?

But poetry is the outcome and flower of circumstance and surroundings as well as of a human being. In his early days, and when under the malign influence of the 'indolent reviewer', Tennyson longed, we know, for the quiet and workaday life of a Lincolnshire yeoman, passing rich with £400 a year—just as Edward Grey pined to flee away from politics and public affairs and be at rest with William Wordsworth.

TENNYSON

Be mine a philosopher's life in the quiet woodland ways,
Where if I cannot be gay let a passionate peace be my lot,
Far-off from the clamour of liars belied in the hubbub of
lies;
From the long-neck'd geese of the world that are ever
hissing dispraise. . . .

A light fierce enough, however flattering, came at length to beat on Farringford. Tennyson detested what must yet at last have become as natural and looked-for a diet as his daily bread—the honeyed adulation which his renown and popularity entailed. Whether an enforced obscurity, narrow means, few and humble friends, freedom from the artificial cares of the too much and the too many, and from the vexations incident to becoming a piece of public property—what effect any such seclusion would have had on his poetry, who can say? The mere profession of poet need, alas, be no irresistible invitation to the Muses. Tennyson, none the less, deliberately destined himself to become a national bard, to write for that rather nebulous norm the general reader and his appreciation. Whatever his success in this ambition may have been, and he had his ups and downs in public esteem, it is difficult to say what and how much he sacrificed in the process. What fraction of his work will eventually survive the perils and privileges of such a career and will continue to be read for its own sake only, what part of it carries the mysterious, inextinguishable lamp of genius beneath the mantle of a classic yet romantic art are questions the critics of a hundred years hence will doubtless answer without presumption, unanimously and with ease. And the critics of the following century may be of quite another mind! Our peculiar respect for posterity, indeed, may suffer a slight eclipse if we remind ourselves that *we* are Tennyson's.

If we turn, however, to the earlier and what in its kind may at last prove to be the most enduring fraction of his work—to the volumes, let us say, whose dates, 1832 and 1842 come as patly to the tongue as that which brought the Conqueror sweeping across the Channel—it is at least possible to distinguish the qualities that will probably tend to endanger and those which may at last ensure Tennyson's assured place among the English poets. Through its whole range, and in all its diversity, his poetry was singularly of a piece. The seal of his intent and individual craftsmanship (which fails of course when the imaginative material is poor or flaccid) is on all his work—from his prize poem on *The Battle of Armageddon*, immortalised as 'Timbuctoo', to that stanza, written within a few years of his death, which is not only signally his own but is also one of the most gravely beautiful in English poetry:

But such a tide as moving seems asleep,
Too full for sound and foam,
When that which drew from out the boundless deep
Turns again home.

The same attachment to a definite kind of experience, the same precision of presentation, repeatedly show themselves. Every facet of the poetic art shines out in these earlier volumes and particularly in the briefer poems that unite the lyrical, the narrative and the dramatic. It was then one of his favourite devices. Nevertheless, he was not a born teller of tales, or freely endowed with that not very unusual faculty, invention. The faintest phantom of a 'story', the barest thread of a plot were made to suffice (as indeed they have sufficed for some of the best fiction in the world), but they were again and again interwoven with that rather shallow and dispiriting theme, the *mésalliance*, a game in which Mammon shuffles a well-thumbed pack of Victorian playing-cards, long familiar to Mrs. Grundy. Money, next to love, the main stand-by perhaps in all its machinations in prose fiction, if not in life itself, is less likely to pay its way in poetry. He sometimes borrowed the themes he elaborated, but in incident and treatment seldom enriched them. Even with a promising nucleus he may not succeed in telling his story well. His endings are often psychologically, and in some of his lyrics are poetically, the weakest parts of the whole.

He studied and analysed men and women, but he cannot perfectly put them together again. Life has flown. His gaze is intent and keen, but the strange power to divine and to become is wanting. His characters, like many of Thomas Hardy's, are the sport of destiny rather than gifted with free will. Unlike Hardy's they have been made, or made up, not born. They serve their maker's purpose but it is not usually a very profound purpose. By sheer lifegiven-ness they do not rise into being, as do even Blake's chimney-sweeps, or Annabel Lee, or the sisters in *Goblin Market*, or George Herbert in *The Collar*; or stalk out of the void with an energy and a mastery that may set a modest reader wondering if he himself has ever really lived. Nor, on the other hand, have they the power of hinting by subtle and cumulative innuendo that actuality itself is nothing more than a disturbed and fragmentary dream.

Nearly all Tennyson's men and women are mainly pictorial—so many minutely observed and depicted mental and bodily traits and features. We see with distinctness enough a Will Waterproof, a Farmer Allen, the fat-faced curate Edward Bull (and apart from 'the clergyman who told' the May Queen 'words of peace', he is not over-indulgent of the Church), a Northern Farmer, a Grandmother, a Sir Galahad, even a Hallam; but do these phantoms of humanity, as do Chaucer's or Wordsworth's, return to memory at the merest hint, animate and haunt us unbidden and unannounced? And how often do they evoke in us that hidden self which may seldom excite our waking attention but yet never sleeps beneath day's restless consciousness? Do we stumble on the secrets of our own hearts in theirs? Even in such a masterly piece of technique as *A Dream of Fair Women* how chill and meagre at times are the uttered words:

I had great beauty: ask thou not my name:
No one can be more wise than destiny.
Many drew swords and died. Where'er I came
I brought calamity.

How statue-like she seems to stand, how cold the agate lamp! Was *this* the face that launch'd a thousand ships, and burnt the topless towers of Ilium? In Tennyson's general treatment of women indeed there is a prevalent strain of the 'yeoman' who coldly scolded Lady Clara Vere de Vere, who appealed against her blue blood to 'the grand old gardener and his wife', and bade her go 'teach the orphan-boy to read, Or teach the orphan-girl to sew'. A suggestion of mock modesty hangs over passages in which even modesty herself might for the time being consent to open her eyes and hold her tongue. Young women encloistered like Mariana (and how vivid and lovely is every natural detail of her stagnant moated grange!); or slowly dying, like his Queen of the May; or dead, like his Lady of Shalott, were assured of his romantic sympathy and sentiment. But he did not stoop to trace his meditations in the sand until Guinevere's accusers had silently withdrawn, and he was, as he intended he should be, to the very last things in humanity quite alone with her. Was he, indeed, ever intensely alone with any of the human creatures, reputable or otherwise, depicted in his verse?

In his private life he detested priggishness; he could speak out bluntly enough in talk; he could splash over the shallow tub of mere conventionalism, and was a man of a broad, masculine humour. And yet in his narrative poems how rare is the pinch of Rabelaisian salt—in precocious evidence in *The Devil and the Lady*—which would have added so appetising a tang to that tantalising niceness, that laborious simplicity. How vainly we usually listen for even the rumble of a voice against which Mrs. Grundy must dutifully stop at least one ear! 'Two notes only', wrote his friend Herbert Warren, 'are absent' from Tennyson's poetry: 'the unkind and the base.' And he adds, a trifle ambiguously, 'Those who knew him realised what he could have done had he yielded to the temptation to strike there also.' He strikes, in another sense, piercingly enough in *The Modern Timon*. Candour is not necessarily detraction, which is unfortunately by far the easiest way of winning a quick hearing; and there is nothing either base or unkind in calling a spade a spade, or meritorious in withholding the usual ha'porth of tar. These disinclinations were certainly not a family failing.* In so many of the longer poems there are traces of that social prudery, and of the genteel, exemplified in the opening line of *Sea Dreams*: 'A city clerk, but gently born and bred.' His salary is referred to as 'gains'. And often when Tennyson mentions the merely ordinary it is with a rather wry effect. It shows in its context like a patch of wool in silk embroidery.

* Frederick Tennyson (no more than Charles, who wrote, with its exquisite finale, *Letty's Globe*) was neither as man nor poet the mere satellite of his famous brother. He referred to himself as 'a person of gloomy insignificance and unsocial monomania'. He was a keen disciple of Swedenborg, hated 'the high-jinks of the high-nosed' or 'Snookdom', and 'the frowsy diatribes of black men in white ties', settled down 1857 in a vast hall designed by Michelangelo, engaged (it was reported) forty fiddlers to sate his love of Mozart, had four children, and that now respected resource of Mother Gamp's, 'an Umbrella'. He had little enthusiasm in general for Other People, but gladly suffered the Brownings. He remarked, however, that 'Mrs B' was 'troubled' like other inspired ladies, with 'a chest', was inclined to agree with Fitzgerald regarding her husband that

It once was the pastoral Cockney,
And now is the Cockney profound,

and dismissed most of his poetic performances as so much 'pure brain-work'.

But may not perhaps the quality of the silk excuse the presence of the worsted?

Walter Bagehot—a critic as original, substantive and provocative as he is exhilarating—divided poetry into three categories: the pure, the ornate, and the grotesque. He consigned Browning's to the third of these, Tennyson's to the second, and, for illustration, used *Enoch Arden*. 'How simple', he comments, 'the story is in itself! A sailor who sells fish, breaks his leg, gets dismal, gives up selling fish, goes to sea, is wrecked on a desert island, stays there for some years, on his return finds his wife married to a miller, speaks to a landlady on the subject, and dies.'

There *may* be a shimmer of irony here; otherwise, perhaps, this summary is hardly fair. A prince, of Denmark, named Hamlet, having been informed by his father's ghost that he was murdered by his own brother, debates whether or not he should and shall avenge him; and finally does. As was not Euclid's way, it reduces the admirable to the absurd. Thus dissecting, are we not disposing of an animated work of art by dealing solely with its bare bones—and that far from the Valley of Jehoshaphat? What of Helen's? Is this the *skull* that launched a thousand ships? Alas, poor Yorick! With any such 'alas' still faltering on our lips we may recall that from a single bone no bigger than that found by the teeny tiny old woman in the churchyard, the great naturalist, Sir Richard Owen, reconstructed in imagination a complete prehistoric monster.

However that may be; having thus dealt with the story or plot of *Enoch Arden*, Bagehot's argument concerning it runs roughly as follows: Poetry, worthy of the name, *must* give us pleasure; 'a sailor who sells fish' cannot possibly be pleasurable company; that being so, all that concerns him in Tennyson's narrative cannot be poetry; Tennyson's description nevertheless of the castaway's island is a model of adorned art; therefore the poem is a little masterpiece of its class. In a later essay, it may be added, Bagehot has quite pleasant things to say (as had William Blake) about a chimney-sweep. But how many fascinating questions spring into view out of this presentation of his case?

Would Enoch have been more agreeable company if he had sold fish wholesale, or if he had become 'a fisher of men'? Where exactly falls the poetic sumptuary line—where sits the salt? Above or below the Ancient Mariner? How far, again, in another art, does the class or occupation of its subject affect the merit of a portrait? Is an artist with a whoreson old sexton for sitter doomed to failure unless he includes in his canvas 'a Mr. Wilkinson, a clergyman' and the rector of the parish to retrieve the balance? Is Hogarth's Shrimp Girl, are Manet's Absinthe Drinkers, are Carpaccio's Venetian Courtesans redeemed by their pictorial setting? Apart again from the fatality of a vulgar calling, what complete ideal of human reality *can* a 'sailor who sells fish' adequately fulfil? How far short of this falls Enoch? Is any obvious deficiency the poet's responsibility; and, if so, was it intentional? And if not, and had his realisation been ample enough, would it have removed this part of the poem into the category designated 'pure'?

But then, are Tennyson's characters in general, his Arthur, his Guinevere, his Knights of the Round Table, his host of the gentry, who one must assume *should* be agreeable company, more real than Enoch? If we have to admit that what is most conspicuous in them is a certain *minus* and a certain *plus* due it would seem to their being so specifically Tennysonian, how does this affect his 'ornate'—the presentation of his marvellously precise and lovely scenery, his exquisite vignettes of the observed and the divined? If these give us pleasure enough (as indeed they do) to ensure their acceptance as 'poetry', the question still remains whether or not that scenery is itself flawlessly real. Or has it too perhaps a tinge of the too idiosyncratic, of the restricted, of what is remote from human nature's daily food? Is it a thought exotic? We think of Chaucer's Nature, of Crabbe's, of Wordsworth's, Vaughan's, and Blake's, and Hardy's; and, grateful to them one and all, may make our choice.

Tennyson himself can hardly have been fully aware that, like Enoch Arden with his 'costly funeral', his plaintive and fated 'little Alice' of *The May Queen* is not only inadequately 'three-dimensional', but—if one watches her a little closely—is also unattractive; or that his Maud never really comes alive. What little 'story' there is in this poem also, so treated, as with *Aylmer's Field*, is simple to the point of insipidity; and the characterisation ranges between the melodramatic and the parochial. But how exquisite at times is the *obbligato* of the voice that tells this tragic, and yet—despite its human sorrow and regret—never acutely moving tale. Again and again the natural magic and music manifest themselves, like the song of some bird of enchantment in an old folk-tale, though seldom of an Ariel or an Israfel.

And now 'twas like all instruments,
Now like a lonely flute;
And now it is an angel's song,
That makes the heavens be mute.

It ceased; yet still the sails made on
A pleasant noise till noon,
A noise like of a hidden brook
In the leafy month of June,
That to the sleeping woods all night
Singeth a quiet tune.

When indeed we think of Tennyson's lifelong and impassioned adoration of *his* Nature, far exceeding in intensity even his concern with things of the intellect, his insight into humanity, his impulse towards introspection and his keen interest in science, all such criticism seems a little graceless and niggardly, if not beside the point.

His first collection of 1830 contains a Song about 'worn Sorrow', and this is its second stanza:

> *Death standeth by;*
> *She will not die;*
> *With glazed eye*
> *She looks at her grave: she cannot sleep;*
> *Ever alone*
> *She maketh her moan:*
> *She cannot speak; she can only weep,*
> *For she will not hope.*
> *The thick snow falls on her flake by flake*
> *The dull wave mourns down the slope,*
> *The world will not change, and her heart will not break.*

In reading these lines is not one conscious of a faint sigh of relief and of renewed interest breathed from the poem itself when that 'thick snow' begins quietly to fall? And did not that dull wave 'mourning down the slope' become in Tennyson's later work a solemn reiterated and endeared refrain? The song recalls Millais' naturalistic picture of nuns digging a grave in the snow of a churchyard; and a lovely woodcut by Arthur Hughes with a similar subject. It recalls too, not Watts, but Christina Rossetti, whose imagination was also haunted by the theme of love and death. It would be quite untrue, however, to suggest that in her poem, *When I am dead, my dearest*, the cypress tree and the green grass, the shadows and the nightingale are its *in*most impulse. The very cadences of her poem deny it. Whereas in Tennyson's song we may feel just the contrary.

Is there not a subtle difference in realization between

> *In the spring a livelier iris changes on the burnished dove,*

and

> *In the spring a young man's fancy lightly turns to thoughts of love?*

This, of course, is merely to say that every poet is only most happily at home *some*where. No mind or heart can be instant tinder to every fortuitous spark; and it may be that no man, from childhood onwards, fails to reveal a pronounced if vacillating inclination to what on earth most fully satisfies for him some permanent, innate or inherited hunger, yearning and desire. A poet, any artist, however versatile, is unlikely to be exceptional in this. He may have many strings to his bow, and a full quiver, but his inward eye is apt to return repeatedly and with a renewed zest to one certain target; and all other aims are of secondary importance and value. Faithful to that, the old mill-horse may die in its tracks, but it has at least laboured to grind the corn prescribed by its secret monitor and master.

'What is Master Awlfred always a-praying for?' enquired the family cook who had heard him clanging out his verses as he paced to and fro at Somersby. Well, if it had been for the power of communicating to the world his worship of beauty, and his zeal for its perfect expression, it would have been a prayer abundantly answered. He stumbles at times simply by reason of his ardour for the last exquisite finish, the golden hair's breadth of precision. Occasionally he detectably inserts among the fresh flowers of a poem a few lines thus elaborated which he had set aside in his pocket-book for future use; occasionally he crystallises what should be fluent and natural with too obviously chosen an epithet; and such passages ('the moan of doves in immemorial elms', for instance) are rather superficially taken as both excellent and characteristic. The verse, too, rather than unveiling its beauty, as may a morning mist the dew and flowers and loveliness of a meadow, is often as sharp and clear-cut as metal or marble. But at his best, Tennyson does not, like William Morris, portray, or, with what seems a chance word, suggest a complete scene of the imagination; he takes his reader up bodily, so to speak, and sets him there in the material midst.

She woke: the babble of the stream
Fell, and, without, the steady glare
Shrank one sick willow sere and small.
The river-bed was dusty-white;
And all the furnace of the light
Struck up against the blinding wall.

We shut the inward eye to escape the glare, and *breathe* that dusty-white. And he succeeds even in lines packed with 'literariness' and the pre-Raphaelite:

Thridding the sombre boskage of the wood,
Toward the morning-star.

It is merely a platitude to repeat that he is the master of one variety of the magic word—whether it was the blissful inspiration of the moment, or far-fetched. In what other poet is so superb so self-evident a magic after so self-evident and eager a search?

Still on the tower stood the vane,
A black yew gloom'd the stagnant air
. . . I lingered there
Till every daisy slept, and Love's white star
Beam'd thro' the thicken'd cedar in the dusk.

Who cannot at once recall or soon recover a score of such exquisitely considered touches as the rabbit's 'harmless face', the 'blue fly' singing on the pane, the 'crackling frost'? Such things as these have long ceased to be vivid images; they are now also enchanted memories. It is difficult to keep back our tears at the verbal truth and the beauty revealed, even in his best-known 'pieces':

When the flowers come again, mother, beneath the waning light
You'll never see me more in the long gray fields at night;
When from the dry dark wold the summer airs blow cool
On the oat-grass and the sword-grass, and the bulrush in the pool.

There is indeed scarcely a lyric of Tennyson's but has for its individual charm not a simple passionate thought, not a mystic allusiveness or a profound human emotion, but some one supremely faithful or significant fragment borrowed from a direct tryst with his Nature. His son has recorded, that however near and dear his companion, Tennyson habitually withdrew himself into a temporary solitude in order to muse upon and perhaps to record what most keenly impressed or deeply affected him in the day's journey. Out of that 'never less alone than when alone' came 'the happy harvest fields', the ship in *Tears, Idle Tears*, the shadow in *St. Agnes' Eve*, the city in *Will*, the wrinkled sea in *The Eagle*, and, again, that miraculous glimpse in the last four lines of *The Captain*. The verse blows salt on our lips, with its roar and hollow crying; and its sea-birds wheel in an abyss of air between eye and printed page. Where else, too, unless in Milton, arches such space and burns and glitters such splendour of moon and sun, of Orion and the Hyades, in a mere leash of words?

All else in his life, so far at least as this is revealed in his poetry (for his wide interests flourished in an ample field), seems to have been to him of secondary import. Beauty—but not specifically the beauty in mystery, or strangeness, or in a fantastic or sinister disguise, or in the perfectly ordinary, or in what is very seldom the concern of art—is the unfailing impulse of his genius, an island of solitude and peace amid the ocean of countless other earthly experiences. And he made, and revealed it as, his own. His interest in Science* was diligent and curious, but that too was in service

* In this he was an innovator, and he would have disdained to take much to heart, however apposite it was to his practice, Bagehot's ironical and by no means unfounded generalization:

'Some people are unfortunately born scientific. They take much interest in the objects of nature. They feel a curiosity about shells, snails, horses, butterflies. They are delighted at an ichthyosaurus, and excited at a polyp; they are learned in to his love of nature. Poets there are whose vision of the world is as far removed from any accepted actuality as was the Lady of Shalott's; they weave the mirror's magic reflections into a web of fantasy: Tennyson from the windows of his eyes, 'dark, powerful, and serene', looked down direct on Camelot.

Inspiration comes and goes. Whether a man toil or tarry in patience or impatience, poetry will not be cajoled, or circumvented, or suffer compulsion; and a lifetime's patient service may be memorably recorded at last only as the outcome of a few supreme moments. Following a merely personal predilection in thought, feeling or imagination, we may set particular store on this or that above all else in our English poets—Donne's brooding intensity, Herrick's detached daintiness, Shelley's raptures, Keats's sensuous loveliness, Coleridge's magic, Wordsworth's impassioned philosophy. Each is the refraction from reality of an individual experience. There remain the virgin riches of a world that would inexhaustibly suffice for theme and inspiration had every man that breathes been born to rhyme. And even from so partial a survey of Tennyson's work as that of these few pages a rare achievement stands out clearly—his intense appreciation—if with out-sight rather than with insight—of what he loved and delighted in; his supreme mastery in the recording of it; and his devotion to an ideal conception of his art to which he remained faithful to the end of his days.

minerals, vegetables, animals; they have skill in fishes, and attain renown in pebbles; in the highest cases they know the great causes of grand phenomena, can indicate the courses of the stars or the current of the waves; but in every case their minds are directed not to the actions of man, but to the scenery amidst which he lives; not to the inhabitants of this world, but to the world itself; not to what most resembles themselves, but to that which is most unlike. What compels men to take an interest in what they do take an interest, is commonly a difficult question—for the most part, indeed, it is an insoluble one; but in this case it would seem to have a negative cause—to result from the absence of an intense and vivid nature.'

The spirit within him was at peace and at home among his native dykes and wolds. Here 'Alfred's mind was moulded in silent sympathy with the everlasting forms of Nature'—a sympathy which failed to impress a fisherman who to the civil greeting of the poet whom he had encountered, sans hat and coat one four-o'clock-in-the-morning pacing his Lincolnshire sea-strand to the music of 'the hollow ocean-ridges roaring into cataracts', replied, 'Thou poor fool, thou doesn't knaw whether it be night or daa!' Official and social obligations and privileges far from conducive to such self-communings were thrust on him, accepted, and, not without intrinsic sacrifice, triumphantly survived. With the encouragement of the wisest king that ever wore a crown, there must have been many in high places who would have agreed with the Laureate's Lincolnshire folk that to 'hev owt' to do with books is a sign of a weak intellect. Nevertheless, to these duties he devoted his great talents; his genius followed its own sweet will.

In *Timbuctoo* Arthur Hallam had seen promise of a unique greatness. The keeping of this promise was summarised by Sir Alfred Lyall; it was Tennyson's 'proud distinction', he declared, 'to have maintained the apostolic succession of our national poetry in a manner not unworthy of those famous men who went immediately before him'. That means perhaps a little less than it seems to say. It might be applied to the author of one faultless lyric. 'Greatness' is a word which, rightly or not, suggests quantity rather than quality: Longfellow rather than Poe; Dryden than Vaughan; Browning than Emily Brontë. Greatness left out of account, Tennyson, purely as a poet, may be justly compared with Coventry Patmore and Christina Rossetti. Their order of merit, which is of little importance compared with the fact that they were without question *poets*, depends on some final definition of poetry itself. But whose? 'The deep saith, It is not in me: and the sea saith, It is not with me.'

Naturalists

'I am going a long journey,' said Frank Buckland on his death-bed, 'a journey where I think I shall see a great many curious animals. That journey I must go alone;' and he set out on it in the belief that God who is 'so very good to the little fishes would not let their inspector suffer shipwreck at last'. It is a more modest, substantive claim than many of Life's sea-farers could establish—except perhaps the stowaways, even if to the orthodox it may hover between the sentimental and the profane. The hymn asks mercy for us worms on earth (and little in my youth did I relish repeating it), but animals, however 'curious', familiar, strange or beautiful, would for most aspiring souls be a saddening substitute for the paradisal harps and the society of the angels. Even if we bear in mind Montaigne's wry admonition that every traveller, whatever his destination, will have himself for company, and an ideal self is not an easy conception, the heavenly Jerusalem is seldom associated with the beasts that perish. A horse, a 'faithful' dog, how welcome the responsive bark or whinny, but even a house-cat edging cautiously on her way through the gates of pearl looks a little odd. And if there shall be no more sea, where then the inspector's fish? He must have hied off to some obscure and peaceful creek, having borrowed one of Charon's old discarded boats.

> . . . *And in that heaven of all their wish*
> *There shall be no more land, say fish.*

Buckland's notion of the Better Land, and few of us would find it easy to be more specific, was an intensification of the happiest and possibly also the busiest of his hours on earth, of a renewed earth, that is, securely possessed of *all* loved, lovely and living things. The man in the street, and there are a great many of him, seldom nowadays even sees a horse. He may visit the Zoo, but that is chiefly for his children's sake; and a bag of buns or nuts is his simple tribute. Humanitarians we may profess to be, even vis-à-vis a leg of mutton; but a robin in a cage is more likely to excite our superstition than our rage; and fine feathers are not yet a disgrace to fine ladies.

True naturalists, patient, ardent, imaginative devotees of that perpetual miracle we so easily dismiss as 'Nature', are rare. The term is more frequently applied to collectors of facts, statistics and carcases. Man, none too happy even among his own kind, kith and kin, has wantonly and to a lamentable degree estranged himself from the fellow-beings who rejoice and share in that Nature: symbols of energy, freedom and strangeness whose only language (and that as yet not confined in any human dictionary) is sweet or raucous noise, or silence. Unlike Selkirk on his island he is flattered rather than shocked by the tameness of the creatures he has '*domesticated*'—a condition not easily distinguishable from a helpless servility. He enters a wood, and instantly a hostile and vigilant hush intensifies its stillness, such as would fall on our modern Gomorrahs at the first windings of the Last Trump.

He is an excellent and sedulous utilitarian, but to his own ends. By unnatural selection he has contorted, dwarfed, fantasticated, or doubled earth's flowers, fruits, animals; has squandered its life in riotous hunting, and has made something of a guy of his original image. Yet he is fairly complacent in his tower of Babel and can still say *bo* to a goose.

'There is no doubt that men are very ignorant about

Nature. . . . We are not *in* Nature; we are out of her, having made our own conditions; and our conditions have reacted upon and made us what we are—artificial creatures. Nature is now something pretty to go and look at occasionally, but not too often nor for too long a time.'

It is W. H. Hudson speaking. And even the primordial spirit in our house-cat, which of all animals profits most self-securely from our artificialities, if given a tongue (though not of the 'Saki' variety), might echo the words which he puts into the mouth of Sir Walter Raleigh, having imagined him come back to earth to inspect our 'modern conveniences':

'Oh, but you have now gone too far in that direction! Your rooms, your tables, all the thousand appointments of your establishment, your own appearance, your hard-scraped skins, your conversation suffocate me. Let me out—let me go back to the place I came from!'

When Hudson confesses himself to be a rank sentimentalist, it is merely to take the words out of his critics' mouths. His heart is hard enough for all honest purposes. He does not tell us to peel off our clothes and go nudist (and protective colouration is usually more congenial and decorative); or to eat nothing but nuts, or to sleep in the snow, or to lead the simpleton's life. In the presence of the vegetarian he muses on the seductions of roast pig. The usual Englishman's idol is a dog. Hudson (and A. C. Bradley seems to have taken some little pleasure in proving that a highly unusual and much-admired Englishman, William Shakespeare, was of the same opinion) flatly refused to bend the knee to this carrion creature. His affection and admiration were for what he deemed finer, cleaner and more intelligent company—'the fairy' marmoset, that 'night wood-ghost' the lemur, the Patagonian dilochotis, the red-gold agouti and that small mountain troglodyte (beloved perhaps of the Incas), the chinchilla. Like Buckland, he too was an absorbed inspector, but of all creatures great and small. His own chosen paradise, we can take it for 'granted (or grunted),' harbours that very sagacious animal the pig; welcomes the serpent; is enjewelled by the toad. No 'Philistine fly-fisher' with his greed for trout will be found therein; but heron and otter, martin and swallow in all abundance; the raven, and the dove.

How is it, then, that even mere literary parasites, denizens by comparison of only a paper ghost-land, who don't know a hawk from a handsaw, call a cockroach a beetle, would cry Profiteer! on the poulterer that asked a ha'penny for three sparrows, and who cannot free themselves from a visiting horsefly by an instinctive appeal to their 'twitching' muscles, how is it that they do not find Hudson's naturalism

pathetically rustical,
Too pointless for the city?

Well, as Burton puts it, the mocker at country life 'may say "Pish!" and frown, and yet read on.' The rest unfalteringly include him in the company of those natural divines and diviners, White—to all eternity 'of Selborne'—and Izaac Walton. With what ingenuous delight we at once renounce the city's 'several gymnics and exercises' for these country 'recreations': when they are shared in an armchair. In Hudson's company we are '*veré Saturnus*'. 'No man ever took more delight in springs, woods, groves, gardens, wells, fishponds, rivers, etc.,' than, with him for philosopher and friend, do we. By some charm, such a charm as he cannot express even in his chapter, 'Advice to Adder-Seekers', he captivates even readers who are scarcely even novices in his themes, utter dunces in his school. And what we win from him is priceless.

Just as, when the white electric glare of a railway carriage fails for a while and out of our small upholstered cage we may see suddenly loom up beyond its smudged oblong of window-glass a wonderland of reality—tree and meadow, hill and water, spectral, lovely, dreamlike in wash of star and moonlight in the deep, spacious night; so any one of his treasured books transitorily illumines and revivifies for us a world to which we are habitually strangers. We all but recover a foregone and secret understanding. Nature is no longer 'something outside ourselves and interesting only to men of curious minds.'

Is it the child in us, the lost or the forsaken youth of the imagination, that Hudson addresses? Such a child as Wordsworth once was, and Traherne and as another referred to in *The Sayings of the Children*, who declared to his mother: 'I can see lots of things with my heart. . . . I've got green trees and a lot of flowers in my heart;' who spoke of a flower as of 'a forgiving blue', and in pacification of his own question, 'Where was I before I came to you?' replied, 'I was a ram upon the hills, and you came and gave me a roseleaf, and I ate it, and became me. . . . I was an eagle, because I've got big thumbs.' Milk for babes; meat for grown men. None the less, is it still perhaps that wraith of the child left in us which in Mr. Hudson's company re-inherits the world?—

'In his nearness to or oneness with Nature, resulting from his mythical faculty, and in the quick response of the organism to every outward change, he is like the animals. . . . Whatever is rare or strange, or outside of Nature's usual order, and opposed to his experience, affects him powerfully and excites the sense of mystery.'

It is, at any rate, this child who never fled from or abandoned him—or whom he won back. He tells how, after killing an adder in the New Forest, a change came over his mental attitude towards living things. Although his chief happiness had until then always been in 'observing their ways', his feeling was suddenly changed for a while to that of the sportsman and collector, intent on killing and corpse-keeping. His mind in this condition could still delight in 'the power, beauty, and grace of the wild creatures', in the imagination of their unceasing adjustment to an ever-changing environment, and of the age-long inheritance through conflict and mutation manifest in the individual of each diverse species. But a rarer sense was forgotten and for the time being lost:

'The main thing had been the wonderfulness and eternal mystery of life itself; this formative, informing energy—this flame that burns in and shines through the case, the habit, which in lighting another dies, and albeit dying yet endures for ever; and the sense, too, that this flame of life was one, and of my kinship with it in all its appearances, in all organic shapes, however different from the human. Nay, the very fact that the forms were unhuman but served to heighten the interest—the roe-deer, the leopard and wild horse, the swallow cleaving the air, the butterfly toying with a flower, and the dragon-fly dreaming on the river; the monster whale, the silver flying fish, and the nautilus, with rose and purple-tinted sails spread to the wind.'

Although, as Hudson says himself, 'what one reads does not inform the mind much, unless one observes and thinks for oneself at the same time,' and although, as William James declares, a generous impulse towards life that is not put into action is a waste of energy and a step towards the formation of a bad habit, and although also even the best of Hudson's books may be only a glass wherein we discern the vividly seen, it none the less enables us to share something of its writer's peace and happiness, his hours of solitary transport. A flower, no less than bird, roe-deer, leopard, nautilus, or 'big game', can confer this rare transitory sense of being '*in* nature' and freed from the conditions which have made us creatures of, if not in positive servitude to artifice and convention. He tells us how, when seeking shelter one morning from the furious Atlantic winds at Zennor (once in Francis Kilvert's words desolate, solitary, bare, dreary . . . a sort of place that might have been quite lately discovered and where 'fragments of forgotten peoples might dwell', but which also resembles a drop-scene between the actual and a further reality), he suddenly chanced on a slope of smooth turf at the foot of the rocks, powdered with the grey-blue of vernal squills—close-clustering, as if in faint reflection of the sky, and almond-scented in the cold April sunshine. That was one such moment. It reminds me of a calm, brilliant Sunday of many years ago when, the dazzling dark-blue sea beneath us, the gulls like snow against the blue above, I was sitting with a beloved friend on another Cornish cliff, also powdered with the grey-blue of vernal squills, and having happened to glance landward, we saw one after another the white blinds being drawn over the windows of a large grey neighbouring farmhouse. Another such ecstatic moment for Hudson was when he chanced suddenly on myriads and myriads of daisies, a band of white, like snow, carpeting the disused Roman road on the downs at Dorchester; and, yet again, the serpentine green of a mile-long British earthwork in Wiltshire crested with the shining yellow of bird's-foot trefoil; and yet again, one of the rarest of English wild flowers, with their serpent-like hieroglyphics, the fritillaries, the chequered daffodils—darkening the earth over an area of about three acres. 'It was a marvellous sight, and a pleasure indescribable to walk about among them.'

Naturalists in general are far less intent on conveying mere feelings. But it is not by accident that there are so many *d*'s in an ironical reference to 'our exceedingly industrious lepidopterists'. The term is as much the halter of a bad name as when he breathes 'canophilist' at the serfs, say, of the parasitic Pekineses, 'weak in their intellectuals.' It is the imagination in such writers as Richard Jefferies and Edward Thomas and Walton, and Traherne, that weaves enchantment into, tinges with magic, the common things which they have seen and describe. The simple and precise prose of the scholarly, contemplative, 'curious' Gilbert White thrills with a perceptible exaltation when he recounts the ravages of the 'rugged Siberian weather' in Selborne during the great frosts of January 1766, and of December 1784:

'Many of the narrow roads were now filled above the tops of the hedges; through which the snow was driven into most romantic and grotesque shapes, so striking to the imagination as not to be seen without wonder and pleasure. The poultry dared not to stir out of their roosting places; for cocks and hens are so dazzled and confounded by the glare of snow that they would soon perish without assistance. The hares also lay sullenly in their seats, and would not move till compelled by hunger.'

The eye as it reads these words is itself dazzled hardly less than were the cocks and hens; the wintry silence and whiteness become all but an hallucination, as they do also in Robert Bridges' 'London Snow'. And what is that 'wonder' but the inarticulate realization of Hudson's 'eternal mystery of life itself'? Poor Robin Herrick exiled from the wits and taverns of the metropolis, objurgated (and languished in) the rusticalities of his 'living' in barbarous Devon. Contrariwise, what a mercy, then, it is for those to whom *Selborne* is an unfailing source of ease and pleasure, that its author was never banished to some eighteenth-century equivalent of our London slums, or buttoned into gaiters and made a dean. His parochial duties can never have been onerous—another blessing; his incumbency of Norton Pinkney was a sinecure.

He had begun his *Garden Kalendar* when he was just over thirty; and he spent the last forty-one years of his seventy-three in the peace and quiet of the place where he was born. Few suns can have risen for him a wink too soon. 'I love all beauteous things, I seek and adore them' might have been his own matter-of-fact summary of his life on earth. Indeed, this faithful old bachelor had only one Platonic mistress, Nature herself. Not the hardy and austere matron which the term usually brings to mind, but a lovely thing—young, 'natural' and a trifle demure. We dip into him, again and again, always pacified, always revived in so doing, and all but solely for the delight he and his chosen company, chiefly 'singing birds sweet', bestow on us. Only incidentally for his facts and information—stiff and starchy terms indeed for his own variety of them.

None the less he felt that his devotion needed a defence and vindication. For one thing, he had the 'gentleman of fortune' in mind; and even in his tryst with Echo of a still clear dewy evening, he had to assure himself that the gravest man need not be ashamed to appear taken with 'such a phenomenon, since it may become the subject of philosophical or mathematical inquiries.' The mere 'nature-lover' whose 'country' is little more than a houseless adjunct of London, whose rustics are 'yokels' and who is himself a kind of week-end migrant, may wilt a little at this reminder. And yet it is the quiet-hearted and the solitary man rather than the light and gay and facetious who more easily 'returns' to nature. A casual observer, however ardent, who habitually wears his heart on his sleeve, or at the faintest note of a decoy flits off into fantasy and rapture, is less likely to add much to our store of knowledge or of accurate observation. Yet an inquirer bereft of imagination, and without that peculiar sense of the 'fantasy' of the God who made the world, is blind in his best eye.

To be specific, there are three W. H. Hudsons present and active in his books, and they may be clumsily denominated as the field naturalist pure and simple, the human-naturalist, and the super-naturalist. As the first of these—like the Gilbert White of the tortoise, the bee-boy, and the goatsucker (or croon-owl or night-jar) that shook with its rattle the straw 'hermitage' in which he and his friends one summer evening sate drinking tea—Hudson watches, scrutinizes, plays 'I spy', and collects. He classifies and experiments. He is a child in the wilds of Nature, and by no means a dreamy child, taking notes. But whether it is the precision of his senses, of eye, ear, nose, hand, and tongue; or the ease with which he places, and bathes, so to speak, the object observed and examined, in its time, space and atmosphere; or the intimate companionableness of his solitude, that makes the reading of him, as compared with most writers of 'nature books', so peculiar a pleasure, it is impossible to say. These qualities are all of them in some degree necessary to any good book of this kind. Rather than any particular one of them being the secret leaven then, it is an elixir distilled from them all that is his own secret. And this is as difficult to analyse as the sheen of a starling's wing, or the dream of Spring upon the 'smiling face' of Winter.

When he speaks of the crystalline sparkle of a perfectly cooked potato; of the pale enamelled turquoise of an adder's belly, such as would have filled with joy and despair the heart of an old Chinese master-potter; or when he plucks rich clusters of elderberries to gratify his friend the pig; or refers casually to the grey of a jackdaw's eye, or to the cries of a heron; or retrieves the tragic fable of a squirrel from his earliest memories and adds to it a gloss out of mature experience; or as placidly and ripplingly as Coleridge's quiet-tuned brook gossips meanderingly on and on of worms and moles and wasps and sheep and foxes and moths and of the disreputable John-go-to-bed-at-noon—well, conjured up by his influence, there steals a spirit into our sophisticated minds that drinks it all in naïvely and wonderingly, and all but makes an 'actual' memory of it. It is then, in a momentary exaltation, that we are tempted to claim to be among the elect who (if not with the microscopical intensity of a

Henri Fabre) are 'accustomed to watch insects closely and note their little acts', and who therefore must be possessed of some small share of 'ladies' brains', seeing that they are 'of a finer quality than men's'.

Children, chameleonic in attention though they may be, are often thus engrossed. Our medicine-man may survey us occasionally with some little attention; the novelist keeps a wary, divining, analytic eye on his fellows; the poet, like Patmore, focuses his gaze perhaps some few inches *beyond* the regarded face; the psychologist is an expert in reactions; the priest is a student of the soul. But how rarely is *any* such student of *humanity* even comparable to a Fabre; how rarely is even the confirmed and incorrigible introvert a Hudson! 'Ladies' brains' are notoriously in close connivance with their owners—according, that is, to man. Their surroundings, physical, social and mental are dyed with themselves. And 'Woman of science' is still a novelty in phrases. So in part then must it be with Hudson and his fellow-devotees. The worms he dug up out of his friend's weedkiller-poisoned lawn are, as with Charles Darwin, red-hot poker in hand, or bassoon at lip, in an odd fashion *his* worms only. The toad, clearly of the same lineage as Gilbert White's, which he watched one day come shambling and panting down the hot stony dusty lane towards the peace, perfect peace, of the pool at its foot, is a toad unique and unprecedented. When he tells us of a pet lamb on the far-away and long-ago farm of his childhood that was wont to sleep and hunt and roister with its eight dogs, or of that adult sheep, also of Patagonia, that would devour tobacco and even books with a gusto shared only by the anatomist of melancholy and the historian of decadent Rome, even although his lamb may be of the species beloved of 'Mary', and his sheep as precisely similar to any other specimen of its species now abroad on the outskirts of Kensington Gardens as trotter is to trotter, yet both of them are as exclusively Hudson's sheep and Hudson's lamb as Alice's sage old bespectacled ewe with her knitting needles in the all-sorts shop was Lewis Carroll's. Even as eventual mutton their flavour, we fancy, would still have been his own. The objects and experiences, that is, which were common in his workaday life as a field-naturalist, however ordinary they may be in themselves (and any lucky anybody's for the asking), are almost always touched with the idiosyncratic. When these experiences, while still of the detective order, are strange and *un*common, he not only conveys them with an easy exactitude, he also dramatizes them. We are in his mind as we read, just as we are in the mind of Jessica sighing her love-reverie, 'In such a night . . .'

In what follows, his tiny dazzling humming bird lives for us as if we ourselves had thridded its native thickets, or as if we had discovered it at liberty in the cage of a poem. Moreover, we survey Hudson's face through *its* eyes:

'I have had one dart at me, invisible owing to the extreme swiftness of its flight, to become visible—to materialize, as it were—only when it suddenly arrested its flight within a few inches of my face, to remain there suspended motionless like a hover-fly on misty wings that produced a loud humming sound; and when thus suspended, it has turned its body to the right, then to the left, then completely round as if to exhibit its beauty—its brilliant scale-like feathers changing their colours in the sunlight as it turned. Then, in a few seconds, its curiosity gratified, it has darted away, barely visible as a faint dark line in the air, and vanished perhaps into the intricate branches of some tree, a black acacia perhaps, bristling with long needle-sharp thorns.'

Again and again he repeats this achievement. As when, in describing the marvellous sixth sense of the bat, he stands, check cap on head, in a sunken lane at evening whirling his light cane around and above his head, while to and fro the flittermice veer and waver, and, in their hawking swoop into and *through* its scarcely-visible rotations, untouched, unscathed, unstartled! Or, again, as when the wife of 'a gentleman in a southern county', with a 'taste for adders and death's-head moths', emptied over him out of her cardboard box 'such as milliners and dressmakers use . . . a shower of living, shivering, fluttering, squeaking or creaking death's-head moths'. 'In a moment,' he says, 'they were all over me, from my head right down to my feet . . . so that I had a bath and feast of them.' Here again, for an instant, we seem to have pierced behind the veil of an alien life; the mere words momentarily illumine it, as may the flame of a singularly clear candle the objects in a dark and beautiful room.

The biographer of Charles Waterton, one of the most original and lovable of our host of English 'characters',*

* 'On the top floor of the house, in the opposite direction to the organ gallery, was the chapel, and a small room which was at once Waterton's study, bird-stuffing workshop, and bed-room, if bed-room it could be called even when there was not any bed. The Wanderer always slept on the boards, wrapped up in a blanket. His pillow was a block of oak, which had been originally rough, and in course of years had become almost polished by use. The entire room revealed at a glance the simple tastes of its occupant. Some prints on the walls, some shelves contained his favourite books, his jug and basin stood on a chair, and he had a little round looking-glass and a table. Over the mantel-piece was an old map of Guiana, a record to him of living scenes and loving memories. For mere ornament's sake, there was nothing. To the sleeping eye all rooms are equally blank. . . .

'His way of life (and he lived to be 83) was primitive. He got up at three, lit his fire, and lay down upon the floor again for half an hour, which he called a half hour of luxury. He had shaved and dressed by four, and from four to five he was upon his knees in the chapel. On his return to his room, he read a chapter in a Spanish life of Saint Francis Xavier, which concluded his early devotions, and he began the secular work of the day with a chapter of Don Quixote in the original. He next wrote letters, or carried on bird-stuffing, till Sir Thomas More's clock struck eight, when, punctual to the moment, the household at Walton sat down to breakfast. His was frugal, and usually consisted of dry toast, watercress, and a cup of weak tea. Breakfast ended, he went out till noon, superintending his farm, mending fences, or speaks of 'the light which sparkles on his pages'. Light, as a matter of fact, is the sovereign grace of every book which has a human imagination in its keeping. It could not be otherwise. The imagination lives on light, as, in the old belief, the bird-of-paradise lived on air and dew. Since light alone not only reveals colour but is an essential element in life itself (and even bodily sleep in a chinkless darkness is frequently *lit* by dreams), no disciple of life can keep its influence out of the words he uses. There are radiant, luminous, scintillating; twilit, gloomy and dark books. Some are of a Stygian darkness, having emanated from darkened minds. A few are written as if in the fabulous gloaming of a moon in her eclipse, and some shed the phosphorescence of decay.

So lucid, lucent, clear and wasteless, so wholly in the service of what it joys in and conveys, is the finer style of such writers as Hudson, Gilbert White, Charles Waterton, Izaac Walton, Edward Thomas (and particularly in his poems), that we may fail to recognise it as a style at all. It partakes not only of the writer himself but of the very objects whose qualities and whose beauties have been transfigured in his mind. It appears as little like a slowly attained acquisition as the pigments of a chaffinch or a sun-beetle or the grace with which a harebell grows. It is then no particular faculty of the intellect that is called upon in reading them—however unusual and acute an intellect may have aided in their making—but our purest senses and a self-

clipping hedges. If the weather was cold he would light a fire in the fields. From noon to dinner, which was at half-past one, he would sit indoors and read or think. Dryden, *Chevy Chase*, Dyer's *Grongar Hill*, *Tristram Shandy*, *The Sentimental Journey*, Goldsmith, White's *Natural History of Selbourne*, and Washington Irving, were his favourite English literature, and what he liked, he read many times over. After dinner he walked in the park, and came in a little before six to tea. He retired early to bed, but if the conversation was interesting he would stay till near ten. He rose at midnight to spend a few minutes in the chapel, and then went back to his wooden bed, and oaken pillow.'

escape for the while from the network of human and social circumstance. The highbrow may smile at one's childish enthusiasm for such books; it is one of his few chances to smile at all. The earnest raise inquisitory eyebrows, and the sophisticated scoff. There are more important and edifying things; more gregarious, social, sociable, civilized, profitable, genteel, smart, witty doings in our personal affairs, both temporal and eternal, than quietly sharing the company of a moth, a robin, a long-tailed tit, an ant, a tortoise, or a toad, even if they are being divined only through words.

But even although our fellow humans possess souls, not always conspicuous, and minds, not invariably attractive, and tongues, at times tedious, they too are only dressed-up mammalia; their habits are familiar. And there is a first nature in us that is not only invoked by the presence of a mountain, but also, it may be, by that of a harvest mouse.

On opening any such book, it is as if out of the heat and dust and noise and shallow fluster of everyday life we had entered into the coolness and quiet of some solitary building, of an age so extreme that it has acquired a natural and living state and beauty; for here every coloured creature, bird, beast, butterfly, leaf and flower and creeping thing in the painted windows, in the capitals, in arch and mullion, niche and corbel, although it be only representative, is alive. The sun streams in; we are alone; but alone in a marvellous small paradise as was the First Man before Eve was taken out of his side. Nor, when we are in serene contemplation of any object, animate or inanimate, are we in that company only. Nor, however simple and common a thing it may be, are its effects and influences on mind and being necessarily rudimentary. That depends on the mind and the being. Monsieur Paul Valéry concludes a profound and fascinating essay entitled 'L'Homme et la Coquille' in *Les Merveilles de la Mer* with these words:

'Je vais rejeter ma trouvaille, comme on rejette une

cigarette consumée. Cette coquille m'a *servi*, excitant tour à tour ce que je suis, ce que je sais, ce que j'ignore. . . . Comme Hamlet ramassant dans la terre grasse un crâne, et l'approchant de sa face vivante, se mire affreusement en quelque manière, et entre dans une méditation sans issue que borne de toutes parts un cercle de stupeur, ainsi, sous le regard humain, ce petit corps calcaire creux et spiral appelle autour de soi quantité de pensées, dont aucune ne s'achève. . .

As with Hudson's moths and birds and adders, so with his fine fawn odd-coloured-eyed horse, Cristiano. This horse was haunted by memories of the wild, and at wail of a plover would start, snort, and stand at gaze, as if mocked by an illusion. His neigh echoingly evokes some remote vestige of ancient memories darkly interred within ourselves, although only Cunninghame Graham, of all our literary acquaintance, could have bitted and mounted him as to the manner born. Cristiano, that is, is tinged not only with the human but with the praeter-human.

So, as if to square the account, Hudson, as *human*-naturalist, touches the people he meets and talks to with his Nature. In the same degree as Cristiano seems to be a somewhat more than normal horse, his human-kind appear to be different from normal humanity; his own father, for instance—master of the potato; the dignified little native girl who, unaccustomed to fine manners and that tuber, put it into her tea; the wife of the old friend already referred to who decanted the death's-head moths; the sisters who cooked the heron; the blind man in Kensington Gardens; and last, Mr. Redburn, the retired bank manager, who took twelve months to discover that his caged thrush—an inimitable mimic—would preen itself the sprucer if cosseted with a daily worm or two, and thereupon became a rook observer, and whose jackdaw, being given its freedom, found a mate, only to perish with her in their tree-top by a celestial stroke of lightning. Of all the English poets perhaps, and Hudson was a poet who merely preferred to express himself in prose, Mr. W. H. Davies is likeliest to confer on those worthy of him a similar fascination. He dyes his objects with himself:

> . . . *It seemed as though I had surprised*
> *And trespassed in a golden world*
> *That should have passed while men still slept!*
> *The joyful birds, the ship of gold,*
> *The horses, kine and sheep did seem*
> *As they would vanish for a dream.*

And, nearer the margin yet:

> . . . *This man had seen the wind blow up a mermaid's hair*
> *Which, like a golden serpent reared and stretched*
> *To feel the air away beyond her head. . . .*

There is nothing, it may be, peculiar about Mr. Redburn except his extraordinary ordinariness; and yet, somehow, he seems to be the heaven-sent nucleus for a detective story by G. K. Chesterton. Hudson confesses, indeed, 'to a De Quincey-like craving to know everything about the life of every person I meet from its birth onwards.' That 'its' may have been an accident, but, whether or not, it is, in its context, nothing but the most delicate compliment he could pay to his fellow humans. On the other hand, his pilgrim toad, 'with yellow eyes on the summit of his head', is, needless to say, 'he' throughout 'his' journey.

And last: 'There is', says Hudson, 'a sense of the *super*-natural in all natural things. . . . We may say, in fact, that unless the soul goes out to meet what we see we do not see it; nothing do we see, not a beetle, not a blade of grass.' It is this sense, above all others, that is the sign manual of all Hudson's writings. All beauty—and in spite of the horrors of life, in spite of the fleetingness of happiness, man has made this supreme discovery—all beauty appeals to our delight in mystery and wonder. Whereas with Fabre we are conscious of a faintly sardonic satisfaction in such phenomena, in Hudson's youth the discovery of the paralysed living larder of the wasp grubs tormented him with the question, How reconcile facts such as these with the idea of a beneficent Being who designed it all? And his Abel, in *Green Mansions*, in his misery cursed God. When, abandoned to a dreadful solitude, he kills the serpent, he dreams in his fantasy that its 'icy-cold, human-like, fiend-like eyes' will for ever haunt him. 'Murderer! murderer! they would say . . . we two were together, alone and apart—you and I, murderer! you and I, murderer!' Then light falls on the body, revealing a lovely play of prismatic colours, and he muses that thus Nature loves all her children, and gives to every one of them beauty little or much, and he comforts himself with the assurance that Rima loved him. What Ariel is, not only to *The Tempest* but in all the Plays, so is the strange, half-earthly, demi-human Rima—'a thing divine, for nothing natural I ever saw so noble'—in all Hudson's writings. And in no chapter in *The Book of a Naturalist* dwells her influence so strangely and magically as on the four concerned with the serpent.

Its manner of progression, the marvellous cryptogrammic patterns of its skin, its fabulous history, its venom, its flickering forked tongue and its enchantments are considered with that closeness of attention and brooding which this observer in a varying degree expended on every other living creature.* Nothing to him in Nature was common, nothing

* Every species [says Charles Waterton] in the great family of animated nature is perfect in its own way, and most admirably adapted to the sphere of life in which an all-ruling Providence has ordered it to move. Could we divest ourselves of the fear which we have of the serpent, and forget for a while the dislike which we invariably show to the toad, both these animals would appear beautiful in our eyes; for, to say nothing of the brilliant colours which adorn the snake, there is wonderful grace and

was unclean except the evil aberrations of mankind. But there haunts here also a peculiar intensity, as if a profoundly concealed innate voice of memory, rather than a novel earthly experience, were struggling to express a secret knowledge. It may seem strange to us that the hoary foe and tempter of Eve, the Serpent, should be thus befriended. But it is the music of the voice of Rima which clear as vibrant glass resounds in this prose, and it is her presence that confronts us at every turn with the conviction of the supernatural. The old Adam, the happy prehistoric child, in every one of us, in response to this incantation harks back in spirit to the garden of his banishment; wherein the divine awaits him, and he can be once more happy and at peace, the veil withdrawn, all old enmities forgiven and forgotten, amid its natural and praeternatural wonders, its abounding life. There is nothing on earth or in Nature that with the voice of Rima will not thus confide its prehistoric call-note to him that hath ears to hear, nothing—no dewfall-hawk or furtive hedgehog, no 'dare-gale skylark', no 'toning of a tear', no 'rope of sand which petty thoughts have made', no 'loaf of bread', nor even so forlorn and so ludicrously un-magical a thing as Hardy's 'last chrysanthemum':

I talk as if the thing were born
With sense to work its mind;
Yet it is but one mask of many worn
By the Great Face behind.

elegance in the gliding progress wherein this reptile's symmetry appears to such great advantage. The supposed horribly fascinating power, said to be possessed by the serpent, through the medium of the eye, has no foundation in truth. We give the snake credit for fixing his eye upon us, when in fact he can do no such thing; for his eye only moves with his body, and . . . the toad, that poor, despised, and harmless reptile, is admirable in its proportions, and has an eye of such transcendent beauty, that when I find one, I place it on my hand, to view it more minutely.

The Thousand and One

Literature, like most things mortal, has survived many mischances—worm and wear, fire and rapine, Censor and Index, Dry-as-Dusts and Commentators, and, not least, the handicap decreed by Babel. One such little mishap is that *The Thousand and One Nights* did not arrive in England well over a century before Antoine Galland's French rendering of the Tales, in twelve crowded volumes—however faulty it may have been. They thus eluded the supreme translators—North, Florio, Philemon Holland, Urquhart and Adlington. And one may just faintly conceive the kind of dramatic companion-piece which the author of the *Venus and Adonis*, of *Twelfth Night* and *The Tempest* might have woven on these threads if any such lavish material as this had happened to come his way. Imagine, indeed, the incredulous delight of some ardent bookworm rummaging in a remote old dark and derelict bookshop and lighting suddenly upon this unique folio; warped, battered, mustily aromatic, with greened copper clasps, a prefatory chart, a little scribbling in the wide margins of egregious notes by fingers now long at rest which need no specification, and with, say, 'S.T.C. from C.L.' scrawled in the left top corner of the title-page. No narrow selection of course can possibly be representative enough; certainly not one of those annual *editions-de-luxe* which contain a dozen or so sumptuous pictures for the enjoyment of 'artistic' aunts and uncles, and a few literary bones for the picking of their nieces and nephews. In some cautious minds it may seem more than doubtful if even that is a really 'nice present for little boys'.

But this is precisely what Burton scornfully asserted the Tales had sunk into being, when he wrote the preface to his own translation. The Arabian elect, it is said, scorn this unclean, unpolished and far too popular classic. It is too loose for words; and reputable literature should edify rather than entertain. Burton contrariwise chafed at the bowdlerized degradation to 'a mere fairy-book' of a work of 'the highest anthropological and ethnographical interest and importance'. And yet, when he recounted the Tales under the effulgent stars of the desert to an entranced Arab audience assembled around his camp-fire, the Sheikhs squatting with outspread skirts, the women and children motionless in the wavering shadows, and all as greedy as nightingales for roses over the succulent repast, and when, again, he tried them on 'the wildlings of Somali-land', it was, surely, nothing merely 'important' but simply the fairy-book side of them that held captive both his listeners' and his own imagination.

No self-respecting editor or translator can whole-heartedly approve of a rival. He may even damn him with faint praise. Burton (after liberally borrowing from John Payne's lavish and accurate version), not only mocked at this 'amiable and devoted Arabist' for pandering to 'a most immodest modern modesty'—arguing with closer truth than logic that what scandalizes us now 'would have been a tame joke *tempore Elisæ*', and that therefore there was nothing to object to in 'the childish crudities and nursery indecencies' of his original. He also censured him for his anglicized Latin, his sesquipedalian and un-English words, and for the stiff and stilted style of half a century ago (1840), 'when our prose was perhaps* the worst in Europe.' None the less, the mere

* This is rather too ample a 'perhaps' if it was intended to exclude the fact that in 1840 Newman was 39; that Lamb and

amateur—who turns to the Tales not, please heaven for 'ology, edification and instruction—but for waking dream and drowsy nightmare, moonshine and delectation, and who is indifferent which or how many of them came from Persia, India, or Arabia, or what precise century finally dished them up—may for once in a way bless the name of Dr. Thomas Bowdler. There is a midden in every farmyard, and it is wholesome enough, but it need not be located under the parlour window. Little indeed of the invaluable essence of the Tales is absent from the text of an edition by the Rev. George Fyler Townsend, even although he so purified it 'that the most innocently-minded maiden may read them aloud to her brothers and sisters without scruple or compunction'—regardless, it seems, of what quite young listeners (who after all, as Freud insists, are born whole) can faintly over-hear and vaguely fathom between the lines.

Burton's exploration of the crudities and indecencies, 'curious' enough, rapidly exceed appetite, and his uncompromising notes become a tedious distraction. In large doses they have an effect similar to that of a midnight séance with the Newgate Calendar and a bottle of grocer's port, and resemble a diet of treacle fortified with some nameless Eastern drug, but sweetened less with the 'perfumes of Arabia' than with civet and patchouli.

As to style, there is a tinge of ye Olde Tea Shoppe in *quoth* and *lief* and *snarked* and *my bonny man.* 'A large gugglet' is not racier English than 'a great jug'. And Sindbad the *Seaman* has more than unfamiliarity against it. Lane can be wooden and wordy, a very different thing from the ornate and unctuous verbosity of his original. But a comparison of the two translations is by no means always to

Hazlitt were but a few years dead; that Dickens had just finished *Nicholas Nickleby* and Macaulay had begun his *History of England*; and that in 1843 the first volume of *Modern Painters* was published.

Burton's advantage; and he may be inaccurate. He revels in an assiduously assonated and alliterated 'Saxon'. 'Presently the Sailor's wife took a great fid of fish and gave it in a gobbet to the Gobbo.' Here one can hardly see the fish for the fid, and the two *gobs* fog the view of both. Any such obvious echo of euphuism is restlessly verbal compared with 'And the Sailor's wife took a large piece of fish, and crammed the humpback with it'. And how pleasingly the latter enhumps the hump! Mannerisms may be amusing in a suitable context; in a romantic story they jolt us out of the pined-for illusion. It is as if we were drowsing down and down into the desired trance (sweeter, surely, than any which even a full eighteenpenny-worth of bhang could produce) when some meddlesome or vociferous canary or tapping busybody jerks us back into sharp and vapid consciousness again.

Lane's despised latinities indeed may be curiously effective. They hang a thin but transparent veil between the imagination and the object. They become cloudy symbols and give distance and perspective to tales whose chief fascination is that they are concerned not only with the bizarre and the macabre, but with the remote. Through them we peer out on Bagdad and Samarcand, the Island of Ebony and the dominions of King Gaiour, much as a small boy gazes through the softly distorting glass of a peepshow or the coloured panes of an old-fashioned conservatory. He has been rapt into another world, far, far away. And he has the Princess of China's talisman in his pocket. The spell is enhanced by the device of the tangled network of tale interwoven within tale. Wonder leads on to wonder, and every guest at every feast, whatever or whoever he be, is the hero or victim of an extortionate adventure. And, noblest or meanest, his is always the gift of the gab.

We open the book at random, and out of a moonlit haze of mystery into the market-place the lady Amina comes shopping. She is followed by the porter she has hired, a fellow (like Yorick, and such as any night-traveller of our own day might encounter, let us say, at Euston) of infinite jest. His great basket is laden with as many enticements for eye and palate (including such substantialities as a jar of excellent wine and five-and-twenty pounds of the finest meat) as there are causes of love-melancholy in Burton. The gate of ivory, opened by Safie, closes behind them. And behold, on a dais in a fountained court of de Quincey-like magnificence, sits the equally peerless Zobeide. The three one-eyed Calenders enter, followed by Haroun-al-Raschid, his grand Vizier and the chief of his household, in their nocturnal disguise. The two black dogs are barbarously beaten with rods, their tears and lamentations are kissed away, the porter, egged on by his betters, addresses but one intrusive little question to the fair ladies, and presto, all but a round dozen of narratives, opening out like incense-breathing water-lilies on some moon-haunted swamp, break one after another into full bloom under our very noses.

Again and again, the very acme of a violent end is postponed for a renewed excursion, and even the Afrite of the coloured fishes, tricked back into his jar, spins thence a yarn. One thing only, as we wander on into these 'tales prodigious and stories extraordinary', does not concern us—whether they are faithful to any conceivable kind of mortal existence, and more especially to that petty and pedestrian variety, whether spent in Peckham or Peking, in Venice or Van Diemen's Land, which is bounded by seven ageing senses and seven and seventy second-hand conventions. It is into a blissful Unreality that Scheherazade allures us, the very materialism of which is more ethereal and hypnotic than our hopes of heaven. Here nothing is usual but the singular and strange. Here stray our viewless enraptured astral bodies amid delights and dangers under the shock and stress of which the mere gross corpus of us would perish in an hour. Just as—dark drawing on to bed-time—the little innocent at his mother's knee greedily whispers, 'Another!', just as these Thousand and One kept Shahriar from his itch to slay and Scheherazade from the risk of slaughter, so, in the words of the mighty, we conjure the garrulous Barber—'Crack our ears with thy ridiculous stories, and continue to us thy disclosure of vices and misdeeds.' We, too, plead for 'nice particulars' and implore him 'to employ exuberance of diction' in his 'relation of these pleasant tales'. For death will come at last, but not, please God, before we are weary of life, and not the mere death of 'casket', hearse and undertaker, but Death, eloquent and mighty, 'the terminator of delights and the separator of companions, the devastator of palaces and houses, and the replenisher of graves.'

'Nice particulars'—they are of the very essence of these Nights, sorcerous, exuberant and otiose. No subtle but possibly tedious analyses of conduct, no fine shades of psychology, or ethical spellicans are here, only the raw crises of mortal existence in their primary colours, and these intensified as if with the aid of the drug from which the word assassin is derived. 'None is accursed', said the sage, 'but he who has a man suspended in his shop.' And this, incidentally, is the borrowed hairspring, not only of 'The Rajah's Diamond', not excluding the young man with the cream tarts, but also of *The Wrong Box*. No man, contrariwise, is truly blessed but he who has stowed away on a dusty shelf some genie's tarnished lamp, or sleeps with a leaden facsimile of King Solomon's Seal under his pillow. Excess, we learn at length, is the secret of felicity, as an implicit trust in fate (of the giddiest alternations) is the reliever of all responsibility. 'So I ate until I was satiated . . . and my soul became at ease.' And as we eat, our eyes dazzle with beauty and magnificence, our hearts melt in us like snow for foreboding and terror. 'I was in his hand, like a little mouthful.' 'I was in the predicament of the mad.'

We may keep our modest and faithful tryst with Henry James, may treasure our Miss Austen; but in books, more frequently than in life, there is a potent rum punch for the asking as well as Château Lafite and Förster Jesuitgarten. All that is necessary when we return to feast once more on these old tales is to enjoy what we expect; with the assurance that however familiar they may have become, they invariably excel the expected when they are ours again. And only in reading do we retrieve their full bouquet. No more than a vision of the night can we fully recall merely in memory these gardens of enchantment ablaze with exotics and bejewelled with magic fruits. Fruits, indeed! Nay, apple-size precious stones—ruby, diamond, emerald, sapphire—heaped up in golden dishes in mockery and cajolery of the sun.

The winner of the first prize in the Calcutta or Irish Sweepstake is unlikely, it seems, to achieve what he hopes for from his money; in consequence he may take to drink, though not that of the Château Lafite. He might much more wisely take to the Thousand and One. In these the inexhaustible spoils of a genie enslaved by ring or lamp never seem to humiliate or debase even the most commonplace of human souls, not even the good-for-nothing Aladdin, whom a wholly unmerited prosperity so rapidly self-educated. It is no less odd and welcome that all this worldly pomp, splendour, egregious wealth and munificence fail to evoke a single gasp of envy, hatred or uncharitableness in our listening and enchanted hearts; whereas in talkie or shocker our hero has only to push through the rotatory doors of some vulgar and pinchbeck Grand Hotel in order to persuade us to turn communist in a trice.* There is, it is

* Few of us indulge in the sort of conscious life depicted in so many Russian novels—that perpetual inward simmering of emotion, pining, regret, remorse, disillusionment, rapture and

true, one kind of egregiousness which Hollywood film and Arabian tale have in common. In both our hero and heroine do not merely fall in love. They crash. The infatuation is mutual and instantaneous. After their first somewhat protracted kiss, however, our film stars usually bethink themselves of the Censor. In the Tales there is a shameless strain of the exotic. Still Eros is by no means the only moral arbiter. We recall Aladdin's sword, and many a guileless Daphnis-and-Chloe-like episode. Besides, as Larousse bids his compatriots pronounce the phrase, here is *häī läīf*; and 'high' has two significations. We are in Cairo or Bagdad or thereabouts; we may mark, without pausing to digest, a thousand allurements, and may escape into the morning fancy-free.

despair. Fewer yet of us could long endure (if merely for lack of nervous stamina), even one of the less exotic and extreme existences depicted in the Tales. Dagoes, gangsters, Mr. Damon Runyon's elect—well, they survive much, for a season. But by comparison with the frequenters of the Nights they resemble galvanised effigies of an indifferent concrete in the glare and shadows of an arc lamp. Compare again the sawn-off shotgun and the electric chair with the nursery simplicity of the bastinado, the exquisite gentility of the silken cord.

Atmosphere, even in a Wilkie Collins novel, is a rarefied and colourless medium by comparison with that which dyes these pages from far Arabia. And Nature concurs. The rivers are deeper and darker; the constellations are more vibrant and menacing, the gazelle-like enchantresses are suffused with a seductiveness alien to anything virgin in Anglo-Saxon. 'Poor Susan', a daisy, a sidesman, Bill Sykes—can one even imagine a single member of this little English quartette intruding on the insomnia of Shahriar? One might as well sip tea from a punch bowl.

Flight for momentary refuge from this present vale of tears and blood is dismissed in the current jargon as escapism, although compared with this year of grace the remote and sullen prison on Dartmoor is a cage with the door left open. And our East, in spite of Rudyard Kipling, is pretty much in the same dismal case as our West. However, so long as we promise ourselves quite faithfully to return again (as do other ghosts), at the stroke of midnight to our natural haunts, in *this* East is a never-failing and transitory refuge—with horrors all its own.

Meanwhile Night—a darkness eastern and wild with stars—has us in her keeping. To taste of these enchantments we need scan only a few titles: 'The Story of Prince Ahmed and the Fairy Pari Banou,' 'The History of Camaralzaman, Prince of the Isle of the Children of Khaledan, and of Badoura Princess of China,' 'The History of Ganem, Son to Abou Ayoub, and known by the surname of Love's Slave.' One chance-seen word even may suffice—talisman, vizier, hummun, alabaster, bezesteen, Zemzem water, the Huma bird, sherif. And how sweetly money talks! Indeed, merely a glance at the best barber in Bagdad is all we need—the barber who, on his own confession, is an experienced physician, a profound chemist, an infallible astrologer, a finished grammarian, a subtle logician—an Oriental Leonardo da Vinci in a word. A spell has fallen upon us. A damsel with a dulcimer is approaching; and yet another Old Man of the Sea, whose elder brother betook himself centuries ago to the mountains, is lurking near. In a moment or two the mood coagulates: 'In this tower was a well, which served in the daytime for a retreat to a certain fairy named Maimoune, daughter of Damriat, king or head of a legion of genies. It was about midnight when Maimoune sprang lightly to the mouth of the well, to wander about the world after her wonted custom.' Maimoune: is *this* the not quite impossible She, playmate of Ariel, handmaid of Psyche, kith of the Sirens, who was frequenting the well springs of our earthly souls before even we were weaned? We stir uneasily in our chair, and glance up from the printed page at our neglected Bradshaw. Whither would *we* wander?

The air is saturated with light and colour—sun, moon, enormous stars. It is dense with the odour of myrtle, jasmine and musk. We swoon with joy—or agony. A giddy exultation whirls us round, but its grip is precarious. We are faint and cadaverous with a futile infatuation to-day; livid and spectral with despair and the certainty of a quick end to-morrow. Contrast is neither less sharp nor radical than that between the happy chance which conveyed Badoura in the arms of the genie to Camaralzaman and the fatality which consigned to the river 'a damsel like molten silver, killed, and cut in pieces'. *Ars longa, vita brevis est*: brief indeed, unless you make full and even improvident use of it.

Distance fairly squanders its enchantment upon us—no mere silly snatch-as-snatch-can distance meted out by telegraph poles and tins of petrol, but to be measured by lunar months of calamitous seafaring or leagues on leagues of sand awaiting a simoom. And although Damascus is next door, that next door may conceal a Princess conversant with 170 modes of enchantment, whose insidious intention in beguiling us to her arms is to fatten us up for the horrific feasts of the Magians. Zobeide may be incredible kindness itself to-day, but, as likely as not, before to-morrow breaks she will have sacrificed not merely our thumbs but our great toes also on the altar of nice table manners. We wiped our garlicked fingers, but failed to wash them. And henceforth forty ablutions with alkali, forty more with its ashes, and a further forty with sandalwood soap can alone suffice to cleanse them. But whatever our rank, class, creed or culture, we shall continue to converse with a perfect urbanity—even after an even bleaker atrocity, that might well have brought tears to the eyes of a Grand Inquisitor.

And who would plead for cold justice in such an environment or for the tepid dews of mercy? 'Mahomet is God's Apostle', and inscrutable are 'the requisitions of Allah'. Extremes adjust the balance.

The Barber's Fourth Brother is beaten almost to a jelly for so venial a folly as having been duped with bad money; the corpse of the Hunchback is reiteratedly re-murdered for no graver misdemeanour than the possession of a hump; while Sindbad the Porter is rewarded with 100 gold pieces per voyage for merely letting his namesake have his will. It is the most unsullied of inhumanities—this of King, Caliph, and Cadi. 'Whoever desireth to amuse himself by seeing the crucifixion of Geifar El-Barmekel . . . let him come forth!' How felt the monarch when he was told that the head of his deliverer from leprosy would speak when it was cut off?—'He shook with delight.' With a like admirable aplomb, Emily replied to Mr. Fairchild when he asked her if she had ever seen a man hanged: 'No, papa, but I would dearly love to.' The sole immutable drawback, indeed, and peculiar to a dead man, even in the Nights, is that *he* alone can tell no tales.

Moreover whatever the learned and sedate detractors of the Tales may maintain, the intention of one of the most selfless and impersonal of the world's story-tellers is a truly moral one. 'The lives of former generations are a lesson to posterity. . . . Be admonished!' Many are the virtues and frailties she exemplifies for reward or correction. On the one hand, courage, prudence, resourcefulness, a head bloody (or even off) but unbowed. Inquisitiveness, loquacity, profanity, the desire for more wives than four, on the other. 'Thou liest, O most ill-omened of mamelukes,' rails his judge, but it is rather the ill-ominousness than the lie which the damsel avenges on Bahadar. 'May God', said I, 'show no mercy to my father for knowing such a man as thou!' The Barber laughed. He was more pious than filial. An unquestioning docility couched in the politest of phrases is the all in all. Even Sindbad was only temporarily 'incorrigible'.

We shall never know, however, whether the insatiable Shahriar at last came to wonder whether his Queen Scheherazade's 'recitations'—'how excellent! and how pretty! and how pleasant! and how sweet!'—were after all only a sort of Caudle curtain lectures in a ravishing disguise. Her voice alone surely must have rivalled the nightingale's, and the motions of her lips and hands the unfolding of the flowers of the lotus. Oddly enough, few Selections of the Tales consent to tell the reader of her reward. It is an eloquent proof of her enterprise, her endurance, and her charms that, during the thousand and one nights (and days) of her reiterated ordeal, she endowed this much-married and hideously disillusioned monarch with three children. What befell them—heirs, or heiresses of her Realm of the Fabulous is now perhaps beyond recovery. Nor is there any Maimoune to help. The two bloods must have made a strange intermingling; and only an artist of the true and ancient Persian tradition could have depicted that rare beauty, dark and still; those eyes like crystal windows looking out on the stars and mysteries of an Eastern summer night. Not that the genie of the tales might not have decreed an unexpected fate for them. Indeed the best and brightest of the three seems to have become a wanderer in the world. Having turned West, he then set out North, for the cold, mountainous and snowy solitudes of Lapland. It thus comes to pass that winter on to winter, Santa Claus never fails to pile up his sled with great bales containing countless copies of the least disreputable and the most romantic masterpieces of that 'matchless raconteuse'. That anything so many centuries old and so lusciously Oriental should have become the literary negus of every English nursery is a destiny strange indeed. That, also, the intoxication may be transitory is suggested by the faces of one's fellow occupants of any First Class railway carriage. In later life literary cocoa of course is more nutritious.

But once. . . . Well, well over fifty years ago, three children, two brothers and a younger sister, much of an age, were presented with a lavish selection of the Tales. Strife and contention for its possession came to such a pitch at length that, in order to avoid further bloodshed, it was agreed that each of them in turn should be left at peace with it for ten minutes by the clock, and should then surrender it to the next claimant. So much for the laity; and could any writer dream of sweeter tribute?

What influence this sweet and heady decoction had on the imaginations of such writers as Poe, Beddoes, Beckford, de Quincey may or may not have been confessed. On Coleridge, according to his own account, it was for the time being at least disastrous. He was about six or seven years old, he tells us, when he secretly admitted himself to these Entertainments. The tale of the man who was compelled to go about the world seeking for a pure virgin 'made so deep an impression on me (I had read it in the evening while my mother was mending stockings), that I was haunted by spectres, whenever I was in the dark: and I distinctly remember the anxious and fearful eagerness with which I used to watch the window in which' the book lay. As soon as the sun shone upon it, he would seize it, 'carry it by the wall, and bask and read.' Having discovered this small addict in the act, his outraged father burned the book. But it was too late. Samuel had already become a '*dreamer*'. From this state it was but a step to that of a slothful solitary, hated and despised by other boys, and equally contemptuous of them. Possessed of 'a memory and understanding forced into almost an unnatural ripeness', he thus became the victim of an inordinate vanity, and at length, at eight, '*a character*'! How far this rapid descent along the road to ruin can be attributed to his infatuation for the pure virgin and how far to a mind precociously capable of it, is a tantalizing question. Here was unique tinder, there the baleful spark. But even tinder needs fanning into a flame.

The naive and ingenious Chinaman who in the innocence of his heart invented gunpowder may very well have intended it as a pretty toy for children. And such it is, as every Guy Fawkes' Day proclaims. This cannot have been the case with the Thousand and One. They can never have been intended as fare for the young. Moreover even for the fully adult Westerner the fascination they distil of the remote and the bizarre must to a large degree be denied to their readers in the East, for whom every breeze is laden with the spices, and other odours, of Arabia. Our human taproots however pierce deeper than the fibres of nationality and race. In Chekhov's enchanting story, *The Steppe*, a group of peasants sit supping round their camp-fire in the silence and solitude of the night—the small boy Yegorushka in their midst. Tales, violent, far-fetched, incredible are exchanged, and Yegorushka believes every word. And the rest?

'Over their porridge they were all silent, thinking of what they had just heard. Life is terrible and marvellous, and so, however terrible a story you tell in Russia, however you embroider it with nests of robbers, long knives and such marvels, it always finds an echo of reality in the soul of the listener, and only a man who has been a good deal affected by education looks askance distrustfully, and even he will be silent. The cross by the wayside, the dark bales of wool, and the lot of the men gathered together by the camp-fire —all this was of itself so marvellous and terrible that the fantastic colours of legend and fairy-tale were pale and blended with life. . . .'

So, in their own fashion, blend the fantastic colours of the Thousand and One, legends marvellous and terrible. And if we cannot persuade ourselves that they evoke any profoundly significant reflections in the mirror of our own souls, then let us lie in wait for the Dark, their appointed habitat. We may rediscover them in our dreams.

Poetry in Prose

There are few tributes to his prose style which a scrupulous writer of the present day would accept with more caution than that it is *poetical*. Even if he were certain that the term was not intended to suggest the merely pretty, the sentimental, the fanciful, or the ornate, he might still remain a trifle dubious and uneasy. But if it can be accepted as a sincere compliment, is it a legitimate compliment? Since from the poetical it is only a step on to the poetic, and only another to poetry itself, can there, then, be such a thing as poetry in prose?

To this question the purist, the precisian would at once reply, No. He would reject the phrase as a confusion in the use of language. Since, he would maintain, the two things in question differ in form, they must also differ in content. They must therefore, if only for clear thinking's sake, be kept severely apart. But even if this is just, is it practicable?

The proper subject-matter of prose, as Wordsworth long ago declared, is Matter of Fact—of Science. Poetry is concerned with the Truths of the Imagination. On this William Blake also insisted, reserving (as for 'vegetable kingdom') his own specific meaning for the word. Cardinal Newman went farther. He refused to concede to the exposition of science even the status of 'literature'. Literature, in his view, is the personal and individual use of language. He suggested, however, no term, I think, for the kind of writing which is appropriate solely to science. It would perhaps be of little service, since there must be many shades of difference between a verbal style that is proper solely to exact science or to expository science, and that excellent use of language which is acceptable as a sound or a fine prose. Can this to any extent be true also of fine prose as compared with poetry? Is fine prose also capable of expressing the truths of the imagination? Has there always been this rigid distinction between them? 'Pherecydes of Syros', says Pliny, 'in the daies of King Cyrus, invented first the writing in prose.' Yet even here, I gather, it was the 'poetic elements' that 'seemed to have held a predominant place'. And Pherecydes was the original spirit who may also have taught his disciple Pythagoras the doctrine of the transmigration of souls.

Prose and Verse

The term prose first appeared in the English language about 1330, but was not, it seems, opposed to poetry until 1561. It was thus used about sixty years afterwards by Milton: 'Sitting here below in the cool element of prose.' He relates too that when in his youth he set himself a task in composition either in English or in another tongue, 'whether prosing or versing, but chiefly the latter, the stile by certain vital signs it had' was deemed 'likely to live'. He makes no sharp distinction between them, then. A century after that, the word took to itself a sorry helpmeet, *prosaic*, signifying drab, commonplace, dull, tame. It is now a loose convenience, covering an immense range of human intercourse—from nursery and nursemaid chatter to *The Advancement of Learning*, from schoolboy jargon to *The Decline and Fall of the Roman Empire*. Indeed the moment the word is uttered, one needs a lynxlike circumspection to avoid referring to Monsieur Jourdain: 'Par ma foi! Il y a plus de quarante ans que je dis de la prose sans que j'en susse rien.'

Since, however, nowadays they are commonly dissociated, even if the division between them is as difficult to specify with complete precision as that between instinct and intelligence, could even a literary anarchist approve the cutting away of any dam, however artificial it may be, that severs the pure mountain tarn called poetry from the vast chaotic sea of prose? Nevertheless, as Sir Philip Hartog in his Essay, *On the Relation of Poetry to Verse*, has intimated, poets and critics so diverse and authoritative as Sidney, Coleridge, Shelley, Mill, and Stevenson have been at least dubious concerning the dam.

And what of the form as distinct from the content—what of the technical differences? Here the only precise antithesis of prose is not poetry but verse—a succession of syllables, that is, forming a perceptible metre. Wordsworth accepted this, prose—verse, as the only 'strict antithesis', although he himself modifies his 'strict'. With one exception, every dictionary I have consulted defines the word prose thus negatively—as language *without* a metrical structure.* The

* Metre itself is declared to be 'any form of poetic rhythm, its kind being determined by the character and number of the feet . . . of which it consists'; or, 'the property of a verse that is divided into a determined number of metrical feet (sometimes quantitative feet), or syllabic groups'; a foot being that which consists 'of a number of syllables, one of which has the ictus or principal stress'. It is unfortunate that the term rhythmical is frequently used to mean 'metrical'. As recently as 1926 Sir Edmund Gosse, in his article on poetry in *Chambers's Encyclopaedia*, so used the word: 'Until the passion and the truth are fused into actual speech, and until that speech takes a rhythmical form, those elements may be as "poetical" as you please, but they do not form poetry.' And in an earlier sentence, 'but to the primitive conception of poetry rhythm is absolutely necessary.' There are definitions more searching and elaborate, but in the presence even of these, the emblem of the serpent with its tail in its mouth slips into the mind. Even the ictus or 'principal stress' in a foot is a term for a phenomenon that is apparently beyond final analysis. Learned and devoted experts continue to disagree, and yet the successful versifier may himself be only five or six years old! Moreover, any sequent metrical 'syllabic groups'—of iambs, trochees, dactyls and so forth—more closely resemble shoes than feet. The prosodist may call the time, whereas the

exception is *The Dialect Dictionary*. Here we are told that the romantic Highlanders once referred to people who merely talked—the despised Sassenachs, no doubt—as 'prose-folk'; and that in days gone by a blockhead in certain parts of England was known as 'prose-hash'—a phrase at whose decease no modest lecturer is likely to grieve.

On the other hand there is an abundance of prose in our superb English that is more simple, sensuous, and passionate than a large quantity of verse in the same tongue, which was, we must charitably assume, at least intended to reveal these rare characteristics. Although then, strictly speaking, poetry must be in verse, by no means everything in verse is poetry. There is indeed no reason, if the man-of-fact can manage it, why science itself—'ascertained' knowledge, that is—should not still be propounded in verse. His medium would then exhibit yet another abstruse, though perhaps only a minor, science. His information might thus far more easily be learned by rote, if not by heart. He would, too, be following the example of Lucretius, Tusser and Erasmus Darwin: even if he were tempted to let *poetry* go hang. Purely instructive rhymes too, one of the minor scourges of childhood, are not only the more easily memorizable for being in verse; they are also little less serviceable if they are wholly prosaic in kind—and none too secure even in their

writer of prose sets his own; only the Pied Piper can choose the tune for either medium and can divinely both pipe and dance.

'Au point de vue poétique', runs the definition of rhythm in *Larousse Universel*, '(dans les vers mesurés ou rhythmiques) comme au point de vue musical, le rythme est constitué par le retour, à intervalles égaux, d'un son (syllabe ou note de musique) plus fortement accentué que les autres et nommé "temps fort". Dans les vers mesurés, par exemple dans la versification française, le rythme repose sur les césures, la longueur et le nombre des différents vers employés. La prose n'est pas non plus dépourvue de rythme: il n'est pas de bon orateur ou de bon écrivain qui ne rythme sa phrase, et chez certains prosateurs, comme Chateaubriand, elle revêt presque une allure poétique.'

grammar. 'Common are to either sex, Artifex and opifex . . .' may remain a rather nebulous statement to any twelve-year-old who fails to catch the signification of 'common' and cannot conceive what connexion there can be between words and sex; but it may none the less save him from an occasional howler, and its consequences, in his prose-hash. Similarly, with 'Thirty days . . .', 'A red sky . . .', and this little dissertation on poisons, which at need may be of sovereign service.

An alkali swallowed!—to make the patient placid
For alkali corrosives give an acid.
An acid swallowed!—then reverse the matter
And give an alkali to kill the latter.
The acid antidotes in household use
Are table vinegar and lemon juice.
What alkalies there are need no revealing—
Take whitewash, chalk, or plaster from the ceiling.

In respect to its skill, variety, finish and value, mere verse may range from a doggerel, flat and empty, to one of the most lively and pregnant means of self-expression. Alert, nimble, witty, cogent, at times humorous or sentimental, occasionally touched with imagination and shot with fancy, the 'light' verse of W. S. Gilbert, for example, was treasure trove to its sister art, light music. He was a master of its craft; but little of it can be confused with what has been called pure poetry. Indeed, a substantial fraction of the 'poetical works' of some of our greater poets, and a still larger fraction of the whole corpus of English verse that is securely in print (and also by reason of the sovereign leaven contained in the lump, is safe at least from oblivion) is in a like case.

If, then, even verse flawless in technique—limerick, rondeau, sonnet, or *ballade royal* let us say—need no more guarantee the presence of poetry than a carved block of stone guarantees the presence of grace and beauty, are we entitled to declare that the difference between a good prose and any order of language which merits the description, 'poetic', may be extreme, but that it may on occasion and in effect be also so slight as to be barely perceptible? That while pure poetry is a sovereign elixir, a tincture of it may also be precious; that neither elixir nor tincture can by any arbitrary edict be restricted to verse; and that, as with all things capable of giving aesthetic pleasure, this is a question of gradation and degree?

It is a familiar and well-worn theme. But if the suggestion is no mere *cul-de-sac*, if it is neither so naïve and obvious as to need no illustration, nor so fallacious as not to warrant any, many other little problems immediately present themselves. Are these degrees of difference marked, obvious and instantaneous, or slight and gradual? Are they both in cause and in effect superficial or virtual? Are they usually the outcome of accident or of design; of effort or impulse? At what stage, if ever, does the poetic in prose, from being in the nature of a tincture, distil itself, as it were, into an essence? Does the modest inquiry to a competent writer, Shall you treat your subject in prose or in verse? imply an attack on his artistry, let alone his conscience, or merely on one's own common sense?* How far, again, can the craftsman of a sound prose venture in manner and matter in the direction of metrical poetry before he risk the charge of having mistaken his medium? And last, are there in fact writers in prose who, alike in what they say and in how they say it, as truly merit the title of poet as certain writers of verse—little in quantity, it may be, but fine in kind—who have justly been awarded this supreme tribute?

* In a preface to *Wessex Poems* Thomas Hardy explains that many of its pieces had been written long ago, and that 'in some few cases the verses were turned into prose and printed as such'. The contrary process is less unusual, I imagine.

These are questions easy to put, but difficult to answer in any fullness; and they immediately usher us into the presence of such consummate men of letters as Sir Thomas Browne, Francis Bacon, Fuller, Jeremy Taylor, Burton, Ruskin, Lamb, all of whom wrote little in verse; and of others—Jonson, Traherne, Milton, Dryden, Landor, Hardy, Doughty, Bridges, who in their several degrees achieved a highly individualized style both in verse and in prose.

Technical Ingredients

But first, what technical characteristics are to be found in good writing of any order—whether it is in verse or in prose, whether it is lyrical or dramatic, whether it is fiction, history or *belles lettres*? All literature consists solely of words in an imposed sequence. The minimum equipment required by an author—a craftsman in words—is an adequate vocabulary, a knowledge of the construction and grammar of the language he uses, and something worth saying. These secured, in all literary composition it is the perfectly rational and lucid arrangement and order of the chosen subject-matter, the attainment of a beginning, a middle and an end, that are the all but insuperable difficulties. Reading without tears is an accomplishment (and one frequently self-taught) which is within the reach even of the youngest of the young; whereas writing (an accomplishment beyond even an Aristotle to impart) without groaning and travailing—is that in any perfection practicable even to a Methuselah? Not unless the testimony of authorities so diverse as Johnson, Rousseau, Flaubert, Darwin, and Newman can be ignored.

Knowledge, memories, ideas, opinions, convictions, speculations, images, fantasies, feelings—their very superabundance may be a writer's most formidable obstacle. To one kind of mind, rational and logical composition is the most natural and least difficult. To another, the creative and imaginative, any thesis or dissertation which involves an argument and proceeds piecemeal and step by step to its conclusion may be hard labour against the grain. A story, a novel, also involves a kind of argument, theme, plan, action, but unless its nucleus, its creative cocoon, as it were, is already more or less complete in the mind, its apt sequence and elaboration are likely to prove all but impracticable. The richer and more individual a writer's mind and heart and the more impulsive his genius, so much the more arduous *may* prove to be the ordeal of communicating them in words, of spinning spider-wise out of his entrails that continuous, tenuous, elastic, vigorous thread and web into a pattern and design that shall best and most fully convey his inmost aim, motive and meaning.

An adequate craft and artistry to this end are equally indispensable in prose and in verse. Every specimen indeed of literature worthy of the name, from a nonsense rhyme 'There was an old man who said "Hush" . . .' to *A Midsummer Night's Dream* or *The Odyssey*, from the briefest of tales or essays to *The Origin of Species* or *The Golden Bowl*, has an imposed and definite structure.

But apart from using words efficiently and effectively, a good writer endeavours to use words well. And this entails attention to the arrangement of verbal sounds. If a writer have no music in his soul, his ear no doubt will be equally defective, and so in this respect will his style be. Otherwise a due heed to verbal harmony and discord is largely the outcome of a natural taste and impulse. Printed words resemble a printed melody in music. They await vocalization. And implied in their use are two sensuous activities, speech and hearing. In English these verbal sounds are numerous enough to afford an inexhaustible variety, and since each such sound either in prose or verse has not only its relative accent, stress, or emphasis, or lack of them, but also its quality, volume, and pitch—its intonation—and is affected by those of its more or less immediate neighbours, this varying harmony, or absence of harmony, is being continually built up and is only in part perishing in memorizing consciousness as we read on. And the making of these sounds may certainly be no *less* an aesthetic pleasure than is the listening to them. Indeed, whether pleasant or otherwise, their effects at least as closely concern the vocal organs as they do the ear. Both sensuous and mental, pleasurable or otherwise, they cannot be avoided. Leagues away from poetry, the most artless speech exhibits them. And although in childhood we had to learn our mother tongue—apting, as Ben Jonson says, our mouths to letters and syllables—any delight we may find in verbal melody, no less than a delight in colour or form, or for that matter in the savoury or the sweet, or even in kisses or crumpets, was ours from birth.

The term poet 'cometh' in Sidney's words, of this word *ποιεῖν*, to make: 'wherein I know not whether by luck or wisdom we English men have mett well the Greeks in calling him a maker.' And maker implies a material, a medium, a vehicle which, before the maker begins to adopt it to his purposes, is in some degree unmade, and also in some degree plastic, workable, adaptable, appropriate, and can be manipulated, dealt with to this extent in accordance with his needs; just as the pictorial artist, having chosen his subject, may render it either with pen or pencil, water-colour or oil, as an aquatint, etching, woodcut or pastel, whichever method he thinks most suitable. Our maker, however, though he needs only writing materials, or, at a pinch, sand and a finger, has ready-made ingredients, verbal units, to deal with. An abundant but not *too* copious choice is afforded him by a grammar intent in particular on English idioms, and by the great English dictionary; and he may eke out the latter with the native and lovely verbal wildflowers to be found in Dr. Joseph Wright's bountiful work on the English dialects. This tribute, 'maker', therefore, is no less the merited privilege of the craftsman in prose than of the craftsman in verse. And—fantastic ideal!—a perfected prose and a perfected verse alike are in varying degree dependent on their word-sounds for a virtual part of any pleasure they bestow. Nor surely need there be any bound to that potential pleasure in prose. In so far as it affects the sense to be conveyed it is essential to it. Otherwise it may be deemed subordinate to other aims. In fine verse at any rate this verbal accord, or 'music', has been generally regarded as indispensable.

But the effect of verbal sounds (no more than those of music) is not solely sensuous. They have and they convey 'meaning'. In this respect they are in varying degree either in or out of keeping with what they signify as symbols. They may, as we say, be good words for what they mean, or, on the contrary, bad; and no synonym, either as sound or symbol, can have precisely the same value as the word it displaces—and this quite apart from its various associations. He hit the deck; he slung his hammock; he went to bed; he retired for the night; he sought his couch; he made essay to woo sweet Hypnos—they all signify much the same thing, but how dissimilar these same things are! The kind of *speaker*, for example, suggested by each phrase in turn.*

* '. . . No one', says Andrew Bradley, 'who understands poetry, it seems to me, would dispute this, were it not that, falling away from his experience, or misled by theory, he takes the word "meaning" in a sense almost ludicrously inapplicable to poetry. People say, for instance, "steed" and "horse" have the same meaning; and in bad poetry they have, but not in poetry that *is* poetry.

> "Bring forth the horse!" The horse was brought:
> In truth he was a noble steed!

says Byron in *Mazeppa*. If the two words mean the same here, transpose them:

> "Bring forth the steed!" The steed was brought:
> In truth he was a noble horse!

In all writing, that is, whether in prose or in verse, and whether by intention or otherwise, if we both repeat and listen to the words of which it is composed, two voices are audible and two meanings are inherent—that of the verbal sounds and that of the verbal symbols. Occasionally in open conflict, though never so in poetry, usually in a more or less amiable relationship, they may also be in a ravishing concord together; and this hardly less in prose than in verse; the one clearly evident, the other remaining extremely elusive however closely we scrutinize it, and ultimately, perhaps, beyond analysis. Indeed, *fully* to explore this connexion between sound and meaning would entail not only herculean labour but also the finest sensibility, particularly if not only our own sovereign language, but others also, living or dead, were, as for this purpose they should be, within the pioneer's range of inquiry.

This implies, naturally, that at any extreme both prose and verse may be falsely or cloyingly melodious, too emphatic, too sonorous, over-sweet, and even pleasing in excess. Too much honey, too little bread. All depends on the fitting relation between the sound and the sense, and the given intention. The meaning of Swinburne's *Hesperia* (an impassioned and remorseful elegy on the theme of love

and ask again if they mean the same. Or let me take a line certainly very free from "poetic diction":

To be or not to be, that is the question.

You may say that this means the same as "What is just now occupying my attention is the comparative disadvantages of continuing to live or putting an end to myself." And for practical purposes—the purpose, for example, of a coroner—it does. But as the second version altogether misrepresents the speaker at that moment of his existence, while the first does represent him, how can they for any but a practical or logical purpose be said to have the same sense? Hamlet was well able to "unpack his heart with words", but he will not unpack it with our paraphrases. . . .' Compare, I once heard Professor Herford suggest, 'Out, out, brief candle!' with *Out, out, short candle!*

and lust) may repeatedly elude us largely on account of its otherwise masterly impetuous emphatic volume of sound. Its vehemence mutes its meaning. As Sir Philip Hartog has said of poetry in general, and his words may be applied to certain kinds of prose, it resembles an incantation, but one that lulls and bemuses a rational attention rather than, as it might, arrests and excites it.

At the other extreme, writings both in prose and verse that may be pregnant with, even if they fail to be delivered of, a meaning of great value, may be in a style so flat, insipid, cacophonous and lifeless that both ear and tongue, and even eye, are in a continual revolt against the duty of transmitting such dismal messages to the mind.

When we give delight without the sacrifice of things more precious, when we enhance the meaning and value of what we say by the charm and grace with which we are saying it —a kind of courtesy and good manners—all this surely is nothing but a gain, whether to prose or to verse. To all devices of verbal music every user of words is entitled to free access, if he can attain it. Failure in this direction is a failure in craftsmanship and art. If indeed one opens any well-written book at random—my own three examples happened to be Henry James's *Letters*, Samuel Butler's *Note-Books* and the *Apocrypha*—it will certainly be found that, within art and reason, alliteration, assonance, chiming, echo and vowel-play are all but as active in prose, though not always so noticeable, as they are in verse. Nor even in prose need positive rhymes ('gewgaw fetters', as Cobbett called them, 'invented by the monks to enslave the people') be by any means outrageous. In verse rhyme serves melody, symmetry, balance. It helps to secure in varying degree a formal pattern, stresses a pause, satisfies expectation, and draws meaning together. Since, too, a rhyming word is in part a repetition of its fellow and in part not so, it confers on its context its own small burden of unity in variety, and of variety in unity. The wings of a building may be said to rhyme, the figures of a dance, the pattern in a Persian rug; the wings of a bird, the leaves on a twig, the markings on an animal, the eyes, brows and ears of a face. In itself—and even poets have disparaged rhyme—it may appear to be a device irrational and childish. That so grave a fellow creature as William Wordsworth, who so far as he could remember had made only one 'joke' in his life, should have *rhymed* about Immortality! None the less only a deaf adder or a puritan aridified by a sense of duty could finally condemn it.

Apart from this, the obligation or choice to rhyme in verse may prove either for a sluggish or a rich mind an aid to the revival, suggestion, or discovery of images and ideas. But since on the other hand certain words in English have no rhymes, and many very few (e.g. in the preceding sentence *from*, *choice*, *either*, *sluggish*, *image*, *idea*), this may prove a hindrance to their use and to that of the words they do rhyme with. The help that rhyming may give, then, must be set against the difficulty of so persuading the suggested word, together with its *relevant* object or image or thought, into the confines of the poem as not even to hint at the process. Few technical defects in verse are more fatal than forced rhymes. They are doubly art-less. When they are forced but obviously intentional and ingenious, as in *Don Juan* and *The Pied Piper*, they are amusing. The jester is ringing his bells. In poetry of another order, *The Grammarian's Funeral* for example, they are out of place because they are out of keeping—like a buttonhole at a funeral.

The prose-writer, on the other hand, neither profits nor loses by the need to find rhymes. But although in a good prose, no regular recurrence of sound is conspicuous, or even noticeable perhaps, that too will echo and resound with assonances and modulations, chimings and rhymings which, in addition to the ease and pleasure they bestow on tongue and ear, also, like alliteration, serve a practical purpose. If they are intended as a mere ornament, they are of course nothing better than the merely ornamental. When they are subtle, apt and intrinsic, they are usually the outcome not of deliberation but of aesthetic instinct and impulse. In the act of composition the inward ear listens intently, the inward voice whispers its counsel, and consciousness obeys. They not only make pattern, design and music wherever they go, but they compact the argument, tie the context together, and enforce the sense. 'The reader who is illuminated', says Mr. H. M. Tomlinson, 'is the poem.' No precise word seems to be available to denote the enlightened reader of Mr. Tomlinson's or any other writer's imaginative *prose*. It would have to be equally complimentary.

'You shall now *see*, then,' to quote Cobbett again—this time from his grammar book for his son, 'what pretty stuff is put together and delivered to the Parliament, under the name of King's sp*ee*ches. The sp*ee*ch which I am about to examine is, ind*ee*d, a sp*ee*ch of the R*e*gent; but I might take any other of th*e*se sp*ee*ches.' This is a deliberately thin flat statement, strummed mainly on one word, in preparation for the flatness of what he is about to quote; the instruction of his little boy being for the moment less in his mind than his hatred of the Whigs.

And Sir Thomas Browne; but with how different an intention and effect—a surface serene, continuous:

'And surely it is not a melancholy conc*e*it to think that w*e* are all asl*ee*p in this world, and that the conc*e*its of this life are as mere dr*e*ams to those of the next as the phantasms of the night to the conc*e*its of the day. There is an *e*qual delusion in both, and the one doth but s*ee*m to b*e* th*e* emblem or picture of th*e* other; w*e* are somewhat more ourselves in our sl*ee*ps, and the slumber of the body s*ee*ms to b*e* but the waking of the soul.'

Lengthen *all* the *e*'s in the last fifteen words, and what havoc it causes to the delicacy of the sense!

And Matthew Arnold:

'The pursuit of perfection, then, is the pursuit of sw*ee*tness and light. H*e* who works for sw*ee*tness works in th*e* end for light also; h*e* who works for light works in th*e* end for sw*ee*tness also. But h*e* who works for sw*ee*tness and l*i*ght un*i*ted, works to make r*e*ason and the will of God prevail. . .'

Such chimings, of course, can be far less open, but by no means for that reason less effective. Sir Philip Sidney:

'Yet confess I always that as the fertilest ground must be manured, so must the highest flying wit have a *Daedalus* to guide him. That *Daedalus*, they say, both in this and in other, hath three wings to bear itself up into the air of due commendation: that is, art, imitation, and exercise.'

Apart here from the play on *i*, *e*, *u*, and *m*, and apart from the excellent truth of this statement, how *convincing* is the effect of the alliteration in its last four words. Pen obeyed idea. And again:

'Of the faculty of these pleasant flowers there is nothing set down in the ancient or later Writers, but [they] are greatly esteemed for the beautifying of our gardens, and the bosoms of the beautiful.'

Do not the delicate assonances and alliterations contrive to make one image, as it were, of the gardens and the ladies so decked—like a thread round a bunch of cowslips?

It is of course destructive of their aptness to over-emphasize or remove such verbal devices as these from their context, but here is another fragment wherein the aptness just (but only just, and how vividly, and ingenuously even) edges into euphuism: 'This undertaking happily perform'd, he re-turn'd with the night; and found Dyonysophanes at his rest; but Daphnis watching, weeping, and waiting in the Walks.'

And again; with an exquisite give and take between *ers* and *o's* and with none between the two *lays*:

'. . . And therefore it was, that great store of winter birds haunted the bush, for want (it seems) of food abroad; many blackbirds, many Thrushes, Stockdoves, and Starlings, with other birds that feed on berries. Under pretext of birding there, Daphnis came out, his Scrip furnished with Country dainties, bringing with him to persuade and affirm his meaning, snares and lime-twigs for the purpose. The place lay off about ten furlongs; and yet the Snow that lay unmelted, found him somewhat to do to passe through it. But all things are pervious to Love, even Fire, Water, and Scythian Snowes. Therefore, plodding through, he came up to the Cottage, and when he had shook the Snow from his thighs, he set his snares, and prickt his lime-twigs. Then he sate down, and thought of nothing carefully, but of Chloe and the birds. . . .'

And here, Lyly himself:

'There is in that Isle salt made, and saffron; there are great quarries of stones for building, sundry minerals of quicksilver, antimony, sulphur, black-lead, and orpiment red and yellow. Also there groweth the finest alum that is, vermilion, bittament, chrisocolla, coperus, the mineral stone whereof petroleum is made, and that which is most strange, the mineral pearl, which as they are for greatness and colour most excellent, so are they digged out of the mainland, in places far distant from the shore.'

In fine verse and in fine prose, again, melody and sense are in so close a communion that they almost defy disintegration. Compare Coleridge's: 'The marble peach feels cold and heavy, and children only put it to their mouths'; and Adlington's: 'Hee himself was of an high and comely stature, grey eyed, his haire yellow, and a beautiful personage'; with this scrap of dictation originated and set by a child only nine years old for the instruction of her sister of six: 'The snow made the downy hills look like a swan's wings, for it was Christmas time.'

That at this 'tender' age it should be possible so to woo an imaginative perception into words as to make their delicate accord the envy of ninety, hints not merely at the debt we owe Pherecydes, but that even in the matter of verbal sounds his Pythagorean doctrine was not wholly a heresy.

Every heedful and well conceived literary composition reveals in its technique a continual subtle verbal mimicry of the objects, images, states of mind and feeling which compose its progressive theme. Clumsy onomatopoeic examples are decisive enough, but fall absurdly short of the full issue. It is by means of the quality and delicacy of this mimicry, as well as of the views and sentiments he is expressing, that we become aware of the self and character of a writer—of his human status and the quality of his mind. And not the least of the achievements of which words and their arrangement may be capable are the secrets they are telling about him of which he himself may be unaware.

It is when consciousness is at an imaginative pitch and in a profound absorption over its task that a writer, whether at work on epic or essay, attains that degree of tension, impulsiveness, perception, apprehension and comprehension, which alone can bid the rock gush out its waters. This is no more likely to be the result solely of a deliberate skill than is the silent manifestation of a genuine mood or emotion—love, delight, generosity, compassion; despair, contempt, hatred. It is far less an affair of art, let alone artifice, than of the artist; and especially if a prolonged apprenticeship to his craft has made of it almost a second nature.

Figures of Speech

What then of the devices, not of language, but of thought, fancy and imagination—metaphor, comparison, simile, synecdoche, metonymy and other figures of speech, expedients much more usual even in ordinary talk than the 'tall, opaque' terms for them would suggest. Like most human blessings, the best in these are probably the unsought. Far-fetched they may be, but even these are more effective and delightful if they appear in their places as naturally as flowers in a meadow, or a smile on a human face. At their best they are evidence of a vivid and richly associated memory that has been fed and nourished on objects and experiences most worth having. 'Nature I loved, and next to Nature Art.' It is love of these, as of everything else, that weaves what they bestow into the very fabric of our minds and imaginations.

Metaphor indeed so densely throngs our daily speech, lurking like a green and tiny moss or creeping lichen in every crevice of it, that, as perhaps with simile also, the vigilant writer's pains are likely to be spent rather on keeping it within bounds than in seeking it out.

Accordant similes and other figures of speech, however, are usually assumed to be not only admirable but indispensable in verse, and as in the nature of a delicacy and indulgence in prose. Nevertheless, and anywhere, they may be not only an enlivening pleasure in themselves, a momentary release from the matter in hand, or little windows revealing a further view, but may serve also as arguments intellectual and cogent, energizing their context by means of analogy as well as example. They resemble the reunion between two charming sisters, whose very unlikenesses to one another give a livelier edge to their resemblances. We may of course prefer a prose, and for that matter a verse also, that is devoid or very sparing of these enticements—but preferences should not be exalted into axioms. It would be folly to lay down any law; since verse of the purest poetry may be all but free from these devices and a good prose liberal in the use of them.

There are, for example, only four similes in so purely poetic and so romantic a poem as *Kubla Khan*, one alone of these being conspicuous, and perhaps extrinsic in origin—that of the flail. There are only three in the first twenty stanzas of *The Rime of the Ancient Mariner*, that of the bride 'red as a rose' standing out (as indeed it should) most clearly; and there are only two in Wordsworth's *Pet Lamb*, a poem wholly simple and tender—over-simple to some tastes, and yet of how delicate a colour and atmosphere. There is only one each in Donne's *Funeral*, in Jonson's *Jealousy*, in Shelley's *The Two Spirits*, in Keats's *La Belle Dame Sans Merci*, and his *Ode to Melancholy*, and there are ten at least in Shelley's *To a Skylark*.

The prose of Donne and Jeremy Taylor on the other hand, abounds in imagery, both simple and complex. Jane Austen's is frugal in this respect, Dryden's imagery is apt as acorn is to cup, De Quincey inclines to be lavish, Dickens is copious in metaphor. Francis Bacon, again, in his essay on Fame, after citing in aid of his theme certain 'flourishes and excellent parables in the poets', suddenly recalls himself and his reader to solid earth: 'But we are being infected', he warns us, with 'the stile of the poets. To continue now in a sad and serious manner.' The infection was recurrent. In his brief and unfinished essay on Vain-Glory there are three similes in a paragraph of only nine lines. But then, as Shelley declared:

'Lord Bacon was a poet. His language has a sweet and majestic rhythm, which satisfies the sense, no less than the almost superhuman wisdom of his philosophy satisfies the intellect. . . . All the authors of revolutions in opinion are not only necessarily poets as they are inventors, nor even as their words unveil the permanent analogy of things by images which participate in the life of truth; but as their periods are harmonious and rhythmical, and contain in themselves the elements of verse; being the echo of the eternal music. . . .'

Opinions more widely conflict regarding poets and the

merits of their prose than regarding certain writers of a fine, sound, or elegant prose and the merit of their verses. Many prose writers, none the less, have borne witness to the advantage of learning in childhood to write verse. Thomas Hardy indeed declares that 'the shortest way to good prose is by the route of good verse'. Hazlitt, on the other hand, maintained that 'while the prose style of poets is sometimes good, nay excellent', it is 'never the better, and generally the worse, from the habit of writing verse'. Although he delighted in begemming his own prose with fragments of borrowed verse, he also facetiously remarked, 'The poet's Muse is like a mistress, whom we keep only while she is young and beautiful. . . . The Muse of prose is like a wife, whom we take during life *for better, for worse.*' The more positive charge is that poets are apt to remain faithful too long to a mistress who, if she is not wantonly guilty of jilting them in their youth, decides that her visits in later life (and after all the Muses themselves age never) shall be few and far between. A whole Flaubertian lifetime may be devoted to the perfecting of a means of communication that must solely in no circumstances conspicuously *scan.* Moreover—marriage-lines apart—it is possible to remain faithful, and at infinite self-sacrifice, to *two* mistresses, if, at any rate, their names are Prose and Verse. Objecting to the florid, Hazlitt preferred a written style 'such as any one would speak in common conversation who had a thorough command and choice of words, or who could discourse with ease, force, and perspicuity.' These are exacting requirements, but not so exacting as to preclude a poet's being possessed of them—Pope, let us say, Cowley, Cowper, Fitzgerald.

Metre

The sole technical feature and device, then, apart from obvious and regular rhyming, that severs verse from prose, and therefore—*if* we accept verse as the only vehicle of poetry—from poetry also, is a certain regular recurrence of rhythm, of elements of verse, in Shelley's phrase, which we call *metre.* Indeed, just as intonation may alter the intended signification of the simplest of sentences, make naïvety reveal itself as irony, and a lie as a lie, so varying and mutable rhythms, the incessant delicate *motion* of words—no less apparent, as Hazlitt implies, in good talk than in good writing—are not only a pleasure to utter and to listen to, but are part and parcel of the meaning of the words and the emotions they convey. They duplicate, so to speak, the meaning, and thus condense it, alike in space and time, and therefore in consciousness. And, apart from any other outcome, metre *manifests* rhythm. It is its primary purpose and effect.

Every metrical recurrence, indeed, by means of varying rhythms, unless it is to dull and deaden the mind, must be continually diversified. A sequence of lines all but regularly metrical is probably the easiest and clumsiest feat of which language is capable. So also a succession of rhythms in prose, which, even if they fall safely short of the metrical, too clearly resemble one another, soon becomes utterly tedious. Language suggestive of the forced and mechanical is devoid of life, feeling and impulse. A prose proceeding in a series of accents and emphases, like the clacking of a rusty chaff-cutting machine, is no less intolerable than an equally execrable verse. In either kind at their best, the rhythms, like the sounds they convey, are in a clear and serene association with their sense. Kindled, various, marked rhythms in any use of language betoken a heightening of the mind. Dead-alive rhythms confess that the fire within has fallen low. The best are those that fully and quietly accord with their creative purpose.

That, moreover, legitimate and charming *elements* of metre also abound in good prose, is beyond question. They lie half-concealed even in ordinary talk. As Dr. D. S. MacColl says, ‘Verse would be a fantastic, if not an impossible imposition upon language, if the collocations of measured feet out of which it builds its lines were not already present in habitual speech. . . . Not only “prose”, but ordinary speech, is rhythmic.’

If we listen to what we are saying—and that, at times, may be a surprising and chastening experience—we shall hear ourselves blithely echoing *Hiawatha* in such statements as: Wóuld you páss the bréad and bútter; Hé is ráther hárd of héaring; Cóme and sée me thén on Mónday. We resort to less simple elements in, Is thís the níne-fiftéen to Lóndon Brídge; in, But you sáid, Mummie déar, there was bácon for bréakfast; in, Now mînd, I wón't have any nôn-sense, Miss; and in, Í shall be láte, my déar, so dón't sit úp. Our excited or exhausted correspondence may begin: Dear Sír, I wríte re yóur demánd for táx / the dócument in blúe; It may echo the Gryphon and the Mock Turtle with, The béef you sent me yésterday was véry far from frésh; and with, I'm véry much afráid, my dear, poor Míllie has the múmps; or it may soar into, Althóugh we now líve in the cóuntry / I can gét to my óffice with éase.

We can hardly open a newspaper without encountering headings and scraps of wholly ingenuous verse, and occasionally verse of a pretty species. ‘And évery dáy new cínemas / can be séen in prócess of búilding’; ‘Fármers Demánds Refúsed; / Exténsion of Stríke Expécted’; ‘Mr.

Sámuel Sámuel Ḿ.P. / múch abóut the sáme'; 'Górdon Ríchards équals Árcher / but rídes fíve lósers.'

A single post recently brought me an election address and an American newspaper. Heart cried to heart with 'Cóme to our Méeting in the Rêst House this évening'; with 'Dón't forgét mass Méeting to-níght, Mónday Novémber 4́'; and with 'Bréaker and Fármer of Hárd Western Sóil'; 'Cásh Plus Tóil Makes Stéel / and the Móney Géts the Rewárds'; 'Wálter Duránty who wrítes Sea Tálks'; 'The Pícture Wórld of Shákespeare's Mínd'. The last was followed by the far more delicate title of the book concerned, Professor Caroline Spurgeon's *Shákespeare's Ímagery ánd What it Télls Us*. The following sentences again, pining, like the Peri, for the paradise of verse, are from a recent letter to *The Times* from Dr. Thomas Bodkin: 'The Mediaeval cathedral was a blaze of colour, inside and out. / The whole west front was washed with ochre. / The niches were painted red, green, and blue. / The statues were separately coloured. / Their crowns and jewels were touched with gold. / The tide of colour and gold rose even over the roofs.' How effective here, if a trifle monotonous, are the emphatic pauses. We look and look, and look again.

Moreover, every good prose will reveal at a heedful reading a marked tendency in its sentence and paragraph construction towards a loosely measurable sequence of a variable pattern, occupying so much time, and therefore its equivalent of sensuous and mental activity—as in a grave and ceremonious minuet. Now, the sentence will fall somewhat short of this vague standard, its pauses completing it; now, the words well over a little, but seldom so far as to overload the interval. There is a perceptible poise, balance, symmetry, proportion, in correspondence with the intermittent progress of the thought and the emotion. The metrical—both sensuous and intellectual—may lurk, then, under a fine prose like the concealed relics of ancient buildings or earthworks, perceptible to the occupant of a balloon, beneath a field of wheat. It is only the more effective for being unapparent. It is, too, in fine prose rather than in fine verse that the poet is likely to discover both novel and subtle rhythms which a little or much delicate contriving will convert into the most promising and seductive of metres. The following, found by pure chance, occur in but one paragraph, the first, in *John Inglesant*:

'*My friend, whose name was Fisher,*
in the lovely summer weather—'

which at once tempts fancy into—

caught a salmon in the Isher
with a fly made of a feather.

Again,

'*form wíde and fértile válleys*
which are watered by pleasant streams.'

And again,

'*forming long lines along the level summits.*'

In this one paragraph Shorthouse even rhymes:

'*In my last long vacation*
I accepted his invitation.'

De Quincey of course is even more enticing:

'*A music such as now | I often heard in sleep*'—

which might be the first two lines of a stanza ending with:

> '*As when Zéphyr in the bóugh*
> *Stirs mídnight dárk and déep*'.

And again:

> '*The undulations of fast-gathering tumults*'.

> '*Ínfinite cavalcádes filing óff, | and the tréad*
> *of innúmerable ârmies*';

And again:

> '*Somewhere, but I knew not where;*
> *somehow, but I knew not how*'—
> *Came a vision heavenly-fair,*
> *Brought its solace to my brow.*

Nor is prose of our own day innocent of these beguile-
ments. In a short story by Mr. Somerset Maugham entitled
Arabesque occur these:

'But rebúffs can déal more déadly blóws than dággers';

'Dárk dárk was the láne outside—and the níght an
obsídian nêt';

'They cóuld indéed forgíve him his síns, but they côuld
not forgíve him his compássions';

and less detectably:

'Cóol it is heré, she sáid, and quiêt, / but tóo dárk evén to
sée your fâce.'

'You are cóld, he whíspered, / toúching her bare néck
with tímid fíngers.'

'It is láte. / Sée how the móon her twílight shéds.'

And here is Miss Rose Macaulay, with all but a lyric in prose—and this thrown off in a debate!

> '*Thís heávenly commódity*
> *ít is a lóvely thíng.*
> *Frêedom;*
> *Leîsure;*
> *Nôbody in thís lífe was éver bóred by líberty.*'

'Good prose', says Landor—and prose, he himself declared, was his 'study and business', poetry only and always his 'amusement'—'good prose, to say nothing of the original thoughts it conveys, may be infinitely varied in modulation. It is only an extension of metres, an amplification of harmonies, of which even the best and most varied poetry admits but few.' An extension of *metres!*

Pronounced verbal rhythms may constantly recur, then, in a plain and, more observably, in an emotional or imaginative prose. Even in our daily talk any emotional incitement, from anger up to joy, adds emphasis to its rhythms, and frequently to a degree bordering on and actually falling into a definite metre.

Prose Numbers

But all this is no more than a superficial reference to an extremely complicated problem. In an essay on *English Prose Numbers* Professor Oliver Elton submits the problem to an indefatigable analysis. A few very inadequate and perhaps even misrepresentative extracts can only suggest its precision and its range. The single feet, the 'foot units' in prose, he tells us, unlike those in verse, which may consist of parts of words (e.g. a gen / tle sun / shine, bless / ing win / ter), are made up of one or more whole words. There are many varieties of these foot units, and most of them are to be found in a sentence quoted from Coleridge: 'What is Greece at this present moment? It is the country of the heroes from Codrus to Philopoemen; and so it would be, though all the sands of Africa should cover its cornfields and olive-gardens, and not a flower were left on Hymettus for a bee to murmur in.' Even the most practised and attentive reader of this attractive and eloquent fragment might fail to perceive, or even perhaps to suspect, that it could be in the manner that follows minutely dissected—without, that is, Professor Elton's help: 'Whát / is Gréece / at this présent / móment /? It is the cóuntry / of the héroes / from Códrus / to Philopóemen /; and só / it wóuld be / , though áll / the sánds of África / should cóver / its córnfìelds / and ólive-gàrdens / , and not a flówer / were léft / on Hyméttus / for a bée / to múrmur in.'

There are, Professor Elton tells us, again, four orders of prose rhythm: rising rhythm, falling rhythm, waved rhythm, and level rhythm, types which 'differ much in *frequency*, *import*, and *emphasis*.' Every prose writer has his favourite variations, which are 'not introduced wantonly, or for the mere ends of convenience, but in correspondence with some transition, in the nature of the imagery or passion.'

In addition to the foot units already referred to, there are also certain classical *cursus* or cadences—sequences, that is, consisting of two or three foot units. These commonly occur in English prose not at fixed intervals but in places where emphasis is required; or they precede a pause. They bring 'the metrical principle into prose'. And there are four or five varieties of them.

Professor Elton takes his examples from De Quincey: (*a*) sérvants depárted, or, tóssing in ánguish; (*b*) bríghtness of thy rísing; (*c*) hínt from the lítany, or, súmmits and declívities; and (*d*) cléan amid áll the gréenness. These classic cadences have long since taken root in English. But in addition there are many native *cursus* of several orders, which (and this might well prove impracticable) have not yet been classified; such as, cólumns of soúnd; trámpled upon eárth; voíces of the choír; strífe of the vócal párts. Others are not, like these, of two but of three units: 'frág-ment or a hínt of such a cloúd', 'hé and his yoúng chíldren', and so forth.

These *cursus* and cadences cut across, as it were, the foot-units. In conclusion, Professor Elton points out that the difference between verse and prose depends not merely on the presence or absence of a regular recurrence of a system of feet. The modulations of verse are due to the attraction of prose rhythms, so that if we listen carefully, 'we confusedly hear the two schemes together'. Similarly, the regular *cursus* and cadences of prose, 'analogous to those of metre though not metrical', in crossing the prose feet also produce a double rhythmical consciousness.

Briefly, our delight in either, if we give it attention, is found to be of an inextricably complex description; and a close examination of anything in nature or art that gives us pleasure confers another kind of pleasure. Moreover, ‘it is a gain to put names and numbers to something of which we already vaguely feel the beauty or the discord. Beauty is form, and number is a constituent of form, and “all things are determined by number”.’

In the course of his essay Professor Elton remarks that the ‘classical *cursus*, in particular, take us away from metre, because they do not enter into any known, or at least into any familiar metre, ancient or modern. So far they sustain the genius of prose.’ Nevertheless with a little patience we may persuade even these into a verse metre which, however crude it may be, may yet not appear to be excessively forced or wholly unfamiliar. E.g.:

Mistress-forsaken,
‘Sérvants depárted’,
‘Tóssing in ánguish’,
Lost, broken-hearted,
Sadly I languish.

Or again:

Cóme, let us bórrow a ‘hínt from the lítany’,
Blest be our table with thyme, sage, and dittany.

And

‘Súmmits and declívities’—
Stárk inhumánities—
Hów compúte the fálls they cáuse, and
Símilar calámities?

And last, and even worst:

Ló, from the crýstal wáters—
Nót as yet fléeced into léanness—
Éwes, with their sóns and dáughters,
‘Cléan amid áll the gréenness’!

In a prose context, such cadences of course are of a much more delicate use and pleasure. To wrench them in this clumsy fashion into metre is only to ruin them.

Longs and Shorts

All metrical and rhythmical verbal scansion, needless to say, is concerned with those elusive and protean phantom entities, called longs and shorts. As abstractions they resemble the grin of the Cheshire cat, 'which remained some time after the rest of it had gone.' How long are they; how short? What precisely distinguishes one from the other—duration, pitch, or energy of sound? And these, singly or in varying combination? Is each of either kind exactly equal in any respect to any other of that kind? What fraction of any long is equal to any short? Is this proportion mutable, and according to taste? And last, to what physical or mental metronome are they more or less obedient?

An intelligent child, if he is asked to read the words lȧ lȧ lȧ, will probably, making a minute pause between each, space the lá's more or less equally, and then, if not before, he may inquire what the dots mean. They mean that each of the three la's may be converted either into:

la lá / la lá / la lá

or

lá la / lá la / lá la

or

lá la la / lá la la / lá la la

or

la lá la / la lá la / la lá la

or

la la lá / la la lá / la la lá

or

lá la / lá la la / lá.

And whatever the vocal and aural difference between a long la and a short la, and whatever fraction of the former the latter may be, the additional shorts will probably approximately conform with the time (in spite of any additional effort) spent in the pauses between his original trio. A ready tongue may venture farther—into a railway rhythm, la la la lá / la la la lá, or la lâ la la / la lâ la la; or, la lâ la la la / la lâ la la la. A close attention to the tappings of a clog dancer, and, beyond *his* skill even, to a patter-dancer—will reveal further possibilities—including syncopation. It is a question of physical skill—tongue *versus* feet; as we perceive if for a short la we substitute, stodg'th—'Stodg'th Blánche / still o'ér / her tásk?'. All this is comparatively simple. But we have already abandoned mere abstractions; and as soon as we abandon also our monotonous la-la-la-ing, the prospect bristles with the problematical. Most verse, we may assume, was intended by its maker (apart from its visual and other imagery) to be listened to; and, an harmonious prose is by this much less enjoyable if (that being possible) eye and mind alone are concerned with it. But, even if reading to oneself proceeds in a silence as profound as that of a lunar landscape, reading aloud involves two aesthetic arbiters, ear and voice, and the latter, as may have been agreed already, is certainly not the less delicate and important of them. Speech is not only a kind of music but, as even a manual on phonetics will demonstrate, it entails exquisitely fine gradations of muscular effort and movement. And, if heaven has given us a passably pleasant voice, even if it be pleasing only to ourselves, we may prefer singing to being sung to. Indeed, when we are merely listening to a musical instrument—flute, clarionet, fiddle, bassoon—some consonant and mimetic activity of the vocal organs seems to be very part and parcel of our response to its strains.

But the intervals of speech are more minute than semitones; its phones are far less precisely measurable than crochets and quavers; we cannot beat time to it; its emphases, accents and stresses are less emphatic. The terms long and short resemble empty boxes, then. *La* is only one of countless kinds and qualities of sound and vocal exercise which we can, so to speak, pack into these boxes. For now we are concerned with words. That being so, not only temporal duration, energy, pitch come into play but volume, timbre, quality, vocal patterning. Verbal sounds uttered by the voice and/or listened to by the ear may in effect be light, heavy, flat, sharp, acute, voluminous, massive, dull, ringing, dark, luminous, brilliant, coloured—and much else. And every such sound, as in those of an orchestra, is in some degree influenced by its near and remoter neighbours.

If a minute and single verbal entity such as la is unique, then, emphatically, any group of verbal units is unique. That la is unique will be evident if we try a few of our railway rhythms with *lass*, *glass*, or *flasks*. The word 'unique' itself, for example, is of a unique verbal and vocal pattern. We can use that pattern only by precisely repeating it. A few words assorted of set intent still further complicate the issue, because a sorter—an individual human being—is now concerned—his tone, his timbre, his level of response, his own personal immediate and remote verbal context. Dull, dissonant and hackneyed a writer's word-sequences may be; still, they are his own; and a close attention and analysis would reveal them as his and his alone. If, on the other hand, his verbal music is markedly idiosyncratic, we can positively recognize his handiwork, revealing his nature, craft and art, in but a few successive words hitherto unencountered. We repeat them, we listen. And, 'O yes, Keats, of course,' we say; or John Donne or William Blake; Swift, Browne or Edward Fitzgerald. 'All in a hot and copper sky'; 'At one stride comes the dark'; 'I watched their rich attire'

—such collocations as these, having been made once, remain immutably themselves and Coleridge's for ever—as does a single flower in the foreground of Leonardo's Madonna of the Rocks, a single fold in the drapery of Michelangelo's Pietà.

This feat—theirs chiefly, but in part also ours in the act of perception and recognition—is, of course, at an almost miraculous extreme, although the fact that it is exceedingly difficult to attend solely to the sound of words and remain unaffected by their sense, must be taken into account. It must be remembered, too, that a sequence of verbal sounds in respect to its rhythm, intonation and meaning, is not a rigid but an elastic entity. It could not be otherwise, since whatever the contents of our boxes called long and short may be, not one kind but many kinds of rhythm are discernible, whether they conform to a metrical basis, as in verse, or to a less evident but dominant pattern, as in prose. In his *English Poesy*, a brief masterpiece in insight, analysis and condensation, Dr. Winslow Hall specifies and exemplifies such varieties of intervolved rhythm as architectonic, phrasal, lineal, sectional, periodic, undulant and numeral. The rippled surface of an Atlantic breaker repelled by the rocks and intermingling with that which has succeeded it is not more diversified. No two readings, then—even one's own—of the same poem can be precisely similar. And no analysis could finally systematize these complexities or their chameleonic resources. The art of a fine literary technique is as far beyond ultimate 'scientific' regimentation as Henry James's psychology was beyond his brother William's. *How* a thing is written is, of course, intrinsic and essential to what it has to say, and what it has to say consists not of inanimate and measurable, but of vital and vitalizing elements. 'Can these dry words live?' 'They are not dead, but sleeping.'

To return for but a moment to our serviceable la's. Take the ballad entitled *The Douglas Tragedy* for one simple example. Here, not only for the realization of a creating impulse and intent, but, at the lowest, for refuge and relief from the monotony of a basal la lá la lá la lá in each fourth line, we have 'Come riding o'er the lea', 'And the sounder I will sleep', 'And put on your armour so bright', 'O whether will ye gang or bide?' 'Slowly they baith rade away', 'For this night my fair lady I've win', and even 'And her father hard fighting who loved her so dear'. As lines of verse, what these have in common, their metre, is in varying degree as plain as it is necessary. As fragments of poetic art and impulse, the differences between them—boxes *and* contents—which are more, or less, in apt mimetic accord with what they mean both intellectually and emotionally, are the touchstone of their success. Only the word infinite seems to be capable of including the potential variations of a rhythmical metre, and only the pen of an angel could so expound the fascinating problems they present as to refrain from repeatedly contradicting himself.

Prosody is to poetry, and, in a similar fashion, to prose also, what the old botany was to a plant and its flower. It is a convenient method of classifying what is in fact unique. But botany, the expert tells us, is now a branch of science with numerous twigs, including cytology, histology, pathology, ecology, and, above all, physiology—life processes. So with metrical verse—rhythmical prose. We may also perhaps be a little burdened with a literary 'paleo-botany'—*fossil* metres, 'quantity' and so forth. The one gift, then, his fairy godmother would refrain from bestowing on a beloved and princely poet in his cradle would be a wholly academic tome on prosody—even although its whole concern is only the simplest of the many elements of his craft.

What doubt is there that our Pherecydes as a child had mimicked or intuited his way into talking long before he had even so much as heard there was a thing called language? 'There is only one school, the universe,' said Landor, 'one only schoolmistress, Nature.' A little girl aged four years and nine months—who had already posed her mother with 'Potatoes, Mother; why *toes*?'—recently heard a small visitor declare that he disliked thin slices of bread and butter. He preferred it in hunks—so wide, so thick. 'And where', inquired her mother, 'did you have them like that?' 'At Eton,' was the reply. Whereupon Miss Four-years-old with a shrewd and pensive glance interposed, 'Were they *eaten*?' It was her first pun; she was radiant; and at once inquired if there were any other words that could be similarly juggled with. She then asked the difference between *shell* and *shall*, having detected that her Nannie preferred, as we most of us do, the former in such phrases as, 'I shell [or sh'll] be along presently.'

When the dark forest glides along,
When midnight's gloom makes everybody still,
The owl flies out,
And the bat stretches his wing;
The lion roars;
The wolf and the tiger prowl about,
And the hyena cries.

At the age of four years and eight months Charles Kingsley composed this scrap of verse, which he entitled 'Night': and only the closest examination will reveal how many delicate technical devices have been put to service in these few immature and no doubt imitative lines. A delight in sound, an interest in words must have been instinctive in both these children, and certainly neither of them had been *taught* how to pun, how to accord speech rhythms and inflexions with sense and meaning, or how to visualize yelping hyenas.

But to return: 'All verse', in the words of Robert Bridges, 'derives its beauty mainly from its speech rhythms, but these are not the prosody, they are the rhythms which are allowed and ordered by the prosody.'

'I invite the reader', writes Dr. MacColl, summarizing his essay, 'to regard Prose and Verse not as sharply-divided entities under separate laws of rhythm, but as, in their characteristic forms, the extremities of a continuous chain, the variation being from freedom of syllable and emphasis towards strictness of foot and metrical pattern.' And between the two extremes, Characteristic Prose and Characteristic Verse, he places, first, Numerous Prose, and next, Verse invaded by Prose emphasis.

Coventry Patmore also simplifies the crucial technical distinction between prose and verse, in an enthusiastic paper on Alice Meynell's Essays:

'. . . The simplest iambic foot of two syllables and one accent is religiously kept to in Mrs. Meynell's Essays, and she never falls into the artistic error, which nearly all other great writers sometimes commit, of changing the unequalled grace of her *walk* into a passage of *dance*; for that is the exact difference between prose, of which the unit is the iambic *foot*, and verse, of which the lowest division is the *metre*, of *two* feet. There are many excellent writers who, like Newman, have adhered strictly to the rule of prose; but such writers have never given, or even perhaps aimed at giving, to prose the greatest artistic beauty, by evoking its proper music, while obeying its primary law. Rare as the most excellent poetry is, the most excellent prose is yet rarer.'

Here is a statement made not only by a fine poet concerning another, but by a sedulous and masterly craftsman. Yet even Patmore, so easily is attention eluded, failed to detect three distinct drifts of the metrical in his last two sentences. First, 'There are mány éxcellent wríters whó'; next, 'by evóking its próper músic, / while obéy / ing its prí / mary láw'; and last, in a merry cantering measure which, I feel certain, he never deliberately deigned to use, and of which at the moment he can certainly not have been conscious:

[*Ladies as lovely there are as my Liz,*
But for beauty of mind she's far fairer.]
'*Rare ás the most éxcellent póetry ís,*
The most éxcellent próse is yet rárer.'

Stevenson (having not apparently accepted Shelley's laudation of language in his *Defence of Poetry*) compared words to bricks, but did not, I fancy, refer to that more elusive thing, the cement which keeps them together. A writer's vocabulary may more frequently resemble ice. It must be thawed of set intent, by feeling, by the desire to express and to communicate, before it will consent to flow. 'I hate', says Landor, 'false words, and seek with care, difficulty and moroseness those that fit the thing.' But even if the thing is clearly and faithfully imaged by the inward eye, the word for it, the unique word—a quarry perhaps too assiduously coveted if three or four apt and available ones will suffice—is the elusive hare. It needs to be hunted. And hunting for words, as for foxes or unicorns, is apt to scare them away. Moreover, like the unicorn, alas, *the* word may prove to be non-existent. Then substitutes must somehow be made to serve. How indeed could any dictionary, even the English, suffice to set down all that is included and implied in any microcosm called Me. Still, language is so rich, supple and plastic a medium that it will accommodate itself to the least change in the user of it, however rare his genius. 'Did you not notice, my friend,' says Socrates to Phaedrus, 'that I am already speaking in hexameters, not mere dithyrambics, even though I am finding fault with the lover? But if I began to praise the non-lover, what kind of a hymn do you suppose I shall raise? I shall surely be possessed of the nymphs to whom you purposely exposed me.' (Needless to say, he presently inverts this attitude.)

An austerely rational, logical, terra-firma prose, regular and leisurely in its progress, and in its sentence and paragraph arrangement, and therefore of little rhythmical and musical variety, is, again, an acutely difficult discipline for a lively spirit. To achieve it he must rein in a natural bent and impulse. He is imposing on himself a method alien to his nature. As soon as the rein is loosed, as soon as fancy or imagination or emotion is the spur, then Pegasus begins to trot, to canter, to gallop; and any verbal rhythms consonant with these charming styles of progress tend towards metre. The problem, yet again, is, if only by a hair's breadth, to shun revealing the tendency. Pegasus must never be allowed to stoop his gentle head and to drink. The paradoxical difficulty, that is, in the writing of any ardent, vehement, sensitive or imaginative prose, is to evade an obvious yet welcome and *helpful* restraint—metre; whereas in the writing of verse, the restraint itself is the means of revealing the subtlest and widest freedom and variety.

Thus far, in their rhythms, prose and verse approximate. But a prose that becomes metrical is almost as unpleasing as a verse that cannot be scanned. Nor is this solely an error in craftsmanship. Why? Is it not because, as Socrates suggests, it has challenged a higher standard—not that of mere verse —but of *poetry* in verse? Poetry of an intensity, that is, which prose itself can rarely achieve. Let the writer print such little oversights as verse, however, and by adding inverted commas, originate, like the Irishman, his own quotations, then his readers will judge them as verse, and he may triumph. If the prose thus far in error persists in that error, it changes its name and becomes verse; it both discards and claims a certain status. So, when a woman marries, she too changes her name, and both discards and claims a certain status. And 'all for love', or because she cannot 'help herself'—whether it be the best *reason* available or not—is at least a pressing incentive. A prosaic loveless mind when it ventures into verse only the more openly announces how prosaic a mind it is. A poetic mind, on the other hand, except of set intent, cannot by merely refraining from metre cast off its own very selfhood and idiosyncrasies. It is that *kind* of mind—including defects and deficiencies perhaps incident to its innate gifts—through and through.

When, then, apart from mere carelessness or artifice, what is intended to be prose lapses into the metrical the secession cannot but imply, we must assume, some minute change of mind, and therefore of matter—the addition of some quality or qualities which *in excelsis* are only to be found in the finest poetry. If the change is warranted, not only has the responsible consciousness altered its orientation, but poetry has crept in. Before venturing farther, then, we can hardly evade some faltering attempt to define the word.

Poetry

What is poetry? More than a score of centuries have fallen into the dust of history since poetry came into full and perfect flower in Greece, and in Palestine. Yet a completely satisfactory answer to this simple question seems to be as forlorn a hope as the lover's, intent on enshrining in mere words his 'not impossible She'. How far indeed is poetry in itself a fixed and changeless mark, and beyond argument; or something dependent on a purely personal and current taste and therefore the sport of changing modes, fashions, intentions, ideals? To what extent are the sounds of fine poetry, like those of music, its essential self; and is all else that is involved in it only invaluable addenda? Is 'poetry' no more than a pure abstraction? If so, should not any attempt to show what it is be confined to the exemplification of it by means of exemplary poems? Would the poets themselves agree that they have in common a certain definite aim, or method, specifiable aspirations and motives? It seems, indeed, a peculiar futility that no final definition should be easily available of what for so many unusual human beings has proved to be the unfailing delight and animation of a lifetime. And yet, as with beauty, happiness, wisdom, innocence, genius, grace—so too with poetry; we may, as of these, have steadily within our minds a vague yet sufficing conception of all that it means for us. It has been derived from a lifelong familiarity. It has been distilled from countless examples; and yet, like the essence of all essences from innumerable flowers, which is itself, I have heard, odourless, it may elude analysis. We may, that is, be aware of what intrinsically we mean by the word, and yet be incapable of expressing that meaning.

Few definitions in actual fact have proved to be of any particular service, not even as an aid in the appreciation of poetry; still less as a recipe for its composition. None that I can recall, apart from any reference to metre, excludes a subtle, spirited, resilient and imaginative prose. There is a recurrent confusion between (*a*) the formless, rapid, multitudinous, volatile mind-stuff and heart-stuff which the poet endeavours to convey by means of words; (*b*) the words themselves, as he is ill or well content to leave them, awaiting his reader's transmutation and revival; and (*c*) the effect they produce on those who can thus revive and transmute them—an effect that cannot but vary with every individual reader and probably at every repeated rendering. It is clearly improbable that any (*c*) should more than approximate to its (*a*).

On the one hand, a purely intellectual search for a definition of poetry may be hindered by lack of experience in the conditions and processes and the kind of experience that go to its conceiving and making. On the other, a poet is apt to cherish an ideal of poetry more or less peculiar to himself, to which he is continually aspiring, although he may never attain it. In face of so many difficulties and dubieties, it is no wonder that definitions range from the touchingly simple to the uselessly abstruse.

'I wish', said Coleridge, 'our clever young poets would remember my homely definitions of prose and poetry; that is, prose—words in their best order;—poetry, the *best* words in the best order.' Proper words, however, in their proper order was Coleridge's original definition of prose. But would even 'proper' placate a Flaubert, a Walter Pater, a Ruskin, a Stevenson, a Henry James? Nothing, of course, short of the best—fittest, that is, for the purpose in view—can be good enough, either in a fine prose or a fine verse; and in neither should that best be too salient, but only uninterchangeable.

Not that a poetic vocabulary may not be markedly original—otherwise Skelton, Donne, Gerard Hopkins, Thomas Hardy, Charles Doughty, T. S. Eliot deserve to be denizens of Plato's Republic—cast forth. Their 'best' is *their* best; and so with the greatest and the least. Poetry, again, has been defined as memorable speech; and as a criticism of life: but doggerel may be vividly memorable, and Paley's *Evidences of Christianity* and Adam Smith's *The Wealth of Nations* are little if they are not in some sort such a criticism.

In his *English Poesy*, already referred to, Dr. Winslow Hall declares that 'three definitions seem necessary'. '1. Poetry is that which transmits emotion beautifully by means of rhythms and words. 2. Poesy is the poet's craft of making. 3. Verse is that form of poetry in which a periodic rhythm is paramount. Next three axioms ought to be laid down:—1. For Poetry no vehicle but voice can be acknowledged. 2. In Poesy the ear is lord. 3. English Poesy must evermore evolve.' They are concise and admirable summaries; but only the third definition with its *paramount* 'periodic rhythm' distinguishes poetry in verse from poetry in prose. Herbert Spencer ventured on a definition of Life itself. It is 'a definite combination of heterogeneous changes, both simultaneous and successive, in correspondence with external coexistences and sequences.' That every funerary urn would supply no less dusty an answer is no refutation of its validity. And, curiously enough, if 'and internal' be inserted before 'coexistences', this might stand also as a definition of the experience involved in the reading of a poem.

Similarly, Wordsworth's familiar statement that 'poetry is the spontaneous overflow of powerful feelings', and 'takes its origin from emotion recollected in tranquillity', applies admirably to his own poetry at its best and purest. Passionate, beyond the conception of poetic natures less profound than his own, the remembered emotion may have been; and this, as he acknowledged, was the state of mind—serene and pleasurable—in which he himself composed. But can we assume it to have been Robert Herrick's state of mind, when, exquisite lens in eye, he seated himself at his lapidary's bench? Intent on refining the verbal setting of some imaginative idea or experience either pleasurable as in his exquisite lyrics, or nauseous, as in his less 'noble numbers', he seems, with a few exceptions, such as his *Litany*, to have been moved by no emotion much sharper or more profound than the goldsmith's zest in that on which he is spending his dearest skill. Nor do many of Edgar Allan Poe's mesmeric 'effusions' appear in origin to have been the *spontaneous* overflow of powerful feelings. By some lovers of poetry—though assuredly not by one whom I know best and only too well—even the finest of them are rejected as crude, artificial and even spurious jingles exhibiting a 'morbid' emotionalism. *The Bells*, far from being spontaneous, was expanded from a few lines written to please a friend into the campanological *tour de force* it became. *The Raven* was of four years' growth. The notion, indeed, that poetry is evolved with ease in a 'fine frenzy' hardly accounts for its extreme rarity.

It might be an aid to its definition, perhaps, to define the word poet. But *his* 'name is Legion': 'For we are many,' as said the evil spirit possessing the man who was always, night and day, among the mountains and the tombs. And it is he whom a facetious Theseus, with the connivance of a self-scanned Shakespeare, consigned to a cell shared by the lunatic and the lover. Compare the English poets one with another—and merely to be English implies much in common between them. They appear, apart from being poets, to be no less diverse in nature, temperament and character than would as many other men classified solely by their professions—whether doctors, lawyers, stock-brokers, publicans, or pugilists. Moreover, as Keats, also looking inward, declared, the poet is of all men the least poetic; and 'to judge of poets is only the faculty of poets, and not of all poets, but the best.' On honey-dew this chameleon may have fed; he may have drunk the milk of paradise; yet his mind in the act of creation must resemble the interior of a hive of bees on the point of swarming—in pursuit of a queen whose name only the Muses themselves could disclose, and which even Solomon kept secret.

All art is learned by art, this art alone
It is a heavenly gift. . . .

'Collect,' says M. Paul Valéry, 'all the facts that can be collected about the life of Racine and you will never learn from them the art of his verse. All criticism is dominated by the outworn theory that the man is the cause of the work as in the eyes of the law the criminal is the cause of the crime. Far rather are they both the effects.'

To those who value it, the one thing certain is that poetry, like wisdom, is a singularly rare thing, that the price of it is above rubies, and that it cannot be gotten for gold. Once given potential life in words, it need never die; an ardent delight in it, and of this, too, there are many degrees, may be not only the joy of childhood, but a supreme and inexhaustible solace to the aged. So long as we ourselves remain faithful, *it* will never prove false.

All men have once been children, and in childhood any innate imaginative power is at its purest. All men have dreamed, and have been conscious of transitory moments of insight and exaltation, for most men have been once or repeatedly in love, whether that love was centred on a woman, on an object, an idea, an ideal, or a God. Experience of this nature, as it is divined, let us say, in the reading of a lyrical poem, is poetic expression; and is so far common to all humanity.

'Love', said Rainer Maria Rilke, 'consists in this, that two solitudes protect and touch and greet each other'; and the words apply equally well to any poet and his true 'sharer'.

In their practice we perceive that all imaginative writers, in varying degree, have the gift of intuition, the faculty of sensuous mental imagery, a certain intellectual energy, the desire and the ability to express themselves in rhythmical language, and to transmute the riches that are signified by the word memory—memory of this life, of the dream life, and possibly of a remoter life yet—into a material *befitting* the imagined. But otherwise?

Alexander Pope, 'the wicked asp of Twickenham', was a hunchback fifty-four inches in height. Shelley, fair, golden, freckled, with his shrill voice and eyes of a very unusual brightness, was compared independently by three of his friends to a flower. Hazel-eyed Keats had a low wide forehead, an unusual and dominant nose, a full-lipped mouth. His face at its most expressive suggested to a friend that he had been 'looking at some glorious sight.' Byron, as a young man, had features of a captivating, if frigid and scornful, attractiveness, and a voice, according to Mrs. Opie, such as the Devil tempted Eve with. His more serious talk was for Shelley 'a sort of intoxication'; his wit reminded Scott of a schoolboy with his pockets stuffed with crackers. So with the rest of the poets: Wordsworth with his long, sombre, pondering countenance; the youthful Coleridge's almost luscious animation and vitality; Chatterton; and Hartley Coleridge's tragically sensitive beauty; Marvell and Milton; Christina Rossetti and Emily Brontë: they differ one from another as much in appearance and character as they differ in the kind and quality of their individual writings. But all of them achieved poetry. In this alone—their devotion to the Muses—they are of one blood. But then, Sir Thomas Browne, Vaughan and Robert Bridges were physicians; Keats and Byron, like Hazlitt, were interested in the Ring; Shakespeare and Coventry Patmore were clear-sighted men of business.

Also, it is as if the universal language that preceded the confusion of Babel were confined to the expression of as ancient a human estate; that deep beneath every human consciousness lies a living relic of this remembrance; and that at a few authentic syllables in echo of it, this remembrance stirs, however faintly, like the bamboo of the Indian magician, into leaf and flower. A paradox then appears. Here it is the manner that is the true and secret communication; the matter may be of comparatively little value, and is only its vehicle, as it were. The phial is of matchless crystal, and comes from afar, its contents may be attar or merely rose-water; the precious or semi-precious stone has its price, but the setting is beyond price.

Yet even if any strict and fool-proof definition of poetry or poet may be impracticable, we can at least attempt to summarize the impressions made on us in the reading of what we ourselves regard and accept as poetry—the poetry we feel upon our pulses, that calls the rarest and strangest of all *Qui Vives?*

In form and expression it is condensed but not congested; it is complex rather than complicated; and even if it be incidentally obscure—by reason of its verbal construction, its references, or its profundity—it is never finally unintelligible. What it tells, while it may be pellucidly clear, is yet deep; it is rational, and yet lies beyond the arbitration of pure reason; and not only will the closest of paraphrases rob it of some vital virtue, but even although it is replete with sense it may be ruined by imposing upon it any detachable and extrinsic meaning. It is lit with beauty, though beauty was not its aim. We know this beauty to be present, but could not prove it to be present. We can scarcely say which entrances us most, the melody it sings or how it sings it; its formal vessel or the nectar it contains; the course it follows or the goal it arrives at. And although we may delight in it as naturally as we delight in water to drink, colours whereon to feast the eye, music to hear, ideas to ponder, human emotions to share, and that region of the imagination to which it admits us; yet its secret and very self, even when it has won in to the aware and engrossed company of our inmost being, may still in some degree elude us.

Statements such as these, of course, are only partial and imperfect descriptions of poetry, not a definition. They are like the specification of an invention unaided by a working model. Ideals may widely differ, the only conclusive revelation of poetry is a fine poem. And any attempt to extract from it everything that it reveals and implies resembles that of a child intent on emptying the sea with his sand-pail. In search of an example I opened an anthology at random and chanced on *A Sonnet of the Moon*. It was a happy chance, as this is a poem almost *in vacuo*, the work of Charles Best, a writer of whom we know nothing except that he was 'flourishing' in 1602, and contributed to Francis Davison's *Poetical Rapsodie* of that year. We cannot then be led astray by the 'personal'.

Look how the pale Queen of the silent night
Doth cause the ocean to attend upon her,
And he, as long as she is in his sight,
With his full tide is ready her to honour:

But when the silver waggon of the Moon
Is mounted up so high he cannot follow,
The sea calls home his crystal waves to moan,
And with low ebb doth manifest his sorrow.

So you, that are the sovereign of my heart,
Have all my joys attending on your will,
My joys low-ebbing when you do depart,
When you return, their tide my heart doth fill.
So as you come, and as you do depart,
Joys ebb and flow within my tender heart.

Apart from its faulty rhyming and repetitions, both of which may easily perhaps pass unnoticed, the most obvious features of this 'Sonnet' are its simplicity, directness, and economy of statement. Although it was written three centuries ago, it contains not a single word that might not be used nowadays in ordinary conversation. There is scarcely a rhythmical phrase—there are few lines even—to be found in it which might not adorn a recent prose romance, or even talk: e.g. 'How strange it is', she whispered, 'that it should be the moon up there in "the silent night" that "doth cause the ocean to attend upon her" ': 'Look, Mother, William's kite "is mounted up so high mine cannot follow" ': 'So, moved by an impulse she refused to examine, Matilda decided to entice him on, "and he, as long as she is in his sight," continued to follow her.' But with how spontaneous a delicacy these verbal rhythms and inflexions are interwoven into the metrical scheme.

There is nothing irrational in the poem, nothing complicated. The first few lines might occur in a (rather unusual) scientific statement in a primer on astronomy. It is natural, its meaning is transparent, the objects it refers to, ocean, silver waggon, crystal waves, and even she to whom it is addressed, are true and lovely in their kind. It is a delight to say and to hear, and as tranquilly lucent in effect as the pale queen herself. Nevertheless its strands of meaning are many, and they are almost inextricably intertwined. It is condensed, but neither congested nor confused. The participants in its mystery, the moon and her tides, sovereignty and its courtiers, enwreathe their mysteries one within the other in the service of the two lovers, to produce at last a profound trinity in unity, a unity in trinity. And when the idea-design and the verbal pattern are completed—the conception come to birth—there follows that tender, artless couplet for postscript; so artless that the poet is content to use two of his rhymes over again! One might as justly belaud a snowdrop for its 'innocence' as tax this sonnet with a moral intention. Nevertheless by comparison with its serene yet impassioned outlook, and with the relation between the lovers—body, mind and spirit—of whom it tells, many of our modern psycho-analysing 'sex' novels take on the appearance of human styes—and roofed in at that.

A poem no less simple at a first reading is this by Mr. Robert Frost, the verbal rhythms of which, I believe, are intentionally and might well be those of daily talk:

I have wished a bird would fly away
And not sing by my house all day;

Have clapped my hands at him from the door
When it seemed as if I could bear no more.

The fault may partly have been in me,
The bird was not to blame for his key.

And of course there must be something wrong
In wanting to silence any song.

The effect of this poem resembles that of the wind's faint ripplings on the surface of some dark quiet lake in the hills, intimating its depth, whispering of its source, and just ruffling its reflections. One could hardly believe that a common little gateway like 'of course' could admit us into so wide a range of contemplation. In this it shares one of the secrets of William Blake.

Reiteratedly in a fine poem this peculiar condensation of 'meaning'—reference, inference, and effect—is revealed. It reminds us of the drowning ship-boy in the ballad, who with his auger 'bored holes two at twice'. What occasions any such pregnant piece of writing is another matter. Anything that is meant by inspiration apart, it seems to proceed from a condition of consciousness compounded in some degree of both dream and wake. It is a state intensely aware yet contemplative, unforeseen, unimposable, infrequent, temporary, and in much all but past analysis. Such metaphors as flash-point, fusion-point, spontaneous combustion, the solitary spot where three roads meet, an island that is the peak of a submarine mountain, clumsy and inadequate though they may be, come into the fancy.

The more 'rapt' the imaginative state of mind, the more effortlessly it will brim its minute verbal phials with a various attar. But so delicately is this secured that even one substituted word can momentarily imperil its influence on the reader. For crude example, we can conceive perhaps the various states and degrees as it were of creativeness between such a prose passage as: 'Two distinct orders of preacher may be distinguished within every presbytery—the ardent and elegant, the substantive and profound. They may be compared to two of our own famous and diverse rivers. I hear, as it were, the *genius loci* of the one addressing that of the other: "Wherefore is it, my friend, that your current flows so tranquilly and quietly?" Whereto, accepting the poetic convention I have ventured to impose on it, the other replies, "Quietly forsooth! That very well may be. Vehement and tumultuous your stream certainly is, and mine slow if not positively sluggish; nevertheless for every single human being whom, without consideration or any trace of compassion, *you* may incontinently overwhelm in your waters, I myself dispose of two at least" '—we can compare that verbose and protracted little disquisition with a lyric, brief, sinister, a minute masterpiece, only the more condensed for the Southerner by its unfamiliar *rin* and *gar*:

Quo' the Tweed to the Till,
'What gars ye gang sae still?'
Quo' the Till to the Tweed,
'Though ye rin wi' speed,
And I rin slaw,
For ilka ane that ye droon,
I droon twa.'

But then, is not prose also fully capable of a fine, pregnant, rational, and imaginative condensation, comparable with that of verse? Listen to the wild and wilful Thomas Nash on 'The Divine Aretine': 'It was one of the wittiest knaves that ever God made. If out of so base a thing as ink there may be extracted a spirit, he writes with nought but the spirit of ink, and his style was the spirituality of art's, and nothing else, whereas all others of his age were but the lay temporality of inkhorn terms. . . . No leaf he wrote on but was like a burning glass to set on fire all his readers. . . .' On the very verge of verse, here and there, this passage is also on the verge of the poetic; and, in its own kind, it would take a rare poet to better it.

And here (again at random) is Mr. By-ends—the genteel nephew of Parson Two-tongues, and the husband of Lady Faining's daughter—now the complete gentleman, even if his great-grandfather was nought 'but a waterman, looking one way, and rowing another'. He is addressing Christian: ''Tis true we somewhat differ in religion from those of the stricter sort, yet but in two small points: First, we never strive against wind and tide. Secondly, we are always most zealous when religion goes in his silver slippers; we love much to walk with him in the street, if the sun shines, and the people applaud it.' With a street and a sun of this order in his repertory, no poet surely would find himself far from home. Everything meretricious in mock piety is poetically packed into those silver slippers; and Traherne himself never saw the sun shine brighter.

And, yet again, Ben Jonson—on style: 'For a man to write well, there are required three necessaries—to read the best authors, observe the best speakers, and much exercise of his own style.' Brevity, hovering again over the borderline of the metrical, is here the winning soul of good sense—but it subserves a rational rather than an imaginative condensation. Presently, after counselling extreme care in seeking the best, in avoiding 'froward conceits', and submitting all to judgment and order, Jonson continues:

'Repeat often what we have formerly written; which beside that it helps the consequence, and makes the juncture better, it quickens the heat of imagination, that often cools the time of setting down, and gives it new strength, as if it grew lustier by the going back; as we see in the contention of leaping, they jump farthest that fetch their race largest; or, as in throwing a dart or javelin, we force back our arms to make our loose the stronger. Yet, if we have a fair gale of wind, I forbid not the steering out of our sail, so the favour of the gale deceive us not. For all that we invent doth please us in conception of birth, else we would never set it down.'

Not only is the imagery telling, it is creative; it knits together the meaning and then intensifies into the poetic with that vanishing glimpse of the solitary in his sailing skiff, skimming in the favour of the 'gale' over the sunny lustre of the sea.

Here, again, is the opening sentence from a chapter in one of Ambrose Bierce's tales: 'To-day I am said to live; to-morrow, here in this room, will lie a senseless shape of clay that all too long was I.' It wouldn't be easy to pack much more meaning into words so few. Metricalize them, and, with a little dilution, add a rhyme-word:

To-day I am said to live;
To-morrow, here in this room,
Will lie a senseless shape of clay
Long-destined to this doom.

How much the *import* of the meaning seems now to have vanished!* So also in mere simple description. John Gerarde's *Herball*, first published in 1597, consists for the most part of brief dissertations on plants, flowers and their properties. Yet even here, in the melody and precision of the language, in the apt infrequent image, in the realization thus conveyed (almost hallucinatory at moments) of the actual living thing described, the poetic creeps in.

'Dwale or sleeping Nightshade hath round blackish stalkes six foot high, whereupon do grow great broad leaves

* Not of course that mere verse as a way of using words and wits is to be decried even if it is as far from poetry as a blackbird's nest in winter is from song. Verse gives an edge and a twist and a tang and a finish not nearly so easily accomplishable in prose. It packs tight, it evokes from memory a more precise and vivacious range of reference, its method is allied to that of music. And if music comparable to *poetry* were alone so labelled, how many delightful voices would fall silent! Take, for example, that genial and jocular Irish fragment, 'My Aunt':

My aunt she died a month ago,
And left me all her riches,
A feather-bed and a wooden leg,
And a pair of calico breeches;
A coffee-pot without a stroup,
And a mug without a handle,
A baccy box without a lid,
And half a farden candle:

One can imagine the prose equivalent of this modest catalogue in the vernacular of half a dozen of Dickens's characters, of Nick Bottom or Trinculo, or of some crony of Gulliver's. It would be no less cogent and concise, but each would lack that little *something* which only the framework of metre and the clinch of unexpected rhyme can bestow.

of a dark green colour; among which grow smal hollow floures bel-fashion, of an overworn purple colour; in the place whereof come forth great round berries of the bignesse of the black chery, green at the first, but when they be ripe of the colour of black jet or burnished horne. . . .

'Banish . . . these pernitious plants out of your gardens, and all places neere to your houses, where children or women with child do resort, which do oftentimes long and lust after things most vile and filthie; and much more after a berry of a bright shining blacke colour, and of such great beautie, as it were able to allure any such to eate thereof.'

Since, as in Charles Best's sonnet, no word here is a mere counter, each object mentioned is slightly heightened in its effect; and *how* vile and filthy is its 'vile and filthie'. Indeed, the sinister berries themselves are thus made the more alluring. Gerarde with his art has silvered his pernicious pills. From the reading even of a prose simple and dutiful as this, may we not derive, if faintly, those odd and pleasing symptoms in skin and diaphragm which Professor Housman discovered to be convincing evidence that poetry has stealthily come in upon us? For mind and body are in no less close an accord than fiddle and music. Nor perhaps will a wise man inquire too closely concerning exact causes, or even effects, provided only the latter triumph.

In the last resort, then, to define poetry or even the poetic seems to remain impracticable, if only because, like the quicksilver in a thermometer, it rises and falls by minute gradations according to the temperature of the reader's mind. 'Even the best of all poems are the best upon innumerable degrees.' We can do little more than attempt to characterize and exemplify these degrees; an enticing and difficult task enough, but one fitful in success; and still more so, if in the course of our enquiry we insist on rejecting prose.

While pondering one day, and as usual all but in vain, on

this richly-recompensing problem, I happened to catch sight of a notice-board behind the spear-headed palisade of a chapel on which were inscribed these words: 'No one can come into Heaven by immediate mercy.'

They were, I think, the translation of an apophthegm of Swedenborg's, and, as it seems to me, they give an example of what we are seeking—the transitional. What characterizes it? It is a sentence in prose. And yet, although it falls short of poetry, is it not in the nature of poetry? How so? It is because the effect on the mind of these nine quite usual words so used resembles that of dropping a pebble into a pool. As does also, 'Oh what can ail thee, knight-at-arms,' or 'Mortality, behold and fear,' or 'When love with unconfined wings,' or 'Gane were but the winter cauld,' or 'Now the day is over,' or 'Here, a little child, I stand.' Like poetry, that is, the sentence cited at once rivets attention. And this, although at first glance, I confess, it seemed to me to be untrue. Offhand I should have assumed that no one can come into Heaven *except* by immediate mercy. However, we may welcome poetry as poetry without (quite apart from its relation to matter of fact) admitting it to be truth, unless it be that imaginative truth which is of a rare order and closely allied with beauty.

Swedenborg's, again, is a statement which, as is so frequently the case with poetry, instantly and repeatedly runs counter to the merely expected and conventional. Word by word we encounter the unforeseen: no one *can* come into Heaven, rather than 'may'; can *come* into Heaven, rather than 'go'; can come *into* Heaven, rather than 'to'. The phrase 'by immediate mercy' also is transparently clear and yet exceedingly condensed. It needs a prolonged exploration. And last, the sentence itself is poised on the very margin of the metrical:

And this my heart avows, that '*no one can*
Come into Heaven by immediate mercy'.

But, as with other fragments of poetic prose when they are forced into metre, the *significant* rhythm, that of the original, is now lost; such a rhythm, that is, as masters an equally meditatable fragment from Keats's *Ode on Melancholy*:

His soul shall taste the sadness of her might,
And be among her cloudy trophies hung.

Only a fine poet could metricalize Swedenborg's sentence without depriving it of an intrinsic grace, even if he might also, perhaps, add his own.

Free Verse

But if even a brief sentence in prose may in technique and effect fall little short of metrical poetry, what is to be said of the two species of writing which, whether rightly or otherwise, openly claim the virtues of both: free verse and prose-poetry?

Both phrases suggest contradictions in terms. No *verse*—imposed metre—any more than a dance made up of certain steps, patterns, and figures can be called free if it is bound by any law or principle, even though that law may be indetectable and is not laid down. Free verse of its own nature resigns many of the rhythms and inflexions, infinite in variety, which are proper to good prose—itself a form that is obedient to many rigorous, accepted, yet unwritten rules. It may succeed in emphasizing significant pauses, but is also apt to isolate metrical fragments which in prose are effective only when they are not self-evident. At the same time it rejects the numerous traditional patterns and designs of metre and stanza. Its gains, then, cannot but be at a severe sacrifice. There are, of course, degrees of freedom as there are degrees of success in every form of art; and a certain novelty of technique is inevitable in any original work. No two leaves on any tree are facsimiles one of the other. Even extreme innovations have only to justify themselves. The process is first a forlorn hope, then a gradual wooing and winning over of opponents, the shedding of inorganic excesses, and a final digestion into the accepted and traditional. Free verse is not yet perhaps out of the balance.

Among the most generous tributes in literature are those which poets have paid one to another. Nevertheless, and whatever penalties the Muses may inflict on them for the treason, they can be inordinately partisan. Some, like the capercailzie, sing best with their eyes shut—blind to all rivals. Others, like the raven (and even lesser birds), resent the presence of any interloper in the sacred territory. They resemble fervid patriots who in their zeal for the fatherland turn to and rend one another. Rival *isms* and schools outfeud the Capulets, heedless of the fact that even if craftsmanship may be in part learned, no art can be taught, and none to any fine purpose deliberately imitated—except perhaps for practice. Each generation in turn, moreover, is apt to fail in sympathy with that which precedes and that which follows it. So also with aim and method. The new wine cannot stand the strain even of neighbouring the old bottles. But time passes, the new grows old, and the great English tradition, refreshed with innovations it can easily engulf, flows tranquilly on. Every such innovation must pave and pay its way.

What at first sight may appear to be free verse is to be found in Coventry Patmore's odes in *The Unknown Eros*. A brief inspection at once reveals their severely metrical and alliterative basis, and that the lines are rhymed. This scrupulous artist could well claim a right to complete freedom; but he used it to impose on himself even more delicate restrictions and thus the more masterfully to triumph over them. That seems to have been Nature's wayward procedure in her long journey towards the anatomy of Man.

Free verse is still in the nature of a novelty; a careful analysis of its technique made by Robert Bridges reveals its dangers.

Prose-Poetry

Prose-poetry, on the other hand, is a use of language discovered centuries before Euphuism and Lyly. It is *fine* writing *in excelsis*, and its most exotic bloom is derided as the purple patch, a phrase at least as remote as Horace. And although there appears to be no specific reference to it in *A Dictionary of Modern English Usage*, the views of the author of this invaluable and intimidating work concerning it will be found scattered among his remarks on genteelisms, gallicisms, poeticisms, purisms, 'the tuppence coloured,' the stylish, and elsewhere. Every imaginative young writer of genuine promise is likely to some extent to fall a prey to this temptation—to be 'literary', that is, precious, elaborate, decorative, to use words for their sounds' sake only, to pose a little, to stylize.

Still, *most* prose poetry is at least innocent in intention. The 'make-up' is intended to improve, not to deceive. It may, too, be the outcome of an extreme sensitiveness, or self-consciousness, of an easily forgivable vanity, or sheer lack of practice. It may also spring out of a genuine delight in the rich, the ornate, the exquisite, and the lavish.

Self-consciousness moreover, all but amounting to the affected, when it is present in moderation, may be a grace note in a valuable prose that manifestly intends it, and may even slightly parade it—Francis Thompson's, or Crashaw's, or Jeremy Taylor's, for example. Every art conceals artifice, and in this, finally, only a virgin naturalness of soul can fully succeed. There is a circuit, too, which highly original minds are apt to make in life—away from a first simplicity, and back to it again.

Apart from the prose-poetry which is indulged in for its

own sweet sake and without ulterior motive, there is a variety that is intended solely as a bait, a decoy. It is a literary bird-lime. The snarer concocts it with the utmost care and if he is to be successful he must be a cunning ornithologist. He has at any rate learned to say Bo to a goose in at least nineteen different keys. His tone is usually genteel and ref*a*ned (but it may be starkly colloquial). His raptures are never careless and usually heartless. He is out to sell—anything whatever, possibly even a pup. The Woman's Page which now provides the sugar and spice even of our sedatest periodicals is only less rich in this commodity than are the advertisement columns of every Lady's Paper. Hosier, haberdasher, corsetière, cosmetician and the rest, one and all they bring forth the best butter in a lordly dish. And it is the tone, not the intent, that differs when this lubricant is supplied by wine-merchant, house-agent, seedsman, tobacconist, purveyor of patent medicines or company promoter.

'Have you ever thought', murmurs the seducer, 'about the enormous amount of printed matter which is published in Britain every year? . . .'—not a little of it consisting of little feministicities like, 'Lady X is an adept in the charming art of hostess-craft, and gives a new angle of human interest to recipes that are commendable in themselves. There is the homely onion broth. . . .' Like, 'Nowhere have I sensed a more welcome air of comfort than that which pervades afternoon tea rites in the drawing-rooms of country houses . . .' and the heady lyricism of:

'You could scarcely help being a siren in——. It holds its shape—at the same time that it holds yours—oh, it's a joy to wear, it's so flexible, so free, and yet so clinging that no lovely line is lost. It is lasting, too . . . smart, shiny, and what the French like to call "sportive".'

But arias of this kind, songs sung *to* the sirens, are as the sands of the sea-shore for multitude. *Man* appears to prefer a rather larger dose of the prosaic with his prose-poetry. He is expected to ease his pocket if he is assured that he is keeping his head.

'Sherry Wine is in every way a Wine suitable for all occasions. Pale amber in colour, with its attractive aroma of the "flor", this sherry possesses the bouquet of a true fino. Light and gentle, it leaves the palate with a dry and refreshing finish. A wine that will not only quench the thirst and give an appetite, but will grace any sideboard.'

Or this, for which even Jenny Wren might jilt her currants:

'Rather distinctive of the Vintage which, on the 'nose', is exceedingly flattering and very pronounced, and on the palate the Wine is far drier than one is led to expect. Very fine luncheon Wine, as it can be served all through the meal; full and of excellent aroma. Showing quality.'

Flowers of speech, again, for flowers from the nurseryman. Two peonies:

'Very rich deep crimson or ruby-red, and the central stamens, which are flattened, are of the same tint, but each one is edged with gold, giving an "effect of light" in the centre, somewhat baffling to describe. The whole forms a glowing mass of colour. Extra. Mid-season. Sold out. . . .'

'Very beautiful. A fine form and most attractive colour; bright rich peach pink, and golden petaloids; it has a high centre of cream coloured short petals, with cockatoo crest of pink tipped with carmine; quite unique and very choice; mid-season to very late; extra.'

The price follows suit.

The expert hopes to persuade; he may even succeed in gulling. His one aim is to be read, marked, digested and acted upon, and he exercises all the cajolery and astuteness which he is capable of: naïvety, wit, fancy, frivolity, sententiousness, solemn humbug. And Autolycus was master of this art: 'Had not the old man come in with a whoo-bub . . .

and scared my choughs from the chaff, I had not left a purse alive in the whole army.' The victim is usually aware of her or his danger, but the singed moth returns again and again to the candle. None the less, this universal lure in pursuit of lucre (and even publishers have a word for it) is nothing better than a pseudo prose-poetry steeped in guile. Nor of course is it confined to advertisers. Don Juan had mastered its rudiments before he went to his dame's school; the coquette, the seductress, while she was still in long clothes.

'Why, my beloved, did you not come to me? Oh, beloved, are you ill? Come to me, sweet one. I waited and waited for you, but you came not. I shall wait again to-morrow night, same hour and arrangement. Do come, sweet love, my own dear love of a sweetheart. Come, beloved, and clasp me to your heart. Come, and we shall be happy. A kiss, fond love. Adieu, with tender embraces, ever believe me to be your own ever dear, fond Mini.'

Here, like the faint vibrant overtones of a glass tumbler or fiddle-string, rings an echo not only of the Song of Solomon but of all the passionate love-letters that were ever written. To scoff at this very brief example merely on that account would imply either a conveniently bad memory, a peculiarly arid career, a cynical disillusionment or a stupid heart. Still, we are entitled to examine it. Here, then, obviously, is a brief prose-poem. Its refrains and assonances—short *u* ('come', 'beloved'), long *a*'s and *e*'s, the alliterative *l* and haunting *m*—recur as if to the manner born. Four or five lines of but just-hidden blank verse are detectable. Of thought there is hardly a vestige; of sentiment and apparent emotion a good deal. But is that emotion perfectly genuine? Are these decoying rhythms spontaneous or habitual or affected? Is there not a repeated note or cadence of falsity throughout, that juts suddenly into full view in the stark 'same hour and arrangement', and in the anti-climax of that single kiss? One wonders. An unbiased reader may come to different conclusions; find only perfect sincerity, intense emotion and a desperate pining in these sentences. I myself was already aware that this letter was written by Madeline Smith a day or two before the death of the unwanted and wearied-of lover whom she was afterwards charged with poisoning? The Scottish verdict was Not Proven; it must apply also perhaps to this indictment of her prose.

Poetic Degrees

As too sensuous, too emotional, or too fanciful a prose is apt to be tinged with purple, so verse with the same weaknesses may be tinged with the puce. They are equally poor extremes. Just, however, as a fine prose may ever and again quietly break into the poetic and in that degree affect us as poetry does, so as fine a verse will reveal *degrees* of poetry also. Is not this true, indeed, of every fine poem? Even the briefest of songs or lyrics is not equally poetic throughout; though what the verbal minimum may be that can enshrine poetry is an extremely nice question. Its completeness *is* the poem; but it shows light and shade, gradation of intensity and condensation—like a smouldering fire again and again breaking into flame. And this, whether it is simple yet condensed, as in Wordsworth; three strands thick with involved meanings, as in Donne; tortuous and agonized, as in *Macbeth*.

Are there not such gradations of the poetic even in *The Ancient Mariner*? It is an acknowledged masterpiece of the purest imaginative genius. Only after the closest scrutiny are we likely to realize to what degree. In Alice Meynell's words: 'It is more full of a certain quality of extreme poetry . . . the most single magic—than any other in our language.' Nevertheless, as she adds, 'the reader must be permitted to call the story silly.' Silly or not, the poem is so far prosaic as to deliver at last a text and to preach a brief sermon. 'He prayeth best who loveth best All things both great and small,' a text which, even although it is one of the very few affirmations in the poetic creed, appears to have been an after-thought, since the statement in the 'argument' of the poem—'How the Ancient Mariner cruelly and in contempt of the laws of hospitality killed a Sea-bird, and how he was followed by many and strange judgements'—was added two years after the poem first appeared, in 1789.

As for its onset:

> *It is an ancient mariner,*
> *And he stoppeth one of three.*
> *'By thy long grey beard and glittering eye,*
> *Now wherefore stopp'st thou me? . . .'*

there could hardly be a more abrupt Sesame. Sindbad has doubled his part with Ali Baba's. What of the treatment of its theme? Certain critics of its day greeted it with derision. And in his *Note-Books* Samuel Butler pilloried its title. A sonneteer himself, and perhaps for this reason, he declared that 'the highest poetry is ineffable'. 'The last thing a great poet will do in these days is to write verses,' since 'versifying' is poetry's 'lowest form'—a paradox which he left naked and unashamed, but which, incidentally, was either a sad slur on the 'days' referred to or a telling tribute to the medium of prose.

His quiz of Coleridge's masterpiece is that it 'would not have *taken* so well if it had been called "The Old Sailor", so that Wardour Street has its uses'. If a tinge of the archaic is the mark of Wardour Street the charge is true—the spelling, such words as eft-soones, and so forth. But then the *Rime* is dateless as well as timeless, and its greybeard loon, Butler notwithstanding, was neither intended to be nor is 'any old' sailor, any 'elderly naval man'—either of the Dibdin or *Treasure Island* or *Nancy Brig* order. He is Coleridge's 'Ancient Mariner', once young, vigorous and venturous, delighting in his cross-bow; now for ever ineffably aged—a sailor whose destiny never was on any earthly sea or shore.

So little concern has he with ordinary human life that—unless I am mistaken—Coleridge tells us neither the name of his ship, nor the port from which she sailed and to which she tragically returned, nor the nature of her cargo. Her steersman is frequently mentioned, but neither her master nor any one of her officers. Nor is any member of her crew spoken of as going below. And would it have been by one iota the better poem if these data had been added to it—or if the star within the crescent's nether tip had been placed well beyond it? One might as well assert that Samuel Butler's *Erewhon*, which begins in a wild entrancing romantic strain and lapses into a fantastic satire, is Wardour Street for Nowhere. In any case it is highly improbable that any child who has feasted his imagination on this matchless poem can have been led astray into such petty entanglements as these.

In spite, however, of its purity as poetry, the Rime enshrines—as Professor Livingstone Lowes has revealed—a multitude of transfigured memories gleaned by Coleridge from scores of books written not in verse but in that plain, faithful, and evocative prose which is almost peculiar to writings in English concerned with the sea and its intrepid seamen (from the days of Noah to Hakluyt, and on to our own). Coleridge had read, marked, and digested; but in that supremely poetic mind this last process, inscrutable transmutation, eventuated in this magical lyric. Its elements, that is, were chiefly borrowed; its essence was solely his own. The poem, then, is founded on facts originally based four-square on a prose foundation. Nevertheless the poem itself is perhaps the most imaginative and romantic in the language, and resembles in its magic an ideal architecture, 'frozen music'.

Further yet. Pondering on his work, it seems, fifteen years after he had completed its first draft—amplifying, refining, enriching, discarding as he went—Coleridge renewed his conception of his theme, and added (what are hardly less remarkable) marginal glosses in prose which at least suggest a motive, that of clarifying and enriching the poem without endangering its poetic effect. Here is a fragment:

'In his loneliness and fixedness [the Mariner] yearneth towards the journeying Moon, and the stars that still sojourn, yet still move onward; and every where the blue sky belongs to them, and is their appointed rest, and their native country and their own natural homes, which they enter unannounced, as lords that are certainly expected and yet there is a silent joy at their arrival.'

In this very unusual and sustained sentence of rhythmical prose we find, as we might well expect, fragments of metrical rhythm:

In his lóneliness and fíxedness he yéarneth;

the haunting hesitant cadence of,

and ís their appóinted rêst;

of,

There is a sílent jôy at their arrívál.

Indeed, the whole tenor of the gloss is far nearer in kind to the poem it annotates than what we commonly mean by prose. And what does it gloss? A verbal wizardry only the more enchanting the more closely it is pondered:

The moving Moon went up the sky,
And no where did abide:
Softly she was going up,
And a star or two beside—

Her beams bemocked the sultry main,
Like April hoar-frost spread;
But where the ship's huge shadow lay
The charmed water burnt alway
A still and awful red.

Beyond the shadow of the ship,
I watched the water-snakes;
They moved in tracks of shining white,
And when they reared, the elfish light
Fell off in hoary flakes.

Within the shadow of the ship
I watched their rich attire:
Blue, glossy green, and velvet black,
They coiled and swam; and every track
Was a flash of golden fire. . . .

The metrical basis of each line in turn exquisitely hovers, as it were, beneath its rhythms, like the shadow of a kestrel above a meadow. As for their longs and shorts, there is not only a continuous fractional variety of measure in every syllable, as there is an intertwining of image, statement, emotion in each line, but the quality, in some indefinable accord, of each several sound (as does the colour) continually varies. Nevertheless and needless to say, the poem is not of an equally fine texture and poetic intensity throughout. How could it possibly be? Its conclusion a little flags, its imaginative coherence wavers. There are tinges of the too fantastic and of the prosaic. Contrariwise, there are scattered stanzas which, although they are external to its own pervasive region of fantasy, and remind us of the familiar and the near, are not only of a singular precision and beauty, but completely apposite—like transfigured objects of the waking senses seen in a dream:

It ceased; yet still the sails made on
A pleasant noise till noon,
A noise like of a hidden brook
In the leafy month of June,
That to the sleeping woods all night
Singeth a quiet tune. . . .

and, again:

Like one that on a lonesome road
Doth walk in fear and dread,
And having once turned round walks on,
And turns no more his head;
Because he knows, a frightful fiend
Doth close behind him tread. . . .

Briefly, then, Coleridge based his poem on borrowed prose; he epitomized it in poetic prose; and its purest poetry reveals itself in it like the wind in a field of wheat, or a flame in a firebrand.

As with poets, so with men in general, and with nations. The great stream of the world's events and achievements flags at times into the languid and shallow, resumes its full and equable flow, or, when the moon and sun in their courses, and the elements in their apparent caprices, combine their influences, its waters overwhelm their banks, the whole countryside is under flood. The sources, energy, and direction even of the human imagination *appear* to be equally capricious.

In his *Guide to Modern English History* William Cory refers to a renewal of these waters, not only in literature, but in English life, and attributes it in part to the influence of two writers. He is speaking of the early years of the nineteenth century:

'In country houses the pleasure of reading was the only pleasure that could compete with field sports. Stupidity or dullness could be lessened only by some excitement. The only literature that could excite was the romantic narrative. By the spirit of romance the sense of duty was heated. Heretofore the fictions tolerated in virtuous parlours had sounded like the purrings of tame cats. In the Waverley period there was heard twice a year a brave man's trumpet, and no one was afraid to listen.

'Of the imaginative literature issued in the same years with the Waverley novels there was a considerable proportion that affected, sooner or later, the character of the people; it was far more effectual than the contemporary music or painting. That which was first in quality, the poetry of Mr. Keats, ripened in a corner, and dropped seeds which twenty years later bore such fruit as no other nation could match. . . .'

He adds, of Wordsworth, 'whom Mr. Keats looked upon as one advanced into a region not yet explored by himself', that he taught his readers 'to recognize beauty in the tranquil affections of plain folks'.

The influences of a book on one's mind may be no less powerful for being stealthy and all but secret. Here Cory specifies as *supreme* influences—not merely on the tastes of a little clan but on the character of a great nation—the prose romances of Scott, the poetry of Keats. Nor, we may be certain, was he precluding the lyrics and narrative poems of Scott, or the letters, matchless in their kind, of Keats. As much as the two men themselves, if one so young as Keats can be so described, these differ in theme, aim, and outlook. But whether in verse or prose, the tales, the lyrics, the letters are pervasively poetic both in principle and in effect.

The Eighteenth Century

And what of the century that preceded the reveille of these brave trumpets?—the literature that was taboo to the tame cats in the virtuous parlours? We are accustomed to regard the Augustan age as the age of prose; even although in music, in painting, in domestic architecture, in furniture and porcelain, in manners and the arts of society it attained an ideal of finish, serenity, seriousness, and charm which we hardly associate with the prosaic and which, alas, has not since then been approached, let alone equalled or excelled. Among its other activities, it ordered, tempered, refined, rationalized, and, in a word, domesticated English prose. Nevertheless, the writers who were responsible for this invaluable achievement, Addison, Gray, Johnson, Defoe, Swift, Goldsmith amongst them, were themselves poets, if poets of varying magnitude. Their prose was of a piece and pitch with their verse. How much a literary fashion and the general trend of the age hindered the full freedom and scope of their imaginations it is difficult to say. However that may be, Gray's description in a letter to a friend of a sunrise—with its wildly vivid, 'and all at once a little line of unsufferable brightness'—is not less poetic in effect than the solemn and deepening twilight of the passing day that tranquilly invades our mind in reading his *Elegy*. Indeed, a grace of the spirit closely related to poetry is more frequent in his correspondence than in his odes. It would be no less difficult, too, to balance the poetic claims of Cowper the letter-writer with those of the author of *The Poplar Field*, *The Nightingale and the Glowworm*, and the tender and natural lines to his mother's picture.

It is, again, the degree rather than the quality of the poetic that distinguishes Goldsmith's *Deserted Village* from *The Vicar of Wakefield*. Walter Scott praised Smollett's *Ode on Independence*. Sir William Blackstone, author of the *Commentaries*, having wedded the Law, bade a fond and tender farewell to his Muse:

> . . . *Lost to the fields, and torn from you—*
> *Farewell!—a long, a last adieu.*
> *Me wrangling courts, and stubborn law,*
> *To smoke, and crowds, and cities draw. . . .*
> *Or, where in silence all is drowned,*
> *Fell Murder walks his lonely round;*
> *No room for peace, no room for you;*
> *Adieu, celestial nymph, adieu!*

Shakespeare, no more, thy sylvan son,
Nor all the art of Addison,
Pope's heaven-strung lyre, nor Waller's ease,
Nor Milton's mighty self must please:
Instead of these, a formal band
In furs and coifs around me stand;
With sounds uncouth and accents dry,
That grate the soul of harmony,
Each pedant sage unlocks his store
Of mystic, dark, discordant lore. . . .

Fielding, too, wrote verse, a lively and sonorous hunting-song, for example, which is at least as full of music as are the horns of the huntsmen, and but one such song is proof enough that its writer is a poet, and is possessed, however intermittently, of the poetic leaven.

Not, needless to say, that any particular writer's prose is necessarily tinged with the poetic because he is an occasional versifier. But most published verse was at least intended by its writer to be poetry; and its achievement entailed a poet's discipline if not his indispensable gifts. It is, again, a discipline that has been repeatedly recommended to would-be writers of good prose. Indeed to practise voice and ear with the essentials of good verse is to ensure a due heed to the verbal music which is the *sine qua non* of poetry itself—and a source of satisfaction and delight in every fine prose.

So, again, with those prose masterpieces, *The Tale of a Tub*, *Gulliver's Travels*, *Robinson Crusoe*, and the earlier *Pilgrim's Progress*. One and all were the work of poets. Defoe himself declared that his Crusoe was an allegory—'sustained metaphor'—and this classification includes within its range *The Divine Comedy* and the *Faërie Queene*. However closely, too, his unwearying romance keeps to actualistic detail, it is yet a work of imaginative invention, as, far more richly and movingly, are the adventures of John Bunyan's pilgrim—yet another allegory. 'During the latter half of the seventeenth century, there were', says Macaulay, 'only two minds which possessed the imaginative faculty in a very eminent degree. One of these minds produced the *Paradise Lost*, the other the *Pilgrim's Progress.*'

Satire and poetry again, the one destructive, the other creative in intent, are usually uneasy bedfellows, but the clarity, vividness and invention (insisted on by all the old critics as requisites in poetry) and the imaginative illusion of the *Travels*, have set Gulliver's adventures—with Alice's in Wonderland—among the nursery classics. Alice, indeed, would soon find herself perfectly at home with good-natured Glumdalclitch, even although she was only of the 'semi-bigness' of a *splacknuck*, and 'not above forty feet high'. It is against the background of Swift's limpid and musical prose that his bitter contempt of the follies and vilenesses of mankind is set; like circling vultures against the harmless blue of the sky. Even at his extreme of poisoned hatred that prose resembles an antiseptic. However 'common' and 'unclean' his objects often are, they are seldom solely that. He suffuses them with his own creative interest, which in itself has an effect resembling that of beauty; just as common pebblestones, while being but pebbles, are more lustrous when under water.

The 'unpleasant animals', for example, encountered by Gulliver when he is set free by the buccaneers in the neighbourhood of Madagascar, are described, as precisely if not so winningly, (with 'anus' and 'excrement' in lieu of seed, root, and fruit) as any flower in the *Herball*; and the horses 'walking softly' in the fields resemble courtiers at a levee, albeit they are as virtuous as they are urbane. Until we learn that the Yahoos are meant for *us*, we shall not be scandalized, and even then may remain amused. So medical works, because their purpose is different, can expatiate on ulcers and emetics far more fully, yet less nauseatingly even than Swift. And *they* need no dulcet verbal allurements for antidote.

Swift, consummate craftsman, in part no doubt intent on his reader's pleasure but chiefly on his own, usually ensures that his honey, even if its nectar originated in aconite or hemlock, shall sweeten his gall; that the most venomous of his gnats shall be enshrined in amber. Indeed, a satirical verse or prose vilely written is merely powder in fermenting jam. It is not in Paradise that we shall listen to bad sermons; and it was only in Paradise *lost* that Adam was compelled to listen to Michael's—'prime Angel bless'd'—on the cogent text of '*not too much*'. With the 'wit' that keeps prose sweet, Swift's, of course, continually scintillates, but the wit itself is often of a faintly poetic cast.

One of the most imaginative fragments, again, in Dryden's work—in its serenity, tone, and atmosphere, is the page or two introducing his *Essay on Dramatic Poesy*. Few scenes in English fiction are so diaphanous in their realization. We ourselves, as we read, sit like phantoms on the thwarts, listening each in turn to these four enquirers into their theme—so tranquil in their views and judgments, whatever enthusiasm may lie beneath them, as they debate in their boat being rowed upon the quiet Thames. In its special graces, the apparently heedless masculine ease and mastery of Dryden's prose at its best is unrivalled, and none but a poetic mind could be capable of it. Even his common sense is gilded with wisdom. Indeed, his verse of the antithetical order, salted with drastic criticism of life and of humanity, must surely have been a more severe restriction to his genius.

Translation

As soon as we find ourselves among the divines, the character writers, the dramatists, the voyagers and the adventurers, and the translators of the earlier centuries, Maundeville, Holland, Adlington, Thornley, Florio, including the miraculous committees who, following chiefly the genius of Tyndale, were responsible for the Authorized Version of the Bible, we are in the presence of a prose of an infinite variety, richly English, noble, exquisite, simple, elaborate, lavish or fastidious, and brimming over with qualities which we always associate with poetry itself.

Translation is one of the fine arts. It entails not merely the mastery of two languages and the comprehension of two orders of mind, but the subtlest intuition, and a commensurate skill in the use of words. From the supreme and condensed simplicity of the first chapter of Genesis to the visionary glories of the Revelation—Isaiah, Ecclesiastes, the Book of Job, the Song of Solomon, the Gospels of St. Luke and St. John, St. Paul's Epistles—the English Bible is of a verbal music and mastery as matchless as its meaning is profound. It is a book not only incomparably poetic, but of an incomparable diversity of the poetic.

'... and the doors shall be shut in the streets, when the sound of the grinding is low, and he shall rise up at the voice of the bird, and all the daughters of musick shall be brought low; also when they shall be afraid of that which is high, and fears shall be in the way, and the almond tree shall flourish, and the grasshopper shall be a burden, and desire shall fail: because man goeth to his long home, and the mourners go about the streets: or ever the silver cord be loosed, or the golden bowl be broken, or the pitcher be broken at the fountain, or the wheel broken at the cistern. Then shall the dust return to the earth as it was: and the spirit shall return unto God who gave it.'

As we read, that spirit within us seems for the moment to have returned to a state of being and to an abode of which the earth with all its loveliness is only a partial and illusive reflection. We awaken from it, as it were; and it is then as if we became conscious that a bird which has been singing in some remote region of the mind has ceased to sing. Tree, bowl, pitcher, wheel, fountain, dust—whatever the origin of this imagery—are objects here lovely and absolute in their kind and in an inscrutable collusion. Like things enchanted they share a secret. When the soul is in eclipse, when love prevails on us, when we are away in dream, the whole of our world is changed. Such poetry as this is a record of similar transmutations.

But the last chapter of Ecclesiastes is one of the most familiar in the Bible; its poetry may appeal to us doubly for this reason; and few mortals are insensitive to its theme. The books of the Apocrypha are for most of us much less familiar. Here, then, for comparison, are a few verses from the second book of Esdras:

'In the thirtieth year after the ruin of the city I was in Babylon, and lay troubled upon my bed, and my thoughts came up over my heart: for I saw the desolation of Sion, and the wealth of them that dwelt in Babylon. And my spirit was sore moved, so that I began to speak words full of fear to the most High.'

The writer then complains bitterly of the captivity of the people of Israel, who, he pleads, in spite of their wickedness, are still the chosen people, and yet are now in subjection to enemies more impious than themselves.

'And the angel that was sent unto me, whose name was Uriel, gave me an answer, and said, Thy heart hath gone too far in this world, and thinkest thou to comprehend the way of the most High?

'Then said I, Yea, my lord. And he answered me, and said, I am sent to shew thee three ways, and to set forth three similitudes before thee: whereof if thou canst declare me one, I will shew thee also the way that thou desirest to see, and I shall shew thee from whence the wicked heart cometh.

'And I said, Tell on, my lord. Then said he unto me, Go thy way, weigh me the weight of the fire, or measure me the blast of the wind, or call me again the day that is past.

'Then answered I and said, What man is able to do that, that thou shouldest ask such things of me? And he said unto me, if I should ask thee how great dwellings are in the midst of the sea, or how many springs are in the beginning of the deep, or how many springs are above the firmament, or which are the outgoings of paradise: peradventure thou wouldest say unto me, I never went down into the deep, nor as yet into hell, neither did I ever climb up into heaven. Nevertheless now have I asked thee but only of the fire and wind, and of the day wherethrough thou hast passed, and of things from which thou canst not be separated, and yet canst thou give me no answer of them. He said moreover unto me, Thine own things, and such as are grown up with thee, canst thou not know; how should thy vessel then be able to comprehend the way of the Highest, and, the world being now outwardly corrupted, to understand the corruption that is evident in my sight? . . . Then said I unto him, It were better that we were not at all, than that we should live still in wickedness, and to suffer, and not to know wherefore.'

This is not a chosen extract, but it is of a rare beauty and solemnity, and also resembles Elihu's reply to Job's challenge against the Almighty, his self-vindication and vow to remain silent. And here, again, is poetry of a rare order, revealed not only in the range and vision of the experience related, but in such simplicities as 'my thoughts came up over my heart', 'thy heart hath gone too far in this world', 'call me again the day that is past', 'which are the outgoings of paradise', 'thy vessel'. The fact that 'incorruption' is given as a marginal gloss to 'corruption', and that certain phrases, in spite of their felicity, suggest a doubt of their complete fidelity to the original text, reveal the problems confronted by the translator. This English prose is a unique *kind* of language. It is touched throughout with a certain strangeness, resembling the half-legible characters of the inscription on some time-worn ancient monument; and assuredly verse could in no virtual respect profoundly better it.

Many of the books in the Old Testament, needless to say, are imitative renderings of Hebrew poetry, although 'if rhyme and metre are considered essential' to poetry, then that poetry 'would have to be denied to the Bible altogether'; its chief characteristics consisting 'in a certain equality, resemblance, or parallelism between the members of each period'. 'This seems to have been the most ancient and original form of poetry,' and no other poetry so easily bears translation.

So also with several passages in the New Testament. If, for example, as Canon J. M. C. Crum has pointed out in a paper on this theme, corresponding sentences in the seventh chapter of St. Matthew's Gospel and the sixth in St. Luke's are compared, one cannot fail to perceive the verbal form that is common to both:

'. . . Therefore whosoever heareth these sayings of mine, and doeth them, I will liken him unto a wise man, which built his house upon a rock: And the rain descended, and the floods came, and the winds blew, and beat upon that house; and it fell not: for it was founded upon a rock. And every one that heareth these sayings of mine, and doeth them not, shall be likened unto a foolish man, which built his house upon the sand: And the rain descended, and the floods came, and the winds blew, and beat upon that house; and it fell: and great was the fall of it.'

And St. Luke:

'. . . Whosoever cometh to me, and heareth my sayings, and doeth them, I will shew you to whom he is like: He is like a man which built an house, and digged deep, and laid the foundations on a rock: and when the flood arose, the stream beat vehemently upon that house, and could not shake it: for it was founded upon a rock. But he that heareth, and doeth not, is like a man that without a foundation built an house upon the earth; against which the stream did beat vehemently, and immediately it fell; and the ruin of that house was great.'

Other scholars, Professor Gurney in particular, have also maintained that these and similar parables in the Gospels were, in their original Aramaic, actually spoken in a simple and familiar metrical form, a form such as could be easily, surely, and truly memorized—got by heart—by those whose ineffable experience it was to listen to them.

Even in our English version the language of the beatitudes is balanced; each exemplifies a verbal design; and none obeys it servilely. To shrink from the assertion that the beatitudes are works of art is natural enough, but would this not be due to a fallacy? The ability to communicate our simplest thoughts and feelings by means of language is acquired only after an infinitude of patience and practice expended from our earliest childhood, and, whatever the extent of that practice, the utmost care and pains are needed to convey them adequately and well. So in an infinitely more delicate degree with the utterance of an innate wisdom, a unique spiritual insight and inspiration. We marvel at the mysteries of the water-diviner. Jesus, as He declared to the woman of Samaria, was a diviner of the waters of life. 'The woman saith unto him, Sir, thou hast nothing to draw with, and the well is deep: from whence then hast thou that living water? . . . Jesus answered and said unto her, Whosoever drinketh of this water shall thirst again: but whosoever drinketh of the water that I shall give him shall never thirst; but the water that I shall give him shall be in him a well of water springing up into everlasting life.'

Even, then, if what is in the mind flows from sources inscrutable, or from a divine wellspring, its expression—by language's very nature—cannot be purely spontaneous, wholly without art. Only a confused conception of art would suggest otherwise, since art is the one achievement of man, which, so far as in him lies, has been consistently faithful to the profoundest of his incentives, and in a world of the transitory is surest of preservation. What has survived of thirty-five centuries of Chinese art is proof enough of that. In no essentials of impulse, conception and aim do its best examples at either extreme differ from one another. And the dilemma of the mystic (as also in a lesser degree of any one who wishes to share his delight in poetry), is not so much that of setting down his mystical experiences in words, as of making his words fully and to their very last echo intelligible to those to whom any such experience is unknown. For words are not in the nature of experience itself, but are only one incompetent means among many of attempting to convey it. A comparison between one's own and a friend's image of Eve in the Garden of Eden, as she is described (and by herself), in the book of Genesis, in *Paradise Lost*, in Charles Doughty's *Adam Cast Forth*, and in Mr. Ralph Hodgson's *Eva*, will reveal not only how diverse are these eight poetic conceptions, but how partial and personal one's translation from words into mental imagery may be.

'What was mere language', in Mr. Odell Shepard's words, speaking of his friend Bliss Carman—and as any two poets would agree, one with the other—

What was mere language to us, after all?
Our toil and trade and art, but not the call
Of one mind to the other, not the blent
Life of our thought, oh, not the thing we meant! . . .

Mr. T. S. Eliot has expressed his admiration for 'a poetry so transparent we should not see the poetry, but that which we are meant to see through the poetry, poetry so transparent that in reading it we are intent on what the poem points out and not on the poetry. . . .' But even this feat, 'to get beyond poetry', is accomplishable only through the medium of words; although all true poetry, and certainly the purest, in the last resort, springs from, and for its communication is dependent on, a rare intuition of the mind and spirit. Our words for ourselves are evocative of the meaning *we* attach to them, and of that only; just as the sound of rippling or falling water may evoke in the mind not only its visual image but much—or little—else; or a bar of shadow, leaning eastward, that of the setting sun and of the night that will follow it; and perhaps, to a child, a dread of that coming night; and to an old or sick man the conviction that his own sun is declining, and may never rise again.

'When [wrote Andrew Bradley] poetry answers to its idea and is purely or almost purely poetic, we find the identity of form and content . . . that embodies in its own irretrievable way something which embodies itself also in other irretrievable ways, such as philosophy or religion. . . . About the best poetry, and not only the best, there floats an atmosphere of infinite suggestion. The poet speaks to us of one thing, but in this one thing there seems to lurk the secret of all . . . which, we feel, would satisfy not only the imagination, but the whole of us. . . .'

The Narrow Bridge

But to return, finally, to the tenuous technical bridge, that spans the interval between a richly rhythmical and imaginative prose and *verse*. We read the Plays and are exhausted with admiration at their verbal mastery. Was it deliberate? Strictly speaking, the question is beside the point. What conscious skill and labour, much or little, went to the actual making of anything may be no more than a wholly deceptive indication of its merit and value. The mushroom in its exquisiteness is the creation of but one day's dark; the cedar broods on in its sombre growth for centuries.

It is the end that matters, not the time spent or the means. That 'energy' which Johnson said was indispensable to genius, and which Matthew Arnold maintained was the dominant mark of the poetic and English mind, may in the act of creation triumph over difficulties with an ease that is beyond both the power and comprehension of those unpossessed of it. We might assume, too, that in mind and spirit the man of genius lives repeatedly if not habitually at a pitch beyond that of his fellows. Yet even at that he may be able to transfuse no more than a mere fraction of his experience into verse. To Shakespeare, verse—and he used it for every conceivable purpose—rhetoric, argument, narrative, wit, humour, gossiping, bawdying, hair-splitting, badinage, fantasy, passion, and, above all, poetry—appears to have become an almost spontaneous language; prose, and as masterly a prose, a departure from it. He must, however, have talked in prose, even if he seldom wrote in it. One of the extremely few fragments of a purely personal character we have of his is the dedication to the *Venus and Adonis*—and that also to *Lucrece*. He himself is speaking here—if somewhat ceremoniously and after the manner of his age. The former dedication consists of 150 words, and, it is amusing to find, some forty of them are all but metrical. He even versifies his subscription: Your hónour's in all dúty Wílliam Shákespeare. Here, also, there are no fewer than three metaphors: heir; prop; barren land and harvest. Similarly, with the dedication of *Lucrece*.

The Tempest—perhaps the last written of his plays—begins in prose; but it is a prose which may be metricalized into:

> *Blow, till thou burst thy wind, if room enough! . . .*
> *What cares these roarers for the name of king? . . .*
> *Cheerly, good hearts!—Out of our way, I say.*

Possibly the complete passage is merely disarranged blank

verse, but verse openly begins only when the desperate 'Mariners' enter:

This wide-chapp'd rascal,—would thou mightst lie drowning
The washing of ten tides!

In the second act Antonio, Sebastian, and Adrian interlard their cynical facetiousness in prose with,

Fie, what a spendthrift is he of his tongue . . .

and with,

Save means to live; of that there's none, or little . . .

When Alonzo enters all talk in verse. Ariel, speech and song, keeps solely to verse; Caliban now to verse, now to prose, and according, it seems, to what company he is in.

Briefly and generally, Shakespeare's kings and queens and the more ceremonious of his noblemen use a highly oratorical blank verse. But not all of them. Duncan is always brief and always a poet; Oberon and Titania learned their English of the bees. The facetious, worldly-minded courtiers converse for the most part in a slightly euphuistic prose, bordering closely on verse, and resembling the letters quoted in the plays. The humorous characters—including even that vast Punchinello of the poetical, Falstaff, the clowns, fools, townsmen, rustics, mechanicals, serving men, assistant murderers, watchmen and gravediggers, keep for the most part to prose, a prose rich, racy, various, condensed, sweet and measured enough to set up in their trade at least a score of young minor poets. And, like Bosola's speeches in *The Duchess of Malfi* on the same theme, one of the most poetic passages in *Hamlet*, the soliloquy on man, is in a highly figured, richly rhythmical and all but metrical prose.

Shakespeare's language, that is, adapts its levels to his own mutable purposes—from the prosaic to the supremely poetic; and this in keeping with the phantasm of his imagination, the character, who is making use of it. And his songs, no less various—in what in the best of them is only a finer music—follow their cue as readily from their context as does a snowdrop blooming in January, 'a bird that talks of the spring.' Let, indeed, the gifted young poet of our own day take, as Shakespeare did so early, to romantic comedy, there should soon be no dearth of neo-Edwardian *song*.

Whether or not, 'as yet a child', he 'lisped in numbers', Shakespeare, like every other poet, must from his cradle have been a perpetually practising novice in the use of words, and afterwards, throughout his life, a confirmed craftsman in them; as Michelangelo was in stone, Rembrandt in paint, and Bach in musical sounds. And although of his daily life and habits, of his speech and gestures, ways of looking and laughing, of spending his solitude, and the private trend of his own spirit, we know much by inference but little for certain, in one thing, as with Coleridge and Keats, we can—and actually pace for pace—trace his footprints in other men's snow. We can, that is, watch this supreme master at work not only in the use he makes of borrowed theme and story, but in the act of edging, persuading, transmuting a borrowed prose into his own superb verse; and this in particular in his Roman plays—*Coriolanus*, *Julius Caesar*, *Antony and Cleopatra*. To any student of verbal art and craft, such passages as these cannot but be of intense interest, since they reveal not only the natural bias and inclination of his mind, but the process of his workmanship. Without this aid, we might have assumed that he can never have failed to improve on his original; that his verse, in its poetical qualities at any rate, must invariably have excelled what he borrowed. But is this so?

In the following passage, Sir Thomas North, translating Plutarch's Greek, chiefly, it seems, through the French of Amyot, is speaking of Cleopatra—and in the most delicate and vigorous rhythms, many of which a slight imposition of emphasis will easily convert into the metrical:

'When she was sent unto by divers letters, both from Antonius himselfe and also from his frendes, she made so light of it, and mocked Antonius so much, that she disdained to set forward otherwise, but to take her barge in the river of Cydnus, the poope whereof was of gold, the sailes of purple, and the owers of silver, which kept stroke in rowing after the sounde of the musicke of flutes, howboyes, citherns, violls, and such other instruments as they played upon in the barge. And now for the person of her self: she was layed under a pavillion of cloth of gold of tissue, apparelled and attired like the goddesse Venus, commonly drawen in picture: and hard by her, on either hand of her, pretie faire boyes apparelled as painters doe set forth god Cupide, with little fannes in their hands, with which they fanned wind upon her. Her ladies and gentlemen also, the fairest of them were apparelled like the nymphes Nereides (which are the mermaides of the waters) and like the Graces, some stearing the helme, others tending the tackle and ropes of the barge, out of which there came a wonderful passing sweete savor of perfumes, that perfumed the wharfes side pestered with innumerable multitudes of people. Some of them followed the barge all alongest the rivers side: others also ranne out of the citie to see her coming in. So that in the end, there ranne such multitudes of people one after an other to see her, that Antonius was left post alone in the market place, in his Imperiall seate to geve audience: and there went a rumor in the peoples mouthes that the goddesse Venus was come to play with the god Bacchus, for the generall good of all Asia. . . .'

Is it possible, one might speculate, that a piece of writing so compact, serene, vivid, musical, and imaginative could by *any* technical device be bettered—given another and richer kind of life? Is it not suffused with poetry, as water may be suffused with wine . . .?

If we watch an ash or a willow tree when its leaves, twigs,

and branches are in a perpetually varying motion in the stream and currents of the wind, we are in the presence of a ravishing natural rhythm—like that of a fine prose. When we realize that this exquisitely coloured, sunlit and shadowy, gentle and deliberate bowing and swaying, surrender and recovery, this continual give and take, these almost oriental obeisances are in obedience to the wind itself, a wind whose currents in turn are themselves obedient to certain states of the atmosphere, our delight in it surely is intensified. The rhythms are now in the nature of those in verse. So with that rather drab-feathered but beguiling little bird, the spotted flycatcher. Not far from his mate in her nest, he perches on a twig made bare by his repeated visitings. And in a moment or two he may describe a series of brief unfaltering fluttering loops, possibly five or even seven in number, and with the last of them he will return once more to his perch. He *appears* to be wholly at liberty—as does the writer in prose, though this, too, is entirely a question of degree. Actually he is confined within the limits of a selected larder; and in this he resembles the writer in verse.

If that is not too poor and trivial a comparison, and North's translation may be taken as the tree and the larder, here are the winds and the wings of Shakespeare. It is Enobarbus who is speaking, until this moment content with prose so little removed from verse as, 'Ay, sir; we did sleep day out of countenance, and made the night light with drinking,' and as, 'when she first met Mark Antony she pursed up his heart, upon the river of Cydnus'; and then, verse deliberate:

'The barge she sat in, like a burnish'd throne,
Burn'd on the water; the poop was beaten gold,
Purple the sails, and so perfumed, that
The winds were love-sick with them, the oars were silver,
Which to the tune of flutes kept stroke, and made
The water which they beat to follow faster,
As amorous of their strokes. For her own person,

It beggar'd all description; she did lie
In her pavilion,—cloth-of-gold of tissue,—
O'er-picturing that Venus where we see
The fancy outwork nature; on each side her
Stood pretty-dimpled boys, like smiling Cupids,
With divers-colour'd fans, whose wind did seem
To glow the delicate cheeks which they did cool,
And what they undid did.'

'*O! rare for Antony.*'

'*Her gentlewomen, like the Nereides,*
So many mermaids, tended her i' the eyes,
And made their bends adornings; at the helm
A seeming mermaid steers; the silken tackle
Swell with the touches of those flower-soft hands,
That yarely frame the office. From the barge
A strange invisible perfume hits the sense
Of the adjacent wharfs. The city cast
Her people out upon her, and Antony,
Enthron'd i' the market-place, did sit alone,
Whistling to the air; which, but for vacancy,
Had gone to gaze on Cleopatra too
And made a gap in nature . . .'

Due allowance having been made for Shakespeare's *debt* to North, and for the difficulty of transmuting what he might more easily have invented, the poet has triumphed. But to what extent, and at what sacrifice? First, of course, he dramatizes the narrative, and embodies a spectator. Next, he makes magnificence of what seemed simple. He adds (for Enobarbus's purposes) his own sensuous nature's art to that of his original. The winds, beaten gently by the fans of the 'pretty-dimpled' boys, become lovesick, the waters are so 'amorous' that they even *follow* faster; even the wharfs are given sensibilities. The cloth-of-gold of tissue is his, the gentlewoman's hands become 'flower-soft', North's wonderful sweet savour of perfumes is now not only invisible but strange. His queen 'beggars description', and over-pictures not merely a natural but an ideal portrayal of Venus. The little fans are now divers-coloured, and, by rosying the delicate cheeks paled with the coolness they bestow, what they do, undo. He silkens the ship's tackle, and twice perfumes the air. He emotionalizes, intensifies, but also beautifies the passage, a process not always equivalent either to improving it or making poetry of it. 'To the tune of flutes', moreover, is not a quite adequate exchange for 'the sound of the music of flutes'. And why flutes only now? The actions of the nymphs and 'prettie faire' boys are slightly confused, and even if we admit that Enobarbus is improvising (he has already described Cleopatra in prose), 'So many mermaids' is little more than stuffing to fill the line, and 'a seeming mermaid' a little flat in effect if not in sound.

But compare North's 'barge' with the similitude of the burning burnished throne; his 'there ran such multitudes of people one after an other to see her', with the even more biblical and condensed, 'the city cast Her people out upon her . . .'; compare these masters, phrase by phrase, down to Shakespeare's 'whistling to the air', an air which—with an astonishing and characteristic and extravagant access of visual genius—he converts into 'an air

> *which* but for vacancy
> *Had gone to gaze on Cleopatra too*
> *And made a gap in* nature.'

Alike in the prose and in the verse, then, of these two passages, there are degrees of the poetic; each one of the two renderings, in turn, and in fragments, falling short of, equalling, or excelling the other.

So also with Milton's rendering of the story of Samson. So with a play whose flattering attribution to Shakespeare is now viewed with 'respectful incredulity'—*The Lamentable and True Tragedie of M. Arden of Feversham.* It resembles many of his own in being based on the *Chronicles.* Holinshed relates in detail the involved plotting, the cold-blooded execution, and the consequences (one of them the haunting of the field in which in darkness and snow the body of the victim was deposited), of a murder for which five men and two women were either burned or hanged. Here again comparison will show that this poetic adaptation frequently falls short of the prose of its original—not only in its general fabric but in certain vividly dramatic episodes: the holding of the candle, for example, to dazzle the victim as he sits intent on his game of draughts or chequers with his rival; and Alice Arden's remorseless 'seven or eight picks into the breast' after the murder has been committed. Holinshed not only gave the poet every impulse he needed (more, indeed, than he could use), including Alice herself—'a gentlewoman, young, tall, and well favoured of shape and countenance'—whom he re-mints and makes from head to foot his own; but even such melodramatic names for his third and fourth murderers as blacke Will and Shakebag! The few fragments of dialogue recorded in the *Chronicles* are not only aptly placed, they not only condense and emphasize both narrative and action, but they are also almost as close to definite verse as prose can tend. ' "Yea (said she)",'—it is Alice Arden secretly debating the subject of poisons with the painter, who, oddly enough, has no part in the play—' "Yea (said she), but I would have such a one made, as should have most vehement and speedie operation to dispatch the eater thereof"; "That can I doo" (quoth he) and forthwith made hir such a one . . .'; ' "Mistresse Ales," says her husband, "what milke have you given me here?" Wherewithall she tilted it over with hir hand, saing, "I weene nothing can please you" '; ' "By his bloud," cries blacke Will, "I know not, nor care not, but set up my staffe, and even as it falleth I go." ' And, again, when Arden, if not his enemy, is intent solely on his game: ' "Now maie I take you sir if I will." "Take me (quoth maister Arden) which waie?" ' And previously to this: 'Then she sent for two Londoners to supper, the one named Prune, and the other Cole, that were grosers, which before the murder was committed, were bidden to supper. When they came, she said: "I marvell where maister Arden is; we will not tarie for him, come ye and sit downe, for he will not be long:" ' i.e.

. . . I
Marvell where maister Arden is; we will
Not tarie for him; come ye and sit downe,
For he will not be long. . . .

And last, that cry of appalled lamentation: 'Oh the bloud of God helpe, for this bloud have I shed. . . .'

Conclusion

To return, finally, from the days of Elizabeth to our own. Poetry, which in its being and creation is the outcome of wonder and delight, seems to have been an element in the very air the Elizabethans breathed. Theirs was an earthly background that had been suddenly renewed and amplified, was largely unexplored and appeared to be inexhaustible. The imagination could range unchecked; and in a boundless freedom that was not without its dangers. The writers of the age, like merchant adventurers haunted by the dream of El Dorado, were in a state of mind eager and vigilant, avid for marvels, for the heroic, the bizarre and the extreme. Theirs was the prose, says W. E. Henley, of adventure and romance, and these 'are the best motives for sound and spirited English'. There is indeed a fulness, ease, flexibility and grace in the words which carry their matter, whether it is concerned with humanity, nature, knowledge or the things of the imagination. It resembles a brimming river bearing a richly-cargoed galleon at the flood. At its best this prose is as faithful to its meaning as is its image to a ship upon the water. In its rhythms, cadences and progression it is a revealing reflection of its sense. It sweeps forward, with recurrent onsets and withdrawals, like the waters of an incoming tide: and the full-rigged ship, in full sail (if our nautical metaphor will stretch to the comparison), returns once more to an even keel.

In self-evident respects it both transcends and falls short of the prose of the Augustan age that followed it, in which the ideals of order, sobriety, rationality and good sense predominate. But it was a 'level of prose far higher than our own'. Why?

Of life's riches and resources, apart from the wear and tear of time, there remains with us nearly everything that these writers exulted in. And we have much else besides. Only the pen of omniscience, endowed with our available vocabulary of five hundred thousand words, compared with the six thousand that sufficed the translators of the Authorized Version of the Bible, could exhaustively expatiate upon it. Yet, as individuals, we can each of us take up his station under this Niagara and, our own small vessel in hand, fill that at least to the brim. If nowadays, however, the possessor of a spirited and vigorous imagination, in the fullness of his heart, and passionately constrained to reveal his gratitude for the riches of life and of the world around him, desires to express himself in words, is an appropriate and *acceptable* language easily at his command? Has there occurred, as it were, another gap—but this in human nature?

We are surrounded with a boundless wilderness of print. It contains refreshing oases, but otherwise, and in general, what terms would be arid enough to describe the sterility, flatness and inanition of its sands? Literature is an art,

English literature is an excellent example of that art. And, however numerous in kind and technique its varieties may be, that art is one. But to how many of the host of books that continually cascade from our presses can the word be justly and fully applied? How many of them are even within call of what concerns the imagination, of poetry?

There is the language of fact and of science, admirable for its purposes but not exactly dancing with life or shot with the magical; there is the language of fiction, but fiction is at present chiefly concerned with naturalism, realism, actualism; there is the current ideal of a belletristic prose—that it shall be plain, direct, concise, restrained; and last, there is verse. In this, it is generally assumed, the poetic imagination, like a bird in the air, can disport itself at ease and with abandon. But although an appetite for rhymes and jingles is no less natural in most young children than that for mud-pies, lollipops and daisy-chains, although the ability to make use of the manifold devices of metre appears to be innate, although a poet is born and is not self-made, the writing of verse is none the less a craft requiring assiduous practice, and an unusual intensity and persistence of impulse. Its rules and restrictions and its concern with poetry cannot but to some extent, even for the skilful, narrow its range of theme. 'With this key Shakespeare unlocked his heart.' Yes, but the sonnet is only a *more* difficult key to manipulate than verse of any other form or pattern; and Shakespeares are few.

The reader of verse, moreover, if it is also to unlock his own heart and mind, must have acquired a certain mastery of its technique more delicate and complex than that needed for the appreciation of prose—which has been familiar to him from his nursery. If, then, poetry is assumed to be confined to verse, there is the danger of restricting its audience, of further narrowing its range, and—as is obvious nowadays—of allowing it to become a precious preserve for the delectation solely of the fastidious, the intellectual and the few. If, on the other hand, in the act of imaginative creation the poetic type of mind is in a condition that differs from the habitual not essentially but only in degree, then it needs for its expression a means, a method, a speech that will adapt itself without excess of friction to every such degree. Will verse suffice?

Let us take a very simple example:

> . . . *Weep not for me when I am gone,*
> *Dear tender one, but hope and smile:*
> *Or, if you cannot choose but weep,*
> *A little while weep on,*
> *Only a little while.*

To alter a syllable of this brief stanza, written when its author was only twenty-two, would be to brush the dyes from a butterfly's wing, to shake out the dew from a wild flower. Its form is itself—that faintly echoing 'on'; the exquisite pause that follows it. And itself was the outcome of how many hours of reverie, foreboding, grief, resignation? A syllable changed, then, and it has lost a drop of the essence that is the spirit of Christina Rossetti. It is verse.

And here are a few lines of a stage direction concerning Napoleon's retreat from Moscow from Hardy's Epic-Drama, *The Dynasts*:

'The scene darkens, and the fires of the bivouacs shine up ruddily, those of the French near at hand, those of the Russians in a long line across the mid-distance, and throwing a flapping glare into the heavens. As the night grows stiller the ballad-singing and laughter from the French mixes with a slow singing of psalms from their adversaries.

'The two multitudes lie down to sleep, and all is quiet but for the sputtering of the green wood fires, which, now that the human tongues are still, seem to hold a conversation of their own.'

This brief passage wells with imaginative evidence of a supremely original poet, brooding—and after what scrupulous attention to the bones of his matter!—on this vast and ominous panorama of the Past. A reader familiar with his work, as with a few lines from a poem of Donne's, or Skelton's, or Herbert's, or Beddoes', might at once recognize the authorship of the first sentence. Certain words thus used—flapping, slow, the two multitudes, tongues, conversation, even the French and the heavens—are made in this context uniquely individual. But is this prose fragment any less poetical than Christina Rossetti's stanza; are any of Hardy's lyrics more *poetically* his own?

Not, yet once again, that prose can achieve that perfection of poetry to which verse at its best and loveliest attains. Nevertheless—and the one modest aim of this prolonged paper has been to suggest a truth all but self-evident!—the realm of poetry extends far beyond the confines of verse. Prose may be a platter of wood compared with that rare crystal, but it is a platter that served not only to present the apple of Eden, but also king Solomon's, and St. Odoric's, in the presence of the Grand Khan. There is a purer and fresher strain of poetry in a few verses of the Bible than in the complete works of the minor Caroline poets; in the prose of Sir Thomas Browne, Jeremy Taylor, Burton, Traherne than in whole poems by Wordsworth, Coleridge, Byron or Gray. Perhaps, now, if these had been written in prose . . .? Shelley, indeed, in attempting to illustrate the meaning which he attached to the word poetry, so expresses himself in prose as to prove how closely and naturally akin it may be even to his own lyrics:

'Poetry is the record of the best and happiest moments of the happiest and best minds. We are aware of evanescent visitations of thought and feeling, sometimes associated with place or person, sometimes regarding our own mind alone, and always arising unforeseen and departing unbidden, but elevating and delightful beyond all expression: so that even in the desire and the regret they leave, there cannot but be pleasure, participating as it does in the nature of its object. It is as it were the interpenetration of a diviner nature through our own; but its footsteps are like those of a wind over the sea, which the morning calm erases, and whose traces remain only, as on the wrinkled sand which paves it. . . .'

Rupert Brooke and the Intellectual Imagination

One evening in 1766, Dr. Johnson being then in his fifty-seventh year, two of his friends, Boswell and Oliver Goldsmith, called on him at his lodgings in Fleet Street. They then endeavoured—and endeavoured in vain—to persuade him to sup with them at the Mitre. But although he was adamant to their cajoleries, he was by no means disinclined for a talk. With true hospitality, since he himself, we are told, had decided to restrict his potations to tea and water, he called for a bottle of port. This his guests proceeded to discuss. While they sipped, the three of them conversed on subjects no less seductive than play-going and poetry.

Goldsmith ventured to refer to the deplorable fact that his old friend and former schoolfellow (already temperate in other respects) had given up the writing of verses. 'Why, sir,' replied Johnson, 'our tastes greatly alter. The lad does not care for the child's rattle. . . . As we advance in the journey of life, we drop some of the things which have pleased us; whether it be that we are fatigued and don't choose to carry so many things any farther, or that we find other things which we like better.'

Boswell persisted. 'But, sir,' said he, 'why don't you give us something in some other way?' 'No, sir,' Johnson replied, 'I am not obliged to do any more. No man is obliged to do as much as he can do. A man is to have part of his life to him-self.' 'But I wonder, sir,' Boswell continued, 'you have not more pleasure in writing than in not writing.' Whereupon descended the crushing retort, 'Sir, you *may* wonder.'

Johnson then proceeded to discuss a little problem which is familiar to but not always soluble by every aspirant to poetry—the making of verses. 'The great difficulty', he observed—alas, how truly, 'is to know when you have made good ones.' Once, he boasted, he had written as many as a full hundred lines a day; but he was then under forty, and had been inspired by no less fertile a theme than that of 'the Vanity of Human Wishes', a poem that, with other prudent counsel, bids the 'young enthusiast' hesitate before deciding to choose literature and learning as a twin spiral staircase up to Fame:

Deign on the passing world to turn thine eyes
And pause a while for Letters, to be wise . . .

Again:

This mournful truth is everywhere confess'd,—
Slow rises worth, by poverty depress'd . . .

And yet again—the poverty surmounted:

Turn from the glittering bribe thy scornful eye,
Nor sell for gold what gold could never buy . . .

Metrical composition had become less abandoned since those halcyon days. None the less, Johnson hastened to assure Goldsmith that his Muse even now that he was nearing sixty had not been wholly mum: 'I am not quite idle; I made one line t'other day; but I made no more.'*

* It is no less interesting that the assiduous if indolent author of the great Dictionary should have remembered having 'made' but a single line of verse and should have implied that a second had been beyond him, than that so stern a moralist should say out that no man is obliged to do as much as he can do. Not that many of us feel habitually so obliged. Even more inviting is the affirmation, 'A man is to have part of his life to himself,' implying that one's being a poet is a more intimate affair than any attempt

'Let us hear it,' cried Goldsmith, 'we'll put a bad one to it!' 'No, sir, I have forgot it.' And so sally succeeded sally.

How much of the virtue of Johnson's talk we are to attribute to Boswell's genius for selection and condensation, and how much to the habitual exercise of his idol's consummate judgment, penetration, humanity and good sense, is a question now beyond a precise answer. One thing however is certain: that, allowance having been made for natural or wilful prejudice, for challenge, caprice and the heat of the moment, Johnson seldom indeed let fall a remark, even at random and merely in passing, which is not worth a sensible man's consideration. He really and truly knew, rare felicity, both how to talk and what he was talking about. However dogmatic, overbearing and partisan he might be, not only in what he is recorded to have said is there always something substantive and four square, but even a quite occasional utterance—as promptly supplied as a ticket from a slot or a child's grace—may stand like a signpost at the crossroads steadfastly imploring the traveller to make further exploration.

'Why, sir, our tastes greatly alter. The lad does not care for the child's rattle.' Here, surely, is one of these signposts, one more incentive to ponder. By rattle, it would seem, Johnson meant not only things childish, but things even childlike. For such things the 'lad' does not merely cease to care. He substitutes for them other things which he likes better. Not that every vestige of charm and sentiment necessarily deserts the rattle, but other delights and interests come into play; and, what is no less important, other facul-

to reveal that one is, even to oneself. Indeed a poem also is born rather than made. Whatever the travail and labour, a living thing has been delivered (though it remains unannounced in the first column of *The Times*), and is henceforth a living thing *apart*. So much so that it may at length even be published, *à la* Rousseau. And yet, 'Never seek to tell thy love! . . .'

ties, hitherto more or less dormant (which perhaps occasion, and will certainly energize those interests), will reveal themselves. Joys and toys there may be, but they will be of another kind. Does not this imply that between childhood and boyhood a change occurs, physical, mental, spiritual; and that in minds, in which the powers and tendencies conspicuous in boyhood, and comparatively latent in earlier years, predominate, those of childhood are apt to fade and fall away?

This is true in degree, I think, of us all, whatever our gifts and graces may be; but it is true apparently in a peculiar extreme of children and boys or lads (and possibly lasses also, although they, fortunately, lie outside this immediate inquiry) who are destined, or doomed, to become poets. Poets, that is, may be divided, for illustration and convenience, into two distinct classes: those who in their dominant inclinations and characteristics resemble children and bring to ripeness the faculties peculiar to childhood; and those who resemble boys. On the one hand is the poet who carries with him through life, in varying vigour and variety, the salient characteristics of childhood, which have been modified and perhaps, but not assuredly, enriched by subsequent activities and experience. On the other is the poet who carries with him throughout his life's work the salient characteristics of boyhood although these in turn are to some extent affected by the influences of his childhood. This is little more than a theory, but it may be worth a passing scrutiny.

What are the salient characteristics of childhood? Children, it may be agreed, live in a world peculiarly their own, so much so that it is doubtful if the adult and the habituated can do more than very fleetingly reoccupy that far-away mind and heart. So too, the world of the grown-up is to children an inexhaustible astonishment and despair. They brood on us. They intently mark, watch, and try to digest us. And often, as their own future will prove, with devastating success. But possessed of tact as well as insight, they hold their peace. Perhaps it is as well that we are not invited to their inward pow-wows, until, at any rate, the hatchet for the hundredth time is re-buried. Children may remind us of butterflies, but they toil with an almost inconceivable assiduity in pursuit of life's scanty pollen and nectar, and yet, by a curious inversion of the processes of nature, they may at length become the half-comatose and purblind chrysalises which too many of us poor mature creatures so ruefully resemble. They are not so closely confined and bound in by their groping senses. Facts to them are the liveliest of chameleons. Between their dreams and their actuality looms no impassable abyss. There is no solitude more secluded than a child's, no absorption more complete, no perception more exquisite and, one might even add, more comprehensive. As we strive to look back and to live our own past again, can we recall any joy, fear, hope or disappointment more extreme and more intensely realized than those of childhood, any love more impulsive and unquestioning, and, alas, any boredom so unmitigated and unutterable?

We call their faith, even in ourselves, credulity; and are grown perhaps so accustomed to life's mysteries that we blanch at their candour. 'I am afraid you cannot understand it, dear,' exclaimed a long-suffering mother, at the end of her resources. 'O yes, I can very well,' was her little boy's reply, 'if only you would not explain.' 'Why is there such a lot of things in the world if no one knows all these things?' ran another small mind's inquiry. And yet another: 'Perhaps the world is a fancy, Mother. Shall I wake from this dream?' And yet another: 'What is the name of the *last* number, Daddy?'

We speak indulgently of childish make-believe, childish fancy. Bret Harte was nearer the truth when he maintained that 'the dominant expression of a child is gravity'. The cold fact is that few of us have the energy to be serious at their pitch. There runs a jingle:

O, whither go all the nights and days?
And where can to-morrow be?
Is anyone there, when I'*m not there?*
And why am I always Me?

With such metaphysical riddles as these—riddles which no philosopher has yet wholly answered to anybody's but his own satisfaction—certain children ease the waking moments of their inward reveries. They are contemplatives, solitaries, fakirs, who sink again and again out of the noise and fever of existence into a waking vision. We can approach them only by way of intuition and remembrance, only by becoming even as one of them; though there are many books—Edmund Gosse's *Father and Son*, for instance, Mr. Forrest Reid's *Apostate*, John Ruskin's *Præterita*, Aksakoff's *Years of Childhood*, W. H. Hudson's *Far Away and Long Ago*, Henry James's *A Small Boy and Others*—which will be a profound and lively help in times of difficulty.

This broken dream, then, this profound self-communion, this innocent peace and wonder make up the secret existence of a really childlike child: while the intellect is only stirring.

Then, suddenly, life flings open the door of the nursery. A masked harlequin springs out of the wings; and at a touch, the child becomes a boy. Not that the transformation is quite as instantaneous as that. But I have watched children on different occasions venture out into the morning for the first time to their first boys' school, and return at evening perceptibly transmogrified, so to speak, into that queer, wild, and (frequently) amiable animal known as a boy. Many fathers—and mothers—must have had a similar experience. Gradually the wholly childlike self retires like a shocked snail into its shell. Like a hermit crab it accumulates defensive and possibly aggressive disguises. Consciousness from being chiefly subjective becomes largely objective. The steam-engine routs Faërie. Actuality breaks in upon dream. Schoolboy traditions, rigid as the laws of the Medes and Persians, adjust the strait waistcoat. Discipline rounds off the glistening angles. The individual is swamped awhile by the collective. Yet the child-mind, the child-imagination persists, and, if powerful, never perishes.

But *here*, as it seems to me, is the dividing line. It is here that the boyish type of mind and imagination, the intellectual analytical type begins to show itself, and to flourish. The boy—I merely refer, if I may be forgiven, to Boy, and far more tentatively to Girl, in the abstract, though, of course, there is no such being—the boy is happy in company. Company sharpens his wits, awakens his rivalry, deepens his responsiveness, enlarges his responsibility, 'stirs him up', as we say. Apron-strings, however dear their contents, were always restrictive. He borrows a pitiless pair of scissors. He, unlike the child told of by Blake and Vaughan and Traherne, had always more or less 'understood this place'. He loves 'a forward motion'—the faster the better. When 'shades of the prison-house' begin to close about him, he immediately sets out to explore the jail. His natural impulse is to discover the thronging, complicated, busy world, to sail out into the West, rather than to dream of a remote Orient. He is a restless, curious, untiring inquirer, although preferably on his own lines rather than on those dictated to him. He wants to test, to examine, to experiment.

We must beware of theories and pigeon-holes. Theory is a bad master, and there is a secret exit to every convenient pigeon-hole. There are child-like children capable of the starkest matter-of-fact; there are typical boys who at times are dreamily matter-of-fancy. But roughly, these are the two diverse phases of man's early life. Surroundings and education may mould and modify, but the inward bent of each one of us is persistent. Can we not, indeed, divide 'grown-ups' into two distinct categories; those in whom the child is most evident, and those resembling the boy? 'Men are but children of a larger growth,' says Dryden. And Praed makes fun of the other saddening fact. 'Bearded men to-day appear just Eton boys grown heavy.' There the insistence is on quality no less than on size. But, in its fight for a place, in its fair play and its foul, in its rigid regulations, in its contest for prizes that are so oddly apt to lose their value as soon as they are won, how like the school of life is to any other school; and how widely opinions differ regarding its rules, its aims, its method, its routine and—its Headmaster.

And the poets? They, too, have attended both schools—the Dame and the High. But what are the faculties and qualities of mind which produce poetry, or which incline us towards it? According to Byron, there are four elements that we are justified in demanding of a poet. He found them, not without a self-complacent satisfaction, more conspicuous in Pope than in his own contemporaries. These elements are sense, learning (in moderation), passion, and invention. Perhaps because he was less rich in it, he omitted a fifth element, by no means the least essential. I mean imagination, the imagination that not merely invents, but that creates, and that pierces to the inmost spirit and being of life, humanity and nature. This poetical imagination also is of two distinct kinds or type: the one divines, the other discovers. The one is intuitive, inductive; the other logical, deductive. The one is visionary, the other intellectual. The one knows that beauty is truth, the other reveals that truth is beauty. And the poet inherits, as it seems to me, the one kind from the child in him, the other from the boy in him. Not that any one poet's imagination is purely and solely of either type. The greatest poets—Shakespeare, Dante, Goethe, for instance, are masters of both. There is a borderland in which dwell Wordsworth, Keats, Patmore, Mr. T. S. Eliot and many others. But the visionaries, the dreamers, the mystics, Plato, Plotinus, the writer of the book of Job, Blake, Vaughan, and, in our own day, W. B. Yeats and John Freeman, may be taken as representative of the one type; Lucretius, Donne, Dryden, Pope, Byron, Browning, Meredith and Alice Meynell, and in our own day, Lascelles Abercrombie, may be taken as representative of the other.

The visionaries, the introverts, those whose eyes are set inward and who delight in the distance, in the beginning and the end, rather than in the assaulting external incidents and excitements of life's journey, have to learn to substantiate their imaginings, to base their fantastic palaces on *terra firma*, to weave their dreams into the fabric of actuality. But the source and origin of their poetry is in the world within. The intellectual imagination, on the other hand, flourishes on knowledge, action and experience. It must first explore before it can analyse, devour before it can digest, the world in which it finds itself. It feeds and feeds upon ideas, but because it is also inventive rather than creative, it expresses them in the usual terms of humanity, of the outward senses and the emotions, makes presentations of 'life' of them, that is. There is less mystery and wonder, less magic in its poetry. It does not demand of its reader so profound or so complete a surrender. But if any boyish youthfulness is left in us, we can ardently welcome its courage, enthusiasm and energy, its zest and enterprise, its penetrating thought, its wit and fervour and arrogance; and we should not find it impossible to sympathize with its revulsions of faith and feeling, its testing and destructive scepticism, its partiality for satire.

Without imagination of the one kind or the other, mortal existence is indeed a dreary and prosaic business. The moment we begin to *live*—when we meet the friend of friends, or fall in love, or think of our children, or make up our minds, or set to the work we burn to do, or make something, or vow a vow, or pause suddenly face to face with beauty—at that moment the imagination in us kindles, begins to flame. Then we actually talk in reviving rhythm. What is genius but the possession of this supreme inward energy, in a rare and intense degree? Illumined by the imagination, our life—whatever its defeats and despairs—is a never-ending, unforeseen strangeness and adventure and mystery. This is the fountain of our faith and of our hope.

And so, by what I am afraid has been a tediously circuitous route, I have come at length to Rupert Brooke and to *his* poetry. His surely was the intellectual imagination possessed in a rare degree. Nothing in his work is more conspicuous than its preoccupation with actual experience, its adventurousness, its daring, its keen curiosity and interest in ideas, its life-giving *youth*fulness. Nothing in his work is more conspicuous by its comparative absence than reverie, a deep still broodingness. The children in his poems are few. They are all seen objectively, from without; though a wistful childlike longing for peace and home and mother dwells in such a poem as 'Retrospect' or 'A Memory'. I am not sure that the word 'dream' occurs in them at all.*

'Don't give away one of the first poets in England,' he says in one of his letters, 'but there is in him still a very, very small portion that's just a little childish.' Surely it was the *boy* in him that boasted in that easy go-ahead fashion, the boy in him that was a little shamefaced to confess to that faint vestige of childishness. Imagine William Blake or

* To my shame, if not consternation, my friend Sir Edward Marsh has pointed out to me that the word 'dream' occurs in no fewer than fifteen. Memory may be a brazen dissembler and this, I hope, will be one more salutary lesson that general impressions are none the worse for being put to a close test. Still, the fact that the peculiar, dreamlike quality and atmosphere which is so prevalent in the poetry of the visionaries is rarely present in Rupert Brooke's will not, I think, be gainsaid.

Traherne being apologetic about it! The general theme of his poems is the life of the mind, the senses, the feelings, life here and now, knocking with the knocker, slamming the door, however impatient he may be with life's limitations. Their longing is for a state of consciousness wherein this kind of life shall be possible without exhaustion, disillusionment, or acute reaction; especially the reactions physical and otherwise of growing old—and that of a second childhood.

His words, too, are for the most part absolute symbols; they mean precisely what they say and only what they say. Whereas the words of the mystics and the poets of a childlike imagination seem chiefly to mean what is left hinted at, rather than expressed. His world stands out sharp and distinct, like the towers and pinnacles of a city under the light of a cloudless sky. Their world, old as Eden and remoter than the Euphrates, lies like the fabric of a vision, bathed in an unearthly atmosphere. He desired, idolized, delighted in, and praised things-in-themselves, for their energy, vividness and naturalness; they do so for some disturbing yet solacing inward and spiritual significance, and for the reality of which things are the painted veil. *They* live or at least desire to live in the quietude of their own spirit, in a region of which a certain order of dream seems to be a reminiscence, in a far-away listening, and they are most happy when at peace, if not passive. He is all questing activity, apprehensiveness.

Nothing pleases him so much as doing things, although, fretted that both body and mind so rapidly weary, he may pine for sleep. His writing, whether in his poems, his study of Webster, or in his letters, is itself a kind of action; and he delights in things touched, smelt and tasted. He delights in them, that is, not merely for their beauty or for any remoter original they may only represent, but for their own sharp sake. He is restless, enquiring, and veers in the wind like a golden weathercock. He is impatient of every vague idealism, as wary as a fox of the faintest sniff of sentimentality. To avoid both (not always quite successfully) he flies to the opposite extreme, and to elude the 'rosy mists of poets' experience he lays emphasis on the unpleasant and sordid aspects of life. At any cost he intends to record fully and concisely the chosen salient instant's actual content—even if that instant was spent in being sea-sick. How appalling to be old *and* amorous! Say so then in a pungent sonnet. It is a poetic duty, and it will be also something of a lark. Truth at all costs: ecstatic, sober, sane or sour; let beauty take care of itself. So he came to write and to defend poems that in his friend's witty and conciliatory phrase one finds it disquieting to read at meals. A child alone, a visionary, lives in eternity; a man in time; a boy in the passing moment. It is the moments that flower for Brooke. What is his poem 'Dining-room Tea' but the lovely cage of an instant when in an ecstasy intellectually observed and analysed time and the world and even the tea streaming out of the teapot stood still?

For truth's sake he has no fear of contradictions. The mood changes, the problem, even the certainty shows itself under different aspects; he will be faithful to each in turn. Obviously he rather enjoyed shocking the stagnant and satisfied, and bating the thin-blooded philosophers, enjoyed indeed shocking and bating himself; but he also delighted, as if it were a sort of mental exercise, in looking, as we say, all round a thing. If, unlike Methuselah, he did not live long enough to see life whole, he at least confronted its parts with a remarkably steady and disconcerting attentiveness. If he was anywhere at ease, it was in 'the little nowhere of the *brain*'. Again and again, for instance, he speculates on the life that follows death. First, (mere chronological order is not absolutely material) he imagines the Heaven of the fish:

Fat caterpillars drift around,
And Paradisal grubs are found;

Unfading moths, immortal flies,
And the worm that never dies.
And in that Heaven of all their wish,
There shall be no more land, say fish.

Next, he laments despairingly in Tahiti, and with a witty, wistful mockery, at the thought of an immortality where all is Platonic abstraction and nothing is individual and real:

And you'll no longer swing and sway
Divinely down the scented shade,
Where feet to Ambulation fade,
And moons are lost in endless Day.
How shall we wind these wreaths of ours,
Where there are neither heads nor flowers? . . .

Next, he wafts himself as it were into the tenuous being of a Shade:

So a poor ghost, beside his misty streams,
Is haunted by strange doubts, evasive dreams,
Hints of a pre-Lethean life, of men,
Stars, rocks, and flesh, things unintelligible,
And light on waving grass, he knows not when;
And feet that ran, but where, he cannot tell.

Next, he deprecates the possibility of a future life even as nebulous as this:

Poor straws! on the dark flood we catch awhile,
Cling, and are borne into the night apart.
The laugh dies with the lips, 'Love' with the lover.

And, last, he is lost in rapture at the possibility which he mocked at in the first poem, sighed at in the second, belittled in the third, and denied in the fourth. And where else but in the following lines, shall we encounter ghosts so rapturously happy, so responsive to every lilt and rhythm and cadence of the words that transport them—as lightly and buoyantly as the airs of dawn the clouds of sunrise? Ghosts too so elated at the assurance of a terrestrial re-embodiment?

Not dead, not undesirous yet,
Still sentient, still unsatisfied,
We'll ride the air, and shine, and flit,
Around the places where we died,

And dance as dust before the sun,
And light of foot, and unconfined,
Hurry from road to road, and run
About the errands of the wind.

And every mote, on earth or air,
Will speed and gleam, down later days,
And like a secret pilgrim fare
By eager and invisible ways,

Nor ever rest, nor ever lie,
Till, beyond thinking, out of view,
One mote of all the dust that's I
Shall meet one atom that was you.

Then in some garden hushed from wind,
Warm in a sunset's afterglow,
The lovers in the flowers will find
A sweet and strange unquiet grow

Upon the peace; and, past desiring,
So high a beauty in the air,
And such a light, and such a quiring,
And such a radiant ecstasy there,

They'll know not if it's fire, or dew,
Or out of earth, or in the height,
Singing, or flame, or scent, or hue,
Or two that pass, in light to light,

Out of the garden, higher, higher. . . ,

Which of these conflicting solutions, we may inquire, to one of Life's obscurest problems are we to accept as finally his own? They are dissolving patterns in the liveliest of kaleidoscopes. Do, or do not, such seductive speculations as these confirm the view expressed by Plato in the *Republic* that the poets undermine the rational principle in the soul? It may be admitted that such poetry as this, in the words of Bacon, 'makes men witty'—far rather than humorous—and is unquestionably a 'criticism of life'. But can it be said to teach—as Wordsworth intended that *his* poetry should; as Dryden said that all poetry does, provided only that the learning is accompanied with delight? Well, when Mrs. Barbauld had the temerity to charge *The Rime of the Ancient Mariner* with two grave misdemeanours; first, that it was improbable, and next, that it had no moral, Coleridge cheerfully pleaded guilty to the first charge, while, as for the other, 'I told her that . . . it had too much —that is, for a work of pure imagination.' Will it satisfy 'serious' inquirers if it be suggested that these poems of Brooke's are manifestations of the intellectual imagination? Probably not. They demand of a poet a definite and explicit philosophy. They desire of him a confirmation, if not of their own faith, then of his. But it cannot be too clearly recognised that the faith of a poet is expressed in *all* that he writes. He cannot, either as a man or as a poet, live without faith; and never does. A few words enshrining whatever is lovely is an expression of faith: so, too, is all love, all desire for truth, all happiness. So too in a negative and minor degree are detestation and contempt for the tepid, the rutted, the sham, the mean and the ugly. If we have any such faith ourselves, and if we search close enough, we shall find a poet's faith expressed implicitly throughout his work.

We must, too, be thankful for many and various mercies, the mercy, for instance so richly conferred on Rupert

Brooke's workaday existence, that here was a man who never spared mind and spirit in the effort to do the best he could, and who was one of the most admirable things any man can be—a craftsman delighting in his job. We cannot demand that he shall answer each of our riddles in turn; 'tidy things up'. He shares our doubts and enigmas, exults in them, and at the same time proves that life in spite of all its duplicity and deceits and horrors, is full of strangeness, mystery, grace and power: is in essence 'good'. This, at any rate, is true of Rupert Brooke. And he knew well enough that the nearer a poet edges towards preaching, the more cautious he should be respecting his pulpit, its appurtenances, and his texts.

As with the life hereafter, so with this life, so with love. The sentimentalist always shy of the real, the cynic always hostile to it, cling to some pleasing dream or ugly nightmare of the real, aware none the less that they are in large part illusions. That is precisely what Brooke, keen, insistent, dissective, refused to do. He pours out his mind and heart for instance in the service of love. The instant that love is dead, he has, to put it politely, very little use for its corpse. He refuses point blank to find happiness in any happy medium, to be a wanderer, as he said, in 'the middle mist'. There are two sides—many more than two, as a matter of fact—to every question. 'Blue Evening' and 'The Voice' prove his competence to see both. At times, indeed, with a kind of boyish waywardness and obstinacy he prefers the other side—the ugliest—of the much-flattered moon. Helen's young face was surpassingly beautiful. True, as time went on, not only must she have lost this youthful fairness; as likely as not she also became repulsive. Well, then, as a poet, hating 'sugared lies', he must say so. And he says so with relish.

It is indeed characteristic of the intellectual imagination to insist on 'life's little ironies'. It destroys in order to rebuild. Every man of science who is not a mere accumulator of specimens and parts, possesses it. Acutely sensitive to the imperfections of the present, his hope is in the future; whereas the visionary, certainly no less conscious of flaw and evil, is happy in his faith in the past, or rather of the eternal now. The one cries 'What shall I do?' the other 'What should I be?' The one, as has been said, would prove that truth is beauty; the other knows that beauty is truth. After all, to gain the *whole* world is to save the soul.

In the lugubrious and exciting moment when Brooke wrote 'Kindliness' and 'Menelaus and Helen', it was not his aim or thought to see that age, certainly no less than youth, is, in his own phrase, '*pitiful* with mortality'. He resented the horror of decay, and associated it with death and evil. For death, whatever else it may do, while revealing the marvel of its anatomy, brings destruction to the beauty of the body; and evil brings the destruction of the spirit which is the life and light and joy of that body. They are the contraries of a true living energy. And because his mind seemed to be indestructible, and his body as intense and urgent with vitality as a racehorse, and love the very lantern of beauty, he not only feared the active passivity of death, but was intolerant of mere tranquillity, even of a quiet and constant friendliness, and, above all, of masking make-believe.

Sometimes, indeed, in his poetry, in his letters, he is not quite just to himself in the past, or even in the present, because he seemed to detect compromise and pretence. 'So the poor love of fool and blind I've proved you, For, fool or lovely, 'twas a fool that loved you.' On the other hand, listen to these fragments quoted in Sir Edward Marsh's vivifying memoir, 'I find myself smiling a dim, gentle, poetic, paternal Jehovah-like smile—over the ultimate excellence of humanity.' 'Dear! dear! it's very trying being so exalted one day, and ever so desperate the next—this self-knowledge! . . .' 'I know what things are good: friendship and work and conversation. These I shall have. . . .' He tells how the day on which he is writing has brought back to him 'that tearing hunger to do and do and do things. I want to walk 1000 miles, and write 1000 plays, and sing 1000 poems, and drink 1000 pots of beer, and kiss 1000 girls, and —oh, a million things! . . . The spring makes me almost ill with excitement. I go round corners on the roads shivering and nearly crying with suspense, as one did as a child, fearing some playmate is waiting to jump out and frighten one. . . .' Between this furious flood and ebb was one fixed assurance. 'The only thing he cared for—or rather he felt he ought to care for—in a man, was the possession of goodness; its absence the one thing he hated. . . . It was the spirit, the passion that counted with him.'

His verse tells the same tale. Life to poetry, poetry back to life again—that is one of the few un-vicious circles. Life and thought to him were an endless adventure. His mind, as he says, was as restless as a scrap of paper in the wind. How seldom is a child's. Changing moods came and went, even while his heart, that busy heart, as he called it, was deeply at rest. Wit to such a mind is a release, a safety-valve; it may be the little whistle which the small boy pipes up for Dutch courage' sake in the dark. Letters and poems flash and tingle with wit—and rare indeed are the poems in our language which, like 'Tiare Tahiti', 'The Funeral of Youth', and 'The Old Vicarage', are both witty and poetic at the same time:

And in that garden, black and white,
Creep whispers through the grass all night;
And spectral dance, before the dawn,
A hundred Vicars down the lawn;
Curates, long dust, will come and go
On lissom, clerical, printless toe;
And oft between the boughs is seen
The sly shade of a Rural Dean . . .

Till, at a shiver in the skies,
Vanishing with Satanic cries,
The prim ecclesiastic rout
Leaves but a startled sleeper-out,
Grey heavens, the first bird's drowsy calls,
The falling house that never falls . . .

Few poets have mocked and made fun and made beauty like that, all in one breath, and certainly not the childlike visionaries, though one of them knew that even by mere playing the innocent may go to heaven. And beneath Brooke's wit, though it was far less active and evident, was humour—the humour that is first cousin at least to the imagination—smiling and laughing out at the world it loves, deprecates and understands.

Byron, too, was witty, mocking, enjoyed turning things inside out and wrong side up, picking ideas to pieces, shocking the timid, the transcendental, the spinners of cocoons; but Brooke, unlike Byron, was never sourly sardonic, never with evil intent morbidly cynical. Simply because he was always testing, analysing, meditating with an intellect bordering as close on his emotions as his emotions bordered on his intellect, he was, again, in the words of the Memoir, self-conscious, self-examining, self-critical, but far less self-absorbed; never an ice-cold egotist, that is, however insistent he may be on his own individuality. More closely than Byron he resembles Mercutio:

If love be rough with you, be rough with love;
Prick love for loving, and you beat love down . . .
If thou art dun, we'll draw thee from the mire
Of this, sir-reverence love, wherein thou stick'st
Up to the ears. Come, we burn daylight, ho! . . .
I mean, sir, in delay
We waste our lights in vain, like lamps by day.
Take our good meaning, for our judgment sits
Five times in that ere once in our five wits.

And in his metaphysical turns, his waywardness, his contradictoriness, his quick revulsions of feeling, he reminds us at times—he reminded even himself (in a moment of exultation)—of the younger Donne.

Although 'magic' in the accepted sense is all but absent from his verse—the magic that transports the imagination clean into another reality, that drenches a word, a phrase, with the light that never shone even on the Hesperides, the Spice Islands or Cathay, he has that other poetic magic that can in a line or two present a portrait, a philosophy, and fill the instant with a changeless grace and truth. It shines out in such fragments, for instance, as:

Beauty *was there,*
Pale in her black; Dry-eyed; she stood alone . . .

or

And turn, and toss your brown delightful head,
Amusedly, among the ancient Dead;

or

And less-than-echoes of remembered tears
Hush all the loud confusion of the heart;

or

There are waters blown by changing winds to laughter
And lit by the rich skies, all day. And after,
Frost, with a gesture, stays the waves that dance
And wandering loveliness. He leaves a white
Unbroken glory, a gathered radiance,
A width, a shining peace, under the night.

What, again, is it but this magic which stills the heart and gives light to the mind, in one of the less well-known, but not the least quiet and tender of his poems, 'Doubts'?

When she sleeps, her soul, I know,
Goes a wanderer on the air,
Wings where I may never go,
Leaves her lying, still and fair,

Waiting, empty, laid aside,
Like a dress upon a chair . . .
This I know, and yet I know
Doubts that will not be denied.

For if the soul be not in place,
What has laid trouble in her face?
And, sits there nothing ware and wise
Behind the curtain of her eyes,
What is it, in the self's eclipse,
Shadows, soft and passingly,
About the corners of her lips,
The smile that is essential she?
And if the spirit be not there,
Why is fragrance in the hair?

Above all, Brooke's poems are charged with, and surrender the magic of what, for want of a better word, we call personality. They seem, as we read them, to bring us into a happy, instant relationship with him, not only ghostly eye to eye, but mind to mind. They tell more than even friendship could discover unaided. They share his secrets with the world—as if a boy had turned out the astonishing contents of his pockets just before going to bed. They share them, too, in that queer paradoxical fashion which makes a published volume of poems an even more secure refuge than lawyer, doctor, or priest.

Many of our fellow-creatures—whether we like or dislike them, approve or disapprove—remain in the last upshot mysterious and problematical. For that reason they are one of the salts of the earth. Even when they most frankly reveal themselves, we are conscious that there is still something beyond and out of direct ken which eludes us—a dream unshared, a reticence unbroken, a fugitive phantom. Have we, indeed, all of us, to the last dim and dusty corner of attic, cellar and corridor, explored ourselves? Because or in spite of his apparent candour, this was to some extent true of Rupert Brooke. Age, in time, scrawls our very selves upon our faces. So at any rate we may fear. Fast-locked, as we suppose, the door of the Self may be, but the key hangs in the porch. Youth (now for obscure reasons a rather insipid term)—youth, on the other hand, and delightful manners may be a mask concealing gravity and deep feeling. And what is one's remembrance of that serenely eager, questing face, stilled, as it were, with the phantom of a smile that might have lingered in the countenance of the Sphinx in her younger days, but that of the very embodiment of youth? We don't often meet people in this world who instantly recall the Golden Age and remind us that the Greek sculptors went to life for their models.* Even Henry James, in his essay on Brooke, not fewer in its translucency than five fathom deep, seems to pause Prospero-like before an Ariel whom he had suddenly encountered in the beautiful setting of the Cambridge backs. With the lingering gusto which an epicure lavishes on a rare old vintage he tastes, and tastes again, and all but hesitates for words to express his precise response and reaction. And to suggest that Henry James was ever at a loss for words is to insinuate that the Mississippi might run short of water.

One was happy in Brooke's company; even if, owing to one's consciousness of the 'prison-house' and of having 'grown heavy' one could not but rather guiltily eye that

* It was a face not in the least feminine (apart perhaps from the slightly tilted nose which redeemed it from being perfect and was borrowed from his mother), but of the rarest beauty. A beauty as remote from the merely handsome as the cheek of an Overbury or a Hardy milkmaid is from rouge. Flamboyantly good-looking men are an outrage on one's sense of decorum. This face you silently surveyed with an interest and admiration as instinctive and unreserved as those you would bestow on the young Greeks and their immortal horses on the frieze of the Parthenon.

gold. Here in laughing, talking actuality was a living witness of what humanity might arrive at when—well, when we tread the streets of Utopia. Happiness is catching. No doubt this admiration sometimes elated him, without his being aware of it. At times, and in certain company, it must have been a pest and vexation. Admiration is a dense medium through which to press to what treasure may be beyond it. Poets, indeed, *un*like children, and for their own sake if not for that of others, may occasionally be heard but should not in general be much seen. And it must have been exceedingly difficult for this poet to take cover, to lie low. He came; *you* saw; he conquered. And afterwards? Like a good child's birthday cake, he proved to be as rich as he looked.

'I never met,' wrote a chance-encountered enthusiast to his mother, 'I never met so entirely likeable a chap. . . . Your son was not merely a genius; what is perhaps more important, he had a charm that was literally like sunshine.' 'Entirely likeable' is a sound tribute from one man to another. And 'not merely a genius' has a wide range of, perhaps, unintended exclusion. The charm was compact of many ingredients—wit, enthusiasm, ideas, raillery, fun, and that sympathetic imagination concerning everybody and everything that he himself said it was the artist's chief duty to exercise. He had, of course, his own terms—critical, and at times exacting. If he suffered a fool, no more than with the rest of his own generation—or with our own—was it with a guileless gladness. He preferred humanity to be not stiff, not stupid, and not dry. Talk he loved; and when he listened, his mind was in his eyes, 'tree whispering to tree without wind, quietly.'

He confronted his fellow-creatures like the sensitive, serious, scrutinizing boy he was, ready to face what and who might come without flinching; smiling lip and steady eye. One was conscious of occasional shynesses and silences, of even a little awkwardness at times that was in itself a grace.

One was still more conscious of an insatiable interest and speculation. His quiet gaze took you in; yours couldn't so easily take him in, in either sense. These are my own remembrances; few, alas, however vivid and unfading: and even at that they are merely those of one of the less responsive sex.

In spite of life's little disillusionments (which, it is prudent to remember, we may cause as well as endure), in spite of passing moods of blackness and revulsion, nothing could be clearer in his poems, in his letters, and in himself, than his zest and happiness. Looking back on his school-days he said that he had been happier then than he could find words to say. How many born *children* would echo that sentiment. What wonder, then, that at twenty he describes himself as in the depths of despondency 'because of my age'? And a little later: 'I am just too old for romance.' What does this mean but that he found life so full and so arresting that he was afraid he might not be able to keep pace with it? It was a needless apprehension. The sea was deep beneath the waves and the foam. If he had lived to be, let us say, forty, he would have come to much the same conclusion, though, perhaps, with more emphasis and with more philosophy. He was never to experience *that* little misfortune! He flung himself into the world—of men, of books, of thought and affairs—as a wasp pounces into a cake-shop, Hotspur into the fighting. When his soul flourished on Walter Pater and Aubrey Beardsley, he thought it a waste of time to walk and swim. When, together with meat and 'alcohol', he gave up these rarified but in their own fashion admirable dainties, and lived, as it is fabulously reported, on milk and honey, it seemed a waste of time to do anything else. He could not be half-hearted. Indeed, in that 'tearing hunger to do things'—working, playing, reading, writing, publishing, travelling, talking, socialism, politics—any one thing seemed a waste of time, because meanwhile the rest of life's feast was kept waiting. 'What an incredibly lovely, superb world!' he exclaims—without in the least reminding anyone who knew him of Emerson or Leigh Hunt. Lovely, superb—what are the substitutes which we ourselves would perhaps prefer? Again, 'it *is* fun going and making thousands of acquaintances.' It must be fun—when you are Rupert Brooke. Frankly, voraciously, that is how he met everything and everybody—from Mrs. Grundy to the Statue of Liberty.

'Happy,' indeed, is the refrain that runs through all his letters. And on his way to the last great adventure of all, 'I have never,' he wrote, 'I have never been so pervasively happy in my life.' It was an acutely conscious and active happiness. But behind all that we say or do, behind even what we think, is the solitude in which dwells what we are. No forest is darker, no water more still, no island more isolated, no time so immutable with the past, so prescient of the future. And for company it has the sublimation of self and the arbiter of eternity. He was no stranger to it, but it was not what called most frequently in him for expression. Because, none the less, each day, in a life so crowded with things and people and interests and activities, was so sharp a tax, however welcome, on mind and body, he sometimes longed for sleep. And here too perhaps the forgotten child that preceded the boy is having its quiet say—as the halcyon visits the wave:

O haven without wave or tide!
Silence, in which all songs have died!
Holy book, where hearts are still!
And home at length under the hill!
O mother quiet, breasts of peace,
Where love itself would faint and cease!
O infinite deep I never knew,
I would come back, come back to you,
Find you as a pool unstirred,
Kneel down by you, and never a word,

Lay my head, and nothing said,
In your hands, ungarlanded;
And a long watch you would keep;
And I should sleep, and I should sleep!

So, again and again, his fancy turns towards death, only in appearance the deepest sleep of all. But then, again, because nothing in life could satisfy such a hunger and aspiration for life, beyond mood and change he longed for a peace 'where sense is with knowing one': and, beyond even this bodiless communion, for the peace that passes understanding:

'*Lost into God, as lights in light, we fly,*
Grown one with will.'

Simply because things as they are are not as they should be, we may take occasional refuge from our defeats and despairs in ridicule and satire, in a passing doubt in man, in goodness, in the heavenly power. So did he. He kept piling up the fuel for those 'flaming brains' of his; took life at the flood. When ashes succeeded the blaze and the tide ran low, and the mud-flats shimmered in the mocking sunshine; why, he could at least be frank. Each in turn he accepted life's promises; when it (or he) broke some of them—as it sometimes must in order to keep the others—he closely examined the pieces, whatever the pang. One such promise, of which his own work was the first fruits, bade fair, had he lived, to be kept. It depended on himself and on the Muses. Widely scorned and neglected, poetry, in A. E. Housman's words, is yet the oldest, rarest and most excellent of the fine arts. Men of the utmost energy of mind, practical ability and acuteness of intellect have delighted in its arduous service.

Keats said, 'The best kind of Poetry—that is all I care for, all I live for.'

Mr. Hilaire Belloc has said: 'It is the best of all trades to make songs, and the second best to sing them.'

And Rupert Brooke: 'There are only three good things in this world: one is to read, one is to write, the other is to live poetry.'

The mastery of the first of these good things is a more unusual feat than is usually realised—if it makes sure of the poetry; attempt to attain the second may prove to be the despair of a lifetime; the last, left a little vague, must be by far the most difficult. And Mrs. Grundy is not uncharmed to discover that not all the poets have proved themselves adepts in this art. But there it is: these are his own words; and he meant what he said.

What, again, if he had survived, he would have actively done in this world, which of his many interests intellectual and practical he would have pursued, is a fascinating but unanswerable question. This only can be ventured: that he would have gone on, and perhaps with increasing condensation and momentum, being himself. Radium is inexhaustible. As we look back across the gulf of the years we see him in vividest outline against that final gloom. Other poets, beloved of the gods, and not unendeared to humanity, have died young, as did he. Indeed, however uncompromising the ill-usage and maltreatment of age may be, every poet, every man in whom smoulders on a few coals of imagination, 'dies young'. But no other English poet of his age has given up his life at a moment more signal and pregnant. That has isolated and set Rupert Brooke apart. No single consciousness can even remotely compute or realise the sacrifice of spirit, mind and intelligence, of life and promise, 'lovely and of good report', which the Great War entailed to England and to the world. His own sacrifice was representative: and the 'incantation of his verse' quickened 'a new birth'; his words have been 'sparks among mankind'.

What place in English literature the caprices of time and taste will at length accord him does not concern us. Let us in our thoughts be as charitable as we can to our posterity, who will have the leisure and confidence to pass judgment, and who can confer that remembrance which fleeting humanity flatters with the term 'immortality'.

Flowers and Poetry

No collection of English verse on the theme of the poetry of flowers could fail to include many flowers of poetry. The very phrase recalls the *Garland* of Meleager—prototype of all anthologies—of precisely two thousand years ago. Meleager's title, however, was metaphorical; he had art and not nature in view; the loveliest poems of his age, that is, including his own. And just as a few—a very few lovers of flowers prefer to leave them all a-blowing and a-growing in their natural haunts rather than to truss them up in buttonholes, nosegays, bunches and bouquets, so to unusually fastidious lovers of poetry there is more than a streak of the barbarous and the absurd in penning in poems between the covers of a book merely because they have in common the same theme. Take for example Milton's lines on Eve with Satan:

Eve separate he spies,
Veiled in a cloud of fragrance, where she stood,
Half-spied, so thick the roses bushing round
About her glowed, oft stooping to support
Each flower of tender stalk, whose head, though gay
Carnation, purple, azure, or specked with gold,
Hung drooping unsustained. . . .

and compare them with Charles Henry Lüders' Myrtilla:

Myrtilla to-night
Wears Jacqueminot roses.
She's the loveliest sight!

Myrtilla to-night:—
Correspondingly light
My pocket-book closes.
Myrtilla to-night
Wears Jacqueminot roses.

Both poets mention roses; but the difference thus revealed between themselves, their verses, and even between their respective roses is as great as that between Alma-Tadema and Albrecht Dürer and between their drawings of one. The argument is that the subject of a poem, as of a picture, or indeed of a conversation, has little to do with its merits: that a panorama of Solomon in all his glory is not in the least likely to be better than a picture (say, by Chardin) of a loaf of bread. How simple otherwise art would be! I recall an anthologist who, having perspicuously and wisely adjudged that the Almighty is pre-eminent in man's small universe, deduced from this conviction that poems about Him must therefore and of necessity be the best poems. He accordingly began his collection with metrical theology. Where he ended—with a Japanese tanka perhaps on the prolification of the exquisite little cups of the lichen—I cannot now remember. But on this theory certain lamentable hymns ancient and modern, excusable only in intention, would take precedence of the *Odyssey*, *Lycidas* and the *Ode to a Nightingale*.

But, said Dr. Johnson, 'the ideas of Christian theology are too simple for eloquence, too sacred for fiction, and too majestic for ornament; to recommend them by tropes and figures, is to magnify by a concave mirror the sidereal hemisphere.'

Nevertheless the theme of a poem cannot but affect our interest and pleasure in it. We may like it purely for its own sake, and for its beauty and workmanship, but we may be attracted and beguiled also and no less by what it is about. An ode addressed to oneself, for example, would have a charm independent of its poetical merits. And since, of the three Kingdoms of the old nursery game, that of the 'Vegetable' is certainly not the least popular, so with poems concerned with it. Confronted, with the titles only, of four new and original lyrics, (*a*) To a Primrose, (*b*) To a Persimmon, (*c*) To a Cauliflower, and (*d*) To a Truffle, which would one turn to first? Authorship apart, subject alone in view, I should for the time being, I think, pass over (*a*), as it has been done before; (*b*) since it has a flavour of the precious; (*c*) as being probably jocular, and should begin with (*d*). Associations count of course, particularly culinary and romantic; but the truffle is a curious and *promising* theme for almost any poet, whether Donne, Dryden, Drayton or Mr. W. H. Davies.

But first, the other two Kingdoms. 'Mineral' is little more than a rag-bag of a word; it will welcome all the left-overs that refuse to be otherwise classified. And while all the precious, and many of the semi-precious stones brood, smoulder, glimmer and coruscate fairly frequently in English verse—and often for their melodious names' sake chiefly;* while mention of that far too rare commodity, gold, a word which rhymes freely, is commoner than silver, a word which rhymes not at all; while iron, steel, brass and bronze have a rather narrow application; zinc, copper, nickel and tin are little more than very occasional helpmeets, and aluminium and even platinum (apart from the famous Limerick) remain, I fancy, as yet unsung.

As for the Animals, English poetry is fairly alive with them, although the range in varieties is not very extensive,

* Ruby, amethyst, emerald, diamond,
Sapphire, sardonyx, fiery-eyed carbuncle,
  Jacynth, jasper, crystal a-sheen;
Topaz, turquoise, tourmaline, opal,
  Beryl, oynx and aquamarine:
Marvel, O mortal!—their hue, lustre, loveliness,
Pure as a flower when its petals unfurl—
Peach-red carnelian, applè-green chrysoprase,
  Amber, and coral, and orient pearl!

and probably no poet still among us could recite the nouns of multitude from the Book of St. Alban's. Few humans are wholly indifferent to the beasts of the field—to the denizens of the Kingdom, that is, of which they themselves also are in certain obvious respects at least the rebellious subjects. We make our choice among them—from Behemoth to 'the little vulgar mouse', from ape to armadillo. And that choice may have something to do with kin and kind. For in a disquietingly large number of human faces the astral physiognomy, so to speak, of a specific beast, bird, or fish is furtively lurking. John Bull has not been given his surname for nothing. A fairly wide acquaintanceship is proof enough of that—or one's own looking-glass perhaps. Any freely-populated railway journey is almost certain to present the observant traveller with one or two examples of the leonine (less common in these whiskerless days than of old), of the ursine, the vulpine, the catlike, the hawklike, the henlike, the codlike, or the froglike; together with more or less remote and dressed-up reminders of horse, dog, sheep, ox, rat, rabbit, ferret, serpent, owl, bullfinch and wren.

To what extent any such similarity may involve both the mind and the character is touched on by that enthusiastic physiognomist, Johann Kaspar Lavater. Feline femininity is notoriously dangerous; and the man that resembles a rat will probably prove to be indifferent company on a sinking ship. Whether henlike old ladies have an exceptional distaste for their foxy-looking fellow creatures, whether the reptilian cast of countenance produces instinctive and instantaneous panic in the froglike, whether an aquiline nose is certain to daunt any sparrow-like little human as yet in the nursery, is an engaging line of enquiry. But whatever our preferences may be based on they are insurmountable, and the devotee of the cat is as unlikely to be a fanatical dog-lover also as he is to share his allegiance equally between fate and free-will, the Romantic and the Realistic, between

Dickens and Thackeray, Keats and Pope. There is an almost universal preference for the young of any species—whether child, cub, lamb, kid, kitten, foal, leveret, chick, duckling or cygnet. It is less general for the ultra-infantine. The 'Finny Tribe', too, like the 'Feathered Creation' has countless advocates and at least one engrossed laureate, Izaac Walton; but the most ardent of these are seldom merely admirers. We treat a frog or a fish only 'as if' we loved it. Poetry more or less faithfully reflects all this—and certainly English poetry. At a venture, the animals most delighted in even by the prosaic are those most frequently found sunning and disporting themselves in rhyme.

Apart from mere preferences, again, an inborn or acquired hatred or even dislike of birds, unless for mercenary or aesthetic or sentimental reasons—owl, vulture, or the hosts of the starlings in their malodorous roosts—is rare. It is not so with insects, even the harmless. The pretty butterfly, the evening moth, the busy bee are insects every one. A cockroach is an unlovesome thing, God wot; a silver-fish to some fancies has a touch of magic. It is nocturnal; it feeds on starch: it is acutely silent. There are eccentrics who blanche at a spider; there are eccentrics who have made poetry out of a fly. In part it is a matter of numbers, in part that of habitat. The human host is usually exquisitely impatient regarding occasional visitors to his person and no less against his pre-ordained parasites. There is the enchantment of childhood in an oak beaded from crown to foot with its cupped and bitter acorns; not so in a rosebush whose every stem is clotted with quivering aphides, or the bare twigs of a willow horrifically astir with the maggots of the green-bottle fly. Life in its profuse and heedless abundance may be no less terrifying than impressive—as Cardinal Newman testified concerning a swarm of locusts. The balance of nature resembles the bed of Procrustes.

But as for flowers?—would even the most outrageous cynic care to confess that he hated the very sight of them—single and isolated or multitudinous, tiny pimpernel to the Rose of Damascus?* 'I shall never be friends again with roses,' sighs the poet of *Les Noyades*, and adds, as though for insult to injury, 'I shall hate sweet music my whole life long.' Could any other declaration be more destructive of any ordinary human being's status? And poets so sadly need one.

None the less, we all have our likes, our less-likes and dislikes even among flowers. A particular joy in the windflower or the wild violet, the cowslip or the single pink need not imply an infatuation for the titivated Japanese chrysanthemum, the blue-red cineraria, stinking mayweed, dog's mercury or bloody-man's-finger. If, too, as John Ruskin declares, an ardent delight in the colour scarlet is proof of a virtuous soul, whereas one for the rarer tints and shades of green, jade or verdigris, may not be, then a craving for gardenia, gloxinia, orchid, magnolia, for the exotic and densely scented had best perhaps be kept to oneself. Swinburne (more than once) refers to the 'lilies' and languor of *virtue*—though the Chalcedonian lily might well have

* And yet how perilous it may be to generalize! Within a little while of venturing on this assertion I chanced once more on Mr. Arthur Symons's *Spiritual Adventures*. Its opening essay is concerned with his childhood:

'I lived in the country, or at all events with lanes and fields about me; I took long walks, and liked walking; but I never was able to distinguish oats from barley, or an oak from a maple; I never cared for flowers, except slightly for their colour, when I saw many of them growing together; I could not distinguish a blackbird from a thrush; I was never conscious in my blood of the difference between spring and autumn. I always loved the winter wind and the sunlight, and to plunge through crisp snow and to watch the rain through leaves. . . .'

His devotion to poetry, on the other hand, is manifest in his own and, for but one example, in his invaluable *Romantic Movement in English Poetry*.

graced Semiramis; while as for his 'roses' and rapture of *vice*, even if the guests of Heliogabalus, who were literally smothered with them at a banquet, would agree to the association, lovers of the damask rose, the Mermaid or the wild—the 'tinted bubble of the hedges, so flitting as scarcely to last the gathering'—would not.

But why, it may be asked concerning flowers in general—since, after all, in the economy of Nature they play no more modest part than did Pandarus on behalf of his niece Criseyde, and are 'out' for a specific and sovereign purpose—why do we most of us ignore their functions in delight of their mere looks? Because we are human; and therefore content not to trouble our minds too much over what so easily pleases our senses. For, whatever other blessings they confer, flowers are cool and soothing to the touch. They are delicate and gentle, and infinitely various and pleasing in pattern and design. They are, unless meddled with, true and pure in colour, hue and brilliance. They are frequently sweet, fragrant or aromatic. Their still, yet active but silent life is full of mystery. They have their many secret enmities and rivalries, but in our own temperate climate, although for human purposes they may flourish too abundantly—heather, bracken, ragwort, bindweed and the rest—foresight and industry and a pitiless vigilance keep them 'in order'. Unlike that of children, their 'wildness' for those who care most for them is their happiest charm, and they need never be *sent* to bed.

How few of them are even self-defensive is suggested by holly, gorse, primula, bramble, nettle and sloe. And even the species rilling with poison in their veins—which in homœopathic doses may be of sovereign efficacy—are apt to breathe *Cave* in their very appearances. A sinister or sullen beauty hints at danger, that mute sister of the potato-plant, belladonna, the dwale or deadly nightshade, for example; metallic-green laburnum, funereal magic-berried yew, fetid henbane, sad-coloured hemlock. But not so the meadow saffron, the poppy, the hellebore, or that dangerous neighbour to horse-radish and parsnip, the monkshood. If we have a little knowledge—instinctive or acquired—for safeguard, even these are innocent of any but a passive mischief; and a host of flowers and plants, as Nicholas Culpeper, 'Student in Physic and Astrology', testifies, are of sovereign value and efficacy. Moreover, our own morals are scarcely at all concerned with them. Although (even if we covet a Naboth's vineyard) we may no more pilfer a neighbour's flowers than we may abduct his children or steal his dog, we may at any rate feast eye and nose on his 'arbaceous' borders from over his garden wall and we may do wholly what we please with 'our own'.

Despite the fact, too, that the first chapter of Genesis altogether refrains from the mention of flowers—it refers only to grass, herb, seed and fruit—so it must have been from the beginning. That, indeed, the beasts and birds of Eden should have been paraded by the Lord God before Adam in order 'to see' what, in a language all his own, and now wholly beyond recovery, 'he should call them', at least suggests that he had already of his own free will and impulse named the Lotus and the Lily, the Myrtle, the Rosemary and the Bay.

There are, then, many good reasons for our taking pleasure in being pacified and solaced by flowers. And even if mere reasons are unnecessary, they may be interesting and helpful. This, for example, is how John Gerard begins the dedication of his famous and immense *Herbal* (a herbal which he frankly confesses on his title page was 'gathered' —i.e. chiefly plagiarized—to 'His Singular good Lord and Master Sir William Cecil, Knight, Baron of Burghley', of whose garden this surgeon-barber was himself the supervisor).

'Among', he says, 'the manifold creatures of God . . . that have all in all ages diversely entertained many excellent wits, and drawn them to the contemplation of the divine wisdome, none have provoked men's studies more, or satisfied their desires so much as plants have done, and that upon just & worthy causes: for if delight may provoke men's labor, what greater delight is there than to behold the earth apparelled with plants, as with a robe of embroidered worke, set with Orient pearles and garnished with great diversitie of rare and costly jewels? If this varietie and perfection of colours may affect the eie, it is such in herbs and floures, that no *Apelles*, no *Zeuxis* ever could by any art expresse the like; if odours or if taste may worke satisfaction, they are both so soveraigne in plants, and so comfortable that no confection of the Apothecaries can equal their excellent vertue. But these delights are in the outward senses: the principal delight is in the mind, singularly enriched with the knowledge of these visible things, setting forth to us the invisible wisdome and admirable workmanship of Almighty God. The light is great, but the use greater, and joyned often with necessitie.'

In a style of this romantic eloquence (although Gerard scorned the 'fantasticall devices invented by poets'), it is easy to miss the argument. *No* costly jewel, it might be said, rivals in colour or radiance a lupin leaf cradling a drop of dew, or a specimen of the common cabbage in the sunshine after rain. Was not Zeuxis renowned (from our early childhood) for a picture of a bunch of grapes so plausible that it deceived the birds into pecking at it. And, *can* use be 'greater' than 'the light'? However that may be, in the descriptions of flowers that follow Gerard's dedication eloquence is rare; precision and simplicity take its place, and with so lovely a naturalness that the image created by the mere words in the mind may even excel the object as we ourselves have seen it, since we have seen it with a less discerning eye. Moreover, even eye apart, the secret of such language as this seems somehow to have been lost.

From flowers to 'botany' is for the amateur an arid journey; from flowers to gardens is only a step, but in certain respects it is a decisive one. The first edition of the *Herbal* appeared the year before Bacon's Essay on Gardens was published, nearly fifty years before John Parkinson's *Paradisi in Sole Paradisus Terrestris*, and about a century before the term *botany* became a necessity—a science that has nowadays at least half a dozen main branches. Bacon's opening sentence echoes Gerard: 'God Almighty first planted a Garden. And indeed it is the purest of human pleasures.'* He does not describe his flowers, he merely names them; but Shakespeare himself could hardly name them more winningly. 'Roses, damask and red, are fast flowers of their smells; so that you may walk by a whole row of them, and find nothing of their sweetness; yea though it be in a morning's dew. Bays likewise yield no smell as they grow, Rosemary little; nor sweet marjoram. That which above all others yields the sweetest smell in the air is the violet, specially the white double violet, which comes twice a year; about the middle of April, and about Bartholomew-tide.' The very melody and rhythm of these few sentences resembles that of a breeze in seeding grasses, an aria of Mozart's. In all, Bacon mentions a few score flowers, and is seeing them in the act; and apart from his chamairis, tulippa, flos Africanus, melocotones and herba muscaria, few are in an alien disguise.

The verdurous hollows of the *Venus and Adonis* more closely resemble a park than open country. Edmund Spenser's 'witch' reclines in a luscious pleasance compared with which the scene in Botticelli's Mars and Venus—'death-pale

* Parkinson likewise begins his *Theater of Plants*: 'From a Paradise of pleasant Flowers, I am fallen (*Adam* like) to a world of Profitable Herbs.'

were they all'—is a desert. Andrew Marvell's garden, on the other hand, where the bee is not merely busy but 'industrious', is, like Lord Burghley's, a true English garden, and one of lordly dimensions. It bestowed on him—and for attractive looks, for poetic quality as compared with quantity, and for a curious, remote yet intimate virginal grace, what poet excels him?—it bestowed on him what no more even than a few rods of ground with an English cottage in the middle may supply: 'Quiet', 'Innocence', delicious solitude. Even one small green tree, indeed, may give a child as close a solitude as the Arab's in his tent, Jonah's under his gourd:

Annihilating all that's made
To a green thought in a green shade.

In his rapture Marvell not only forsook the paths of his garden, but strayed over the beds:

Stumbling on melons, as I pass,
Ensnared with flowers, I fall on grass.

And his memory—as with Gerard and Bacon—returns to the oldest garden of all, and one without, as yet, its Eve:

Two paradises 'twere in one
To live in Paradise alone.

His other 'Garden'—'written after the Civil Wars'—comes nowadays even nearer home:

Unhappy! shall we never more
That sweet militia restore,
When gardens only had their towers,
And all the garrisons were flowers;
When roses only arms might bear
And men did rosy garlands wear?

The lines are artificial to the last degree, and yet not so in their complete effect.

As with most things in this world, man may look even on flowers with a divided mind; and yet, to win our purest pleasure from them, we need no more knowledge of their use and purpose, their species, rarity, cost and origin than our various senses can supply. And of these, very young ones will suffice. The commonest favourites among them—the old-fashioned ones—Sweet-William, snapdragon, Old Man, heart's-ease, stocks (ten-week and Virginia) and fretted pinks—are those, indeed, which most closely haunted our childhood. Even a chance and unexpected glimpse of these may recall for a moment a phantom of that lost visionary beauty. Both in stature and spirit we were closer to these earth-neighbours then: and what we love early, we love late.

At a little country birthday-party which I was sharing a year or two ago, a fair-haired child came running out of the house helter-skelter into the sunshine, and instantly stooped herself double to pick a daisy. 'She must be', the shade of Sherlock Holmes murmured in my ear, 'a London child.' She reminded me of another child who, although she lived not a stone's-throw from Paddington railway station, enquired, on being taken into Hyde Park for the first time a few summers ago, what that 'yellow flower' was called—a buttercup! And of another who, at the sight of the Round Pond, exclaimed, 'Please, Teacher, is that the sea?' Their delight was as instinctive as that in a box of coloured beads or a sugar stick. And so it may continue to be with the grown-up—until perhaps he begins to buy daffodil bulbs at £5 apiece, despises 'common' varieties, craves for alien exotics, *insists* on calling a larkspur a delphinium, a columbine an aquilegia, a snapdragon an antirrhinum, becomes the slave of the greenhouse, and grows roses for show.

It is not as if England, in spite of her Black Country and her vast acreage of bricks and mortar, were an island green but sterile, and had only Kent for a garden. What could be lovelier and less uncommon than her traveller's joy and her honey-suckle, her bryony, her convolvulus; her bramble, willow-herb, sea-pink and bugloss; her hemp agrimony, parsley and gorse? It is said of Linnaeus that when he first saw the furze in blossom in England he fell on his knees and thanked God for the beauty of it. To have paused to day-dream in a dell of the Alps is to covet even a glimpse of the foothills of the Himalayas, and but one prolonged, incredulous gaze, as from a balloon, upon the matted flowers that canopy the forests of Brazil, and Borneo, and Ceylon. Yet, as for the glories of the tropics, 'I have never seen there', quotes Canon Ellacombe from Wallace, 'such brilliant masses of colour as even England can show in her furze-clad commons, her glades of wild hyacinths, her fields of poppies, her meadows of buttercups and orchises, carpets of yellow, purple, azure blue, and fiery crimson, which the tropics can rarely exhibit. We have smaller masses of colour in our hawthorns and crab trees, our holly and mountain ash, our broom, foxgloves, primroses and purple vetches, which clothe with gay colours the length and breadth of the land.'

The child's daisy had usurped an English lawn, and a lawn (which, apart from clover and uninvited visitors, consists, of course, of the leaves of grasses that have been forbidden to flower and seed) is part of a garden. And in a garden even a daisy, even a pimpernel, an eyebright, a celandine, or a buttercup, whose multitudes—spared in spite of her honey-coloured butter by the gentle cow—are the glory of an English meadow in June, is a *weed*. And weeds to the gardener are what poachers are to a game-keeper, coiners to the Keeper of the Mint, fleas to a dog. Nevertheless, every weed, great and small, plain or pretty, is one of Nature's love-children, and many cultivated flowers, like certain animal pets and natural objects, are little better than humanized bastards, and spoilt at that.

To and in poetry, at any rate, although it welcomes wild flowers in all abundance, none of them is by any possibility merely a weed. By Chaucer, our daisy, *bellis perennis* (or bairn-wort or bruise-wort or benner-gowan or herb Margaret), was so dearly beloved that he would rise soon after daybreak, he tells us, to walk in the dewy meadows and there kneel down in the 'small soft sweet grass' to watch it spread its petals to the sun; and he would return at evening again to see 'how it will go to rest'—'for fear of night'. A charming little creature it looks, too, its petals pushed up for ruff and nightcap above—not its head, but its heart. Canon Ellacombe, in spite of Shakespeare's comparative neglect of it (and Spenser's and Milton's) gives it an epilogue in his *Plant Lore* all to itself.

It has also an odd little problem all to itself. A poet in the Middle Ages in praise of his mistress would compare her to a rose; or rather, the one lovely image evoked the other. And the comparison became a commonplace. At length, however, as Professor Livingstone Lowes points out in his *Convention and Revolt in Poetry*, 'Through the celebration by a group of French poets of the charms of certain ladies whose name was Marguerite, the *daisy* became the fashionable symbol for the poet's mistress. What happened? The wealth of conventions that had gathered about the rose was transferred, through the accident of a lady's name, *in toto* to the *marguerite*'—nowadays an imported bane to American farmers. 'And that carried with it a rather astonishing result. The marguerite falls heir to the possessions of the rose; the rose is endowed with fragrance; *ergo*, the daisy, which now represents the lady must possess it too. And so it follows that the *marguerite*, in Machaut,

Par excellence est garnie d'odour:

and Chaucer in his rapture goes so far as to assert that in sweetness and odour it excels every gum or herb or tree.'

And yet, every herbalist, every unbiassed nose declares that, however quaint the daisy may be, it is 'smell-less'.

Well, is it? Sweet, no; but hasn't it a minute earthy dusty whisper of an odour all its own? Enquire of Miss Seven-year-old. But even her yes would still leave the riddle unanswered. There appears, alas, to be nothing to show that the daisy ever had (or needed) a fragrance comparable to that of a damask rose. In this, the poet, intent on his mistress who has, even if only her lapdog be aware of it, a unique fragrance of *her* own, does not count. And yet, I myself can recall the musk that was once the secret joy of my nose in childhood, and not of my nose only. Why has the magician deprived that demure blossom of a gift so captivating?

It is to Fletcher that we owe that highly original 'smell-less'. That Shakespeare, too, had signally perceived the daisy with his own unfailing eye is shown by his reference to it in *Lucrece:*

> *Without the bed her other fair hand was,*
> *On the green coverlet, whose perfect white*
> *Showed like an April daisy on the grass.*

Robert Burns, having ploughed up this 'bonnie gem' and grieved over it, gave it 'celebrity'. 'It is scarcely too much to say', writes Canon Ellacombe, that since Burns's and Wordsworth's time 'not an English poet has failed to pay his homage' to the daisy's 'humble beauty'. Moreover, not even Wordsworth himself—'The Daisy by the shadow that it casts protects the lingering dew-drop from the sun'—has bestowed on it a more exquisite niche than Beddoes, who, in *The Second Brother*, speaks of the daisy 'in Noah's meadow' whereon the 'foremost drop of rail Fell warm and soft at evening'—the first and foremost drop before the Flood.

This perhaps is the chief difference between the flowers that flourish in poetry and the flowers that are made to disport themselves in our 'beds' and herbaceous borders, or are listed at so much a dozen or hundred in a catalogue, or that we buy in a shop. For the poets (at least in their imaginative hours) there is no division whatever in essence between the wild and the cultivated; no faintest stigma is implied in the term 'weed'. In this, as in some other respects, they resemble children. As with animals, months, metaphors and their fellow creatures they may have their favourites; but all their flowers are *flowers*. And for sheer abundance in this respect, Shakespeare, as in much else, easily surpasses every rival.

The names of no fewer than some 170 different flowers and plants occur in the Plays and the Poems. He uses them Nature's way. They spring up sweet and natural in his mind and memory, precisely as and when he has need of them—much as many even of his own songs seem to have done; of pure impulse. None, apparently, was sought for or thought for as an adornment either of his ideas or his verses, or is torn up by the roots. Fifty-seven several times he mentions the rose; and fifteen times the briar;* and both are usually 'sweet' and 'red'. Even the sour, dusty and frowning nettle—which, according to Camden, the Romans brought to Britain as a chafe to warm up their bodies against our northern cold, and which Pepys enjoyed dressed as a porridge—is twelve times referred to. To judge from this and from the rest of English poetry, and apart from the hospitable, first-hand, vividly noted assemblages of them to be found in *The Seasons*, in Shelley's *The Question* and in

* Corn and wheat score 30, the oak 26, the lily and the vine 25 each, the apple 24, grass 21, the thorn and the violet 18 each, the rush 16, the fig and the hazel 12 each, the plum 11. Of the rest, the aspen, the apricot and clover find two niches each; parsley, poppy, camomile and columbine, among others, and like cabbage and coloquintida, only one. Of the common flowers, only the snowdrop, the forget-me-not, the foxglove, the lily-of-the-valley and the dandelion have been left blooming *apparently* unheeded. Statistics may be dead-alive enough, but these give a hint of the wealth and activity of that supreme mind.

Robert Bridges' *Idle Flowers,** it is clear that the flowers dearest to poetry are also the most usual, and that while to every poet any primrose must of necessity a yellow primrose be, it is seldom nothing more. It is pale and faint for Shakespeare; pale and soft and silken for Milton; flaming for Giles and Phineas Fletcher. Not that Wordsworth's 'yellow' is precisely 'on the gold'. 'So ethereal is the primrose', says Miss Casta Sturge in *Thoughts*, a little book as remarkable as it is rare, 'that its tint is not yellow, but a light suggestion of it; its texture is hardly material, but just a whispered hint of the fabrics of a spirit-world; its scent is not a scent, but a waft we know not whence. We only know that the scent, the sight, the touch of a primrose brings over the spirit the pain of a great nostalgia. We sit among the primroses to think, to wonder, to dream. If the mere semblance of Life as it reveals itself in a flower is so overwhelming in its beauty, what must be the unveiled Beauty? Some think to close their eyes on the primrose when they die; nay, but shall we not rather open them on the "something more" that lies hidden in its heart?'

But whether flowers appear in poetry at hazard, for ornament, for edification, or as metaphor or simile, there seems to be no one way of regarding them that is exclusively

* . . . High on the downs so bare,
Where thou dost love to climb,
Pink Thrift and Milkwort are,
Lotus and scented Thyme;

And in the shady lanes
Bold Arum's hood of green,
Herb Robert, Violet,
Starwort and Celandine;

And by the dusty road
Bedstraw and Mullein tall,
With red Valerian
And Toadflax on the wall . . .

and how many others. One chosen word and the flower itself is visible and placed.

'poetical'; either in respect to their kinds, appearances, qualities or associations—Erasmus Darwin's *The Loves of the Plants* being in a class by itself. Inaccurate, even contradictory statements concerning them may still be poetic.

Full many a flower is born to blush unseen
And waste its sweetness on the desert air.

No one would question the presence of poetry in these two lines from Gray's *Elegy*—a poem that has made at least as many converts as any other in the language. In spite of it, to Alice Meynell they were inescapable evidence of 'mediocrity'. The Elegy is a poem, she decided, deserving only of being put at the top of the second class. Indeed, for all its serenity, grace and finish, it cannot escape the charge of being a trifle priggish. We might (at our peril) hesitate to agree with this verdict on Gray's lines if, for fatal foil, she had not placed beside them Shakeapeare's

The summer flower is to the summer sweet
Though to itself it only live or die;

and a presence seems to haunt that 'summer' less material but no less real to the imagination than that of Autumn 'drows'd with the fume of poppies' in Keats's Ode.

And again:

The canker blooms have full as deep a dye
As the perfumed tincture of the roses
. . . but they
Die to themselves—sweet roses do not so;
Of their sweet deaths are sweetest odours made.

And again:

But earthlier happy is the rose distilled
Than that which, withering on the virgin thorn,
Grows, lives and dies in single blessedness.

The astounding precision, wisdom, beauty and perfect pattern of it all! Shakespeare is, of course, matchless for imaginative exactitude; his daffodils that begin to *peer*, that 'take the winds of March with beauty'; his daisies, violets, lady-smocks and cuckoo-buds (buttercups) 'that paint the meadows with delight'; his 'azured harebell'; and 'vagabond flag' 'lackeying the varying tide, To rot itself with motion.'

Not, again, that exactitude of observation is essential to the poetic, although imagination is. I am, for example, pretty sure, in spite of what he says to the contrary, that Mr. William Davies's delightful bees, gold-dusty with pollen and tipsy with nectar, do sometimes visit Chaucer's daisies; indeed, I have seen the whole small flower toppling on its stalk with the weight of its visitor. Was, again, Prior justified in comparing the crocus to a 'bell, whose spire Rocks in the grassy leaves, like wire'; or Thomas Moore in suggesting that the jasmine exhales its cool and sweet and liquid odour only at night; although then, of course, we are more likely to perceive it, as we do the nightingale's song? Clare, too, a countryman born and bred, echoes Gray when he says that the evening primrose 'wastes its fair bloom upon the night', when, in fact, I suppose, she is then likely to waste it least, since it is in the cool of the dew that the prowling moths sally out in search of drowsy syrups.

But while a poem or even a simile need certainly be no worse for being completely accurate, hasty observation need not imply that to its maker 'the meanest flower that blows' is not suggestive of thoughts and feelings which had lain too deep for tears; and which therefore could only be hinted at in his verse. And although (until Alice can share her mushroom with us or we can persuade the tiger-lily to talk, and Amphion will teach us how to make trees dance) scientific proof of Wordsworth's 'faith' may be wanting, there must be very few poets who do not share with him the belief that every flower 'enjoys the air it breathes'. And this is a statement that was made, not regarding the water-lily or the Crown Imperial, but the trailing wreaths of blue-eyed periwinkle among tufts of primroses.

What condition of the human consciousness this enjoyment is comparable with is a further question. But if it resembles the delight which its fellow living-creature, a man, may experience as he stands beneath an apple-tree arrayed in the Spring in its first pale-green leaves and myriad flowers of snow and rose, and sonorous with the murmuration of almost as many bees; or when in October its branches are stooping with their burden of seeded fruit which are scarcely less lovely than the blossom which produced them and of no less vital and essential a virtue—then it is a joy which the young and beautiful and the old and wise can equally share. A life, an order of being, so complex and exquisite, utterly devoid of self-realization would be a problem dark indeed. If the Lord God alone enjoyed that first earthly garden 'eastward in Eden', and of all service and delight, it is well; if Adam within his human scope enjoyed it with Him, it is better; but it would be sheer Eureka if all three, as the poets almost universally assume, were in this in the closest of companionships.

Consistency, however, is far less usual in man than in an apple-tree. And if a poet is also a gardener he is at least tempted—although it may be dead against his own inmost voice and conviction—to root up in it every speedwell, celandine, buttercup, willow-herb, pimpernel, eyebright, bindweed and chickweed; the last perhaps, with that of the grass and moss, the most magical of all flowers, since its supremely little is representative of so much. And, having fallen to this temptation overnight, the very next morning, as likely as not, his heart will leap up, as if at a rainbow, at some unexpected glimpse of any one of them in hedge or ditch or down or cornfield or patch of waste land.

A very mild enigma by comparison is concerned with the

picking of a flower. It is recorded of Walter Savage Landor that (presumably after his childhood was over) he disdained this barbarous custom. He confesses it, not without a trace of complacency. Angered one day beyond endurance with a manservant, he threw him headlong out of the window; and immediately thrust out his head after him in consternation, with the lamentable cry, 'My god, my violets!' I have read somewhere, too, that Coventry Patmore and Ruskin, when on a walk together at Coniston one fine morning, chanced on a rock in whose crevices a wild strawberry plant was in exquisite flower and fruit. They drank in its miracle of beauty, and turned away. There was a pause. 'Do you know, Patmore,' said Ruskin at length, 'I fancy we are the only two people in England who would not have eaten those berries?' Again there was a pause. And then, 'Do you know, Ruskin,' replied Patmore, 'I fancy you are the only man in Christendom who would even have thought of such a thing?'

These are fine shades of feeling, concerning which poems about flowers would naturally be eloquent. And to some minds a hungry and perhaps ragged armful of bluebells dragged up inches out of the ground heedless of their future is a much more easily forgiven offence than to turn a flower into a text for a sermon in verse. None the less, this moralizing on flowers is far from infrequent even in poets who flourished well after the eighteenth century. Crocus, daisy, dandelion, the 'pretty' or 'obsequious' marigold, the 'fair' daffodil, the 'modest' violet, the 'meek' primrose, the 'flaunting' sunflower, the 'chaste' lily—all these have served this purpose, and many of them have, unreproachingly, served it well. And yet, one hesitates. There are better things than sermons to be found even in stones. 'Poetry', said Dryden, 'instructs as it delights.' Its delight *is* its instruction. Occasionally, it is true, a poem succeeds in being almost equally didactic and delightful. In 'Gather ye rosebuds', for example, Herrick so enchants voice and ear and eye that we may completely fail, first, to notice that he is in Hymen's pulpit, and next, that his text, irrespective of its dubious ethics, is a little commonplace. Apart from the degree of enchantment, this applies to most poetical moralizings on flowers.

If in the palm of one's hand one examines 'with a serious musing' a daisy, the flower itself, its dark, bluish-green, rounded leaves; its multitudinous rootlets—reminding one that what is hidden in the unconscious may be of a deeper intrinsic virtue and 'nature' than the daylong flowering of it which we call Self—it is not what it looks like or even what one feels about it, but what it *is*, that baffles both one's understanding and imagination. What Tennyson says of the flower in the crannied wall, Alice Meynell has said more fully and profoundly:

Slight as thou art thou art enough to hide
Like all created things secrets from me,
And stand a barrier to eternity. . . .

In one of his parochial sermons, 'The Invisible World', Cardinal Newman speaks of animals:

'Can any thing be more marvellous or startling, unless we were used to it, than that we should have a race of beings about us whom we do but see, and as little know their state, or can describe their interests, or their destiny, as we can tell of the inhabitants of the sun and moon? It is indeed a very overpowering thought . . . that we familiarly use, I may say hold intercourse with creatures who are as much strangers to us, as mysterious, as if they were the fabulous, unearthly beings, more powerful than man, and yet his slaves, which Eastern superstitions have invented. . . . Cast your thoughts abroad on the whole number of them, large and small, in vast forests, or in the water, or in the air; and then say whether the presence of such countless multitudes, so various in their natures, so strange and wild in their shapes, living on the earth without ascertainable object, is not as mysterious as any thing which Scripture says about the Angels.'

Word for word almost, this measured and unusual statement—suggesting a Thomas Traherne come to 'reason' as it were—might have been made concerning flowers. We may vaunt the possession of a green thumb, or hope 'the gardener' is thus gifted. We wander in our small demesne; we glance, we sniff, we observe, we day-dream perhaps, we at least enjoy *our* flowers. (Their corollas chiefly, that is, and their calixes.) But how seldom we most of us look close. Take, even yet again, that 'unassuming Commonplace of Nature', the daisy. 'It is a white floure inclining to red'; 'its yellow cup being 'crowned as it were with a garland consisting of five and fifty little leaves, set round about it in manner of fine pales.' We are told it is a perennial. It continues, that is, to live, as we do ourselves, from year to year; discarding, as the seasons range on, what of itself it does not need for itself, until at last its life is over. We take this 'composite', mute, cold little creature into the palm of our hand and examine it; and Jean Jacques Rousseau in one of his letters on botany, quoted by Professor Boulger in *British Flowering Plants*, will tell us what we shall see:

'Take', he says, 'one of those little flowers, which cover all the pastures, and which every one knows by the name of Daisy. Look at it well, for I am sure you would never have guessed from its appearance that this flower, which is so small and delicate, is really composed of between two and three hundred other flowers, all of them perfect, that is, each of them having its corolla, stamens, pistil and fruit; in a word, as perfect in its species as a flower of the hyacinth or lily. Every one of these leaves, which are white above and red underneath, and form a kind of crown round the flower, appearing to be nothing more than little petals, are in reality so many true flowers; and every one of those tiny yellow things also which you see in the centre, and which at first you have perhaps taken for nothing but stamens, are real flowers. . . . Pull out one of the white leaves of the flower: you will think at first that it is flat from one end to the other, but look carefully at the end by which it was fastened to the flower, and you will see that this end is not flat, but round and hollow in the form of a tube, and that a little thread ending in two horns issues from the tube. This thread is the forked style of the flower, which, as you now see, is flat only at the top. Next look at the little yellow things in the middle of the flower, and which, as I have told you, are all so many flowers; if the flower is sufficiently advanced, you will see some of them open in the middle and even cut into several parts. These are monopetalous corollas, which expand; and a glass will easily discover in them the pistil, and even the anthers with which it is surrounded. Commonly the yellow florets towards the centre are still rounded and closed. These, however, are flowers like the others, but not yet open, for they expand successively from the edge inwards.'

Much, thus aided, concerning our daisy, we have now shared with Rousseau, but, as poets repeatedly urge, we are no nearer the secret of its very being, of its 'life', of its unique individuality, of the intention of its creation, and of the ultimate destiny and appearance and purpose of its children's children to the n-th generation than, apart from what our faith and reason declare, we are concerning our own.

It remains: exquisitely, complexly, simply constructed; and in its marvellous ingenuity infinitely beyond the most perfect little thing of use or beauty ever made by man. The few moments of consciousness so occupied may have evoked our mere curiosity, our serious interest, our rapture, or a fleeting glimpse into what appears to be some other order of being. But any communication entailed has been—but *has* it been?—completely one-sided.

A character in *A Diagnosis of Death* (a story by Ambrose Bierce) who has invented and constructed a grisly automaton chess-player—another Frankenstein—declares that just as 'intelligent co-operation' is conceivable even among the 'constituent elements of the crystals'—those of frozen moisture for example, selecting the beautiful forms of snow flakes, so a machine may become capable of thought; and also a plant. ' "And what pray", enquires his sceptical friend, "does it think with in the absence of a brain?" '

' "Perhaps", he replied, "you may be able to infer their convictions from their acts. I will spare you the familiar examples of the sensitive mimosa, the several insectivorous flowers and those whose stamens bend down and shake their pollen upon the entering bee in order that he may fertilize their distant mates. But observe this. In an open spot in my garden I planted a climbing vine. When it was barely above the surface I set a stake into the soil a yard away. The vine at once made for it, but as it was about to reach it after several days I removed it a few feet. The vine at once altered its course, making an acute angle, and again made for the stake. This manoeuvre was repeated several times, but finally, as if discouraged, the vine abandoned the pursuit and ignoring further attempts to divert it travelled to a small tree, further away, which it climbed.

' "Roots of the eucalyptus will prolong themselves incredibly in search of moisture. A well-known horticulturist relates that one entered an old drain pipe and followed it until it came to a break, where a section of the pipe had been removed to make way for a stone wall that had been built across its course. The root left the drain and followed the wall until it found an opening where a stone had fallen out. It crept through and following the other side of the wall back to the drain, entered the unexplored part and resumed its journey."

' "And all this?"

' "Can you miss the significance of it? It shows the consciousness of plants. It proves that they think." '

'Think' may be rather too extreme a term to use; but the character in the story was a victim of insomnia. 'Consciousness' may be a more acceptable one.* An indefatigable botanist and observer of plants, Sir Jagadis Chandra Bose, has declared that they are demonstrably sensitive to the presence of human visitants, whether such visitants are themselves

* . . . 'In animals,' says Dr. Millingen, the author of *Curiosities of Medical Experience*, which was published in 1837, 'the very laws of nature are not unfrequently unheeded; and in these instances natural instincts appear less powerful than the mechanical discrimination that we witness in vegetable life, where germs, and molecules, and fibrils not only select each other, according to nature's harmonic institutions, but actually attract each other from distant situations. This attractive power is beautifully illustrated in the mysterious vegetation of the *vallisneria spiralis*, an aquatic plant, in which the male and female are distinct individuals. The organisation of the male qualifies it to adapt itself to the surface of the water, from the bottom of which the plant shoots forth, and to float in the middle of the deep and rapid tide. The female, on the contrary, is only found in shallow waters, or on shores where the tide exerts but little influence. Thus differently formed and situated, how does their union take place? It is a wonderful mystery. As soon as the male flower is perfect, the spiral stem dries away, and the flower thus separated sails away towards the shore in pursuit of the female, for the most part driven by a current of wind or the stream; yet as soon as it arrives near its destination it obeys a new influence, and is attracted towards the object of its pursuit, despite the powers of that wind and tide which until then directed it.'

A mystery indeed, and one, not only of many, but very similar to that set us by the human lover. By mere chance as it would seem, he meets his 'elective affinity', is in an instant infatuated (and not necessarily either by her goodness or beauty or understanding) and is as obviously possessed by her memory and the desire for her company as a flower is by its fragrance, or the child Samuel by the Angel of the Lord.

sensitive or otherwise, and that, like them, they have their detectible moment of death. In any case, as Miss Sturge expresses it,

'Flowers are tremulous with Life, which vibrates in every atom that composes them, and Life which moulds itself differently for every kind of flower. We cannot see the Energy moving, we cannot hear it, we cannot imagine it; it is wonderful beyond what eye can see or ear hear.'

Even a daisy then remains an enigma. And no poet, no botanist can more than stammer his few ardent or measured words in recognition of what may so easily exhaust his wonder and his praise. He salutes it, and passes on.

Lessons, morals and metaphysics apart, and whatever the intention of any particular poem may be, it cannot but have two subjects: one of them, the poet himself; the other, that which it is about; a flower, let us say. How shall we decide which contributes to it the larger share? It is at any rate the closest, widest and deepest imaginative association between them that produces the purest poetry; whether that poetry is Herrick's, Shelley's or D. H. Lawrence's.

Blake's flowers, of all the English poets, are perhaps the loveliest and most ethereal, Vaughan's the most visionary, Shelley's the most romantic, Keats's the richest, Shakespeare's the most signal and natural, Chaucer's the most personal (and certainly not the least beloved), Wordsworth's the most deliberately edifying, Milton's and Swinburne's the least individualized and 'real'. As with any other object, essential poetry may be revealed in but a single line or sentence concerning a flower, even when that has been torn from its context: 'For I maun crush amang the stoure Thy slender stem'; 'Drooping its beauty o'er the watery clearness'; 'And floating water-lilies, broad and bright, Which lit the oak that overhung the hedge'; 'Yet will they open when they see the sun'; 'O Rose, thou art sick! The invisible worm . . .';

'Ah, Sun-Flower! weary of time'; 'And duller should'st thou be than the fat weed That rots it self in ease, on Lethe Wharf. . . .'

But although in English poetry flowers abound (and what wonder, since even the dullest, drabbest and dingiest of Englishmen's castles skulking under 'a sky the colour of anthracite' is seldom without its back yard, and that without its hollyhocks and marigolds?) its positive range in this respect is neither very rich nor wide. As with our English birds, many flowers—which we might assume could not but enravish any intent eye, serene or 'frenzied'—are seldom mentioned; and some, apparently, never. References also to seed and berry, to root and branch and leaf, to pattern and design, are rare. Yet it is the form and shape of a flower, simple or complex, no less than its colour, and this especially if it is seen against the newly risen or declining sun, which is of endless beauty, variety and interest. Moreover (although it is wise, before deciding on the pattern and beauty of minute flowers, to use a magnifying glass), not only are certain trees and plants more attractive in their leaves than in their flowers—the acacia and the beech, for example, the holly, arbutus and yew—but the flowers themselves are in the closest congruity with their buds, stems, leaves, twigs, branches: with the complete plant that is. (So too with our own faces, hands and bodies. Alike in the very young and in the aged, and apart from any question of beauty, eccentricity, habit or occupation, this in-keepingness and accord, this repetition of the unique and the characteristic, are inexhaustibly interesting.) In proof of it, one has merely to recall in memory a leafing or flowering or fruited spray or twig of whitebeam or of the spindle-tree, of clematis, primula, convolvulus, moss, jasmine, pointed ivy, of beech, acacia, or moonlight-coloured may. A few curious exceptions may come to mind, when we pit our own taste against nature's; but in general it is the contrast and harmony between flower and stalk and leaf and bark and thorn, bough and bole, and their way of life, that is so strangely engrossing and attractive.

As for smell, scent, perfume, fragrance, aroma—no perfect gentleman, of course, would acknowledge that he has inherited or been given a nose for any other purpose than the enjoyment of his Stilton or his pheasant or his tweeds; his claret and old brandy and perhaps his China tea. It is effeminate to rhapsodize on scents and odours. That being so, most of the poets, unhappily enough, who have written about flowers have proved to be gentlemen. Nevertheless faint, sweet, fresh, sour, dry, hot, aromatic, liquid, composite are words that come trippingly enough to the tongue *via* that nose when, gentility either lacking or forgotten, one happens to be straying through even the smallest of gardens in the spring or summer. Indeed, in any season, hour or weather.

But the smell of many flowers and of most herbs is as exquisitely difficult of analysis as is that of the dust after rain, or of mown grass in a meadow. One must pause, heed and ponder—curiouser and curiouser: Old Man or southernwood, rue, 'wine-sweet musk rose', rosemary, fennel, spiced gillyflower, balm, the little thyme, verbena, geranium, tansy, jasmine, camphor, menthol, wormwood, sage, mint and peppermint, hawthorn, lilac, chives, carrot, juniper, cowslip, spurge. Are these, as we read them in this haphazard list, only mere names of the irrecallable, or does the most nebulous ghost of their originals and their soft incense haunt the printed page?

In the actual company of the flowers themselves, morning or evening, how many hours, I wonder, should we need to spend in merely recording the effects of these perfumes and odours on senses, mind and spirit? The gods, we are told, enjoy even burnt offerings, snuff up greedily that appalling smoke! 'He leads a dog's life' need not, then, be a wholly disparaging statement.*

* Smell, indeed, as Jason Hill, the author of *The Curious Gardener* declares, has become the Cinderella of the senses; although she flaunts herself in my lady's chamber; and is of much more service than we suspect. To her we owe all tastes and savours except four: the salt, the sweet, the acid and the bitter; the tip of the tongue notifying salt and sweet, its edges, acid, and its further reaches the bitter. She is, moreover, in the closest *rapport* and accord with memory; and memory is the mistress of self and of sanity. The reader of *The Curious Gardener* will be introduced into what Jason Hill calls the 'invisible' garden. The terms he uses for various scents—cold, intense, complex, evocative, interesting, hearty, luscious—suggest how discerning a Cinderella must be his. What follows, I imagine, will put most noses to shame:

'The scent which seems, more than all others, to have an independent existence is that of "strawberry leaves dying with an excellent cordial smell"; in fact, when I met it for the first time, as I was walking along a country lane in winter, I felt sure that some violets were flowering before their time in the hedge-bank, and when I found nothing among the dead leaves to account for the unexpected scent, I was inclined to put it down as an hallucination. There is a distinct note of violet, or rather of orris root in it, together with cedar wood and something like the dry, earthy fragrance of ambergris; and, because all scents of the musk and violet group fatigue our sense of smell very quickly, it seems to fade away almost as soon as you perceive it. . . . A variation on the violet theme is played by Mignonette, which introduces a note—a dusty odour of antiquity—that is almost peculiar to itself, though it occurs again, I think, in the subtle chord struck by the flowers of the Vine and of the Climbing Asparagus. . . . There is a trace of sharpness in the scent which drifts, on a hot day, from the glandular stems of *Rubus odoratus*; but here the impression is chiefly that of a mixture of resin and cedar wood with a slight hint of pineapple. . . . The most powerful and far-reaching scent in the garden by daylight is given off by *Humea elegans*, not only by the flowers—plumes of chestnut-coloured Pampas grass—but also by the stems and leaves. It resembles incense so closely that it once caused a country vicar to be suspected of ritualistic practices; and one day, as I was walking down Victoria Street, some hours after handling a leaf of it at Vincent Square, a friend who was with me remarked, "What a long way the smell of incense carries from Westminster Cathedral!" . . .'

But even if the mention of flowers were no more than incidental in poetry, delight in them need by no means imply either a close acquaintance, or the ability to give them their proper names. A little problem of technique arises here. *Cerastrium tomentosum*, *Helosciadium* (*Sium*) *nodiflorum*—however pleasing these flowers themselves may be, their designations are rather stubborn to manage in English rhyme and metre—

Sweet as thyself thy flowers to me!—
They banish all that's woesome:
Even the tiny chickweed, love—
Cerastrium tomentosum ;

whereas Snow-in-Summer and Fool's Water-cress are likelier than not to be wanting in one's everyday repertory of recognizable wildflowers. Of the four hundred-odd English-named varieties of grass, of the eight hundred species of moss, how many could I instantly name? Perhaps, ten! 'I am no great Nebuchadnezzar, Sir,' says the Clown in the play, 'I have not much skill in grass.'

And last, how will flowers fare in the poetry of the future? 'Th' exulting Florist' of to-day, in spite of his apparent ignorance of the 'language of flowers', now deemed Victorian and demoded, nevertheless implores his clients to 'say it with flowers'. He may be less eager to cajole or instruct the 'Botanic Muse'. She appears, moreover, to be proving a hesitant pupil. Whatever its other characteristics may be, one conspicuous tendency in English verse for the time being is *away* from Nature. There are young poets who have all but abandoned the Vegetable Kingdom. 'No flowers, by request.' There is nothing to intimate, however, that the trend of the English people is in the same direction. The general exodus nowadays, with dire consequences in certain respects, is away from the towns and into the country. Nor is it by any means the poet cooped up in bricks and mortar who is least likely to pine for a water meadow or for the peace of Innisfree.

So, even if England is destined never again to be a nest of *singing* birds, or doomed even to languish at last without a living poet to her name, there is copious evidence that her folk, her people, in spite of 'wanting the accomplishment of verse', have not only loved and delighted in flowers, but, knowing them by heart, have lavished on their country names for them their sentiment, humour, wit, fancy, insight and imagination. The delicate, shade-loving, night-folding *Oxalis acetosella*, whose snowy flowers are at times 'dashed over with a small show of bluish', and whose sour relishing juice 'maketh a most dainty clear syrup', is, for convenience and botanical purposes the *Oxalis acetosella*, and it is nothing more. In rural polyonymosity it is hailed as sheep-sorrel, cuckoo-spice, hallelujah, ladies' cakes, and God Amighty's bread-and-cheese. Need it be added that it is also St. Patrick's one true shamrock? If this widespread genius not only for naming but for accepting such names for one of the aconites as bear's-foot, helmet-flower, Turk's-cap, Monk's-cowl, Luckie's mutch and wolf's-bane; and, for sub-christening one of the *Galiums*, catch-weed, cleavers, hair-eve, mutton-chops, love-man, goose-bill and geckdor—*if* this genius for a sort of wayside poetry continues to flourish—and, alas, it has many unintentional enemies nowadays—there will be little basis for the charge that the ancient fountain has run dry. Meanwhile let the intellectualist who sneers at the 'folk', a word which after all is honest old Anglo-Saxon for the French-derived *people*, be reminded of the Spanish proverb: 'He who spits at the whirlwind spits in his own face.'

London may still remain of 'townes *A per se* . . . the floure of Cities all', even if, nowadays, it is somewhat overblown. But what Cowley said in his essay 'Of My self' remains true of most imaginative and meditative minds. They hope to find their peace and solitude beyond its straggling, ragged outskirts, even although the restless hum of the vast hive may occasionally incite to honey the bees (perhaps from Innisfree) in their own bonnets. On the other hand, there are Elians, and cronies of the Mitre. Cowley himself, even at 'the Court of one of the best Princesses of the World', wearied of much company and no small business; of the daily sight of Greatness; of the Paint of that kind of Life; of that Beauty which is not real but Adulterate.

His Majesty happily restored, he refused to attempt to compass any extraordinary fortune that might well have come his way; and withdrew:

Content thy self with the small barren praise
Which neglected Verse does raise . . .

But God [he goes on] 'laughs at a Man, who sayes to his Soul, *Take thy ease*: I met presently not onely with many little encumbrances and impediments, but with so much sickness (a new misfortune to me) as would have spoiled the happiness of an Emperour as well as mine: Yet I do neither repent nor alter my course. *Non ego perfidum Dixi Sacramentum*; Nothing shall separate me from a mistress, which I have loved so long, and have now at last married; though she neither has brought me a rich Portion, nor lived yet so quietly with me as I hoped from her. . . .

Nor by me ere shall you,
You of all Names the sweetest, and the best,
You Muses, Books, and Liberty and Rest;
You Gardens, Fields, and Woods forsaken be,
As long as Life it self forsakes not me.'

Some Women Novelists

As any particular period of time steadily recedes into the past, its content in human memory passes through a series of gradual or rapid and inevitable transmutations. By far the greater part of it is immediately obliterated. The rest fades in patches, changes colour, lightens in one place, darkens in another. It becomes contorted, distorted, shrunken; here it is flattered in retrospect; there, belittled, misunderstood, or defamed. How extravagantly partial, inadequate, condensed, yet for the most part superficial is the record of any twenty-four hours in the next morning's newspaper! How few of the myriads of mankind find the minutest niche in history beyond that afforded by a mouldering grave-stone! Though the whole of the past, we vaguely suppose, is still 'there', as precisely fitting its original receptacle as a nut fits its shell, even of the personally experienced only scattered, disjointed and momentary fragments are recoverable, and they not as they actually were, but as they now look to be. For the rest we must depend upon memorials in print or writing, in stone or wood or canvas, and attempt to translate them into something resembling the original. But many even of these memorials have been the outcome of a close or heedless sifting, selection or condensation, and they cannot but be modified or falsified in some degree by the perspective of the present, in meaning and impressiveness.

So with that brief section of time known as the 'seventies. From our crow's nest of the passing hour we gaze out in its direction over the sundering flood in search of landfall and sea-mark. It is a period for many of us (a many rapidly dwindling to a few) just remote and just retrievable enough to be singularly beguiling. What was its general appearance? Who and what was 'going on'? Only a faltering bird's-eye view is practicable.

During the last few days of 1869 a thaw had set in after a hard frost, and readers of the 'agony column' in *The Times* were greeted on New Year's Day with this message: 'R—D to B—S. Thanks dearest. Delighted. All right. 6. 8. 10. 11 will suit—not 7, prefer 6. Your own R':—a simple utterance that might at any moment be addressed by humanity itself to the fatal Sisters. As for larger affairs, Europe was on the verge of the Franco-Prussian War—a fiery Phoenix that of late returned to the sole Arabian tree. On the 8th of June Charles Dickens, that supreme magician, then fifty-nine, after working all day on *The Mystery of Edwin Drood* died suddenly of a stroke. The School Boards were established in the same year, and Thomas Huxley was one of the original members for London. The Bank Holiday Act, Darwin's *Descent of Man*, Ruskin's *Fors Clavigera* and Guild of St George ('Food can only be got out of the ground and happiness out of honesty'), and *The Adventures of Harry Richmond* were of 1871, a year before *Erewhon*; *The Ring and the Book* having completed its publication in '69. In '71 Henry Irving opened at the Lyceum with *The Bells*; in '71 T. W. Robertson died, in '73 Lord Lytton, in '75 Charles Kingsley, in '76 Harriet Martineau. In '74 Whistler exhibited his portrait of Thomas Carlyle. And precisely midway in our period 'A Young Lady' implored the Editor of *The Times*, the great Delane, to lend his aid in the releasing of ladies from segregation when travelling by train. The doors and windows, she said, were obstinate. She had hurt her hands and ruined her gloves in the attempt to open them. 'Men and women', ran her challenging postscript, 'are meant to go through life together, to separate them is a poor way of getting over any difficulties there may be.'

Though Girton College had been founded in '69 and Bedford College had come into being ten years afterwards, the 'Girton Girl' (who 'views with horror a slim ankle and a pointed toe') was still an object of derision to Mr. Punch even in '86, the year of the establishment of the 'National Society for Women's Suffrage'. Four years afterwards he began to ogle the 'Undomestic Daughter'. In '78 England secured 'peace with honour' at the Congress of Berlin, Parnell became the uncrowned king of Ireland, *H.M.S. Pinafore* was produced. In '79 John Henry Newman received the cardinal's hat. In 1880, a year before his death, Benjamin Disraeli's last novel, *Endymion*, was published.

In the 'seventies the rich and various work of the great English illustrators—how rich and various Mr. Forrest Reid has lately revealed—began to decline. And it would be difficult to say how much in form and design they owed to the happy accident that the feminine attire of the time was a rather full skirt and a rather tight bodice with natural sleeves, and a tendency to shawls. Shallow, brimmed hats, or ovals of fur or velvet, crowned heads with the hair bunched out behind in a chignon. Between these and the ferocious English sun a little fringed parasol afforded a pleasing, tinted and becoming shade. In the following years monstrous flounces began to multiply, the train to expand, the 'waist' to contract. Indoors was awaiting a cap (or 'lappets') to ensure respect for the matron of thirty and upwards, who, says Mrs. Alexander, might still be called charming even at that advanced age; and who might then solace herself at the pianoforte with such sentimental ballads, I fancy, as *Love's Old Sweet Song* or *In the Gloaming, O my Darling*.

About 1880, whiskers, curly or weeping-willow-wise, and, if need be, dyed, were vanishing from the scene, together with that 'fantastic velvet vestment', the smoking jacket. The crinolette was 'in'. I recall, too, a sort of tongs which were worn dangling from the hips to keep the train from out of the dust. Little 'buses, with a conductor hanging from a strap behind, or with a hole in the roof for the collection of fares, and with straw in the interior, roamed the streets, which rang merrily with the strains of the butcher boy whistling *Tiddy-fol-loll* or *Tommy, make room for your Uncle!* A few years later he began shrilling *We don't want to fight....*

The bell of the horse tram had first tinkled in London in '71; Charles Peace—who preferred the solitude of a gig—met his end in '79. The lamp-lighter with his little ladder still went his dusk and daybreak round—even in Holywell St. and Seven Dials; and Valentines, exquisite and otherwise, burdened the peak-capped postman's back on the 14th of February. Jack-in-the-Green jigged through the streets on May Day, and occasional roving Frenchmen scared every horse within scent of them with their dancing bear. Third-class railway passengers after dark took their ease on narrow wooden seats under a single oil lamp, its ooze softly swinging to and fro in a glass container over their heads. Smoke as of the infernal regions asphyxiated the hardy subterranean adventurer whose route lay from Bishop's Road to Farringdon St.; the merry-go-round of the Inner Circle having not as yet been completed.

The typewriter, friend of the printer, was of '73; the telephone, foe of the unready, of '76; and the phonograph, a rich blessing though one then in disguise, was patented by Mr. Edison in '77. Life was in process of being mechanised, 'speeded up', made noisy and malodorous—though in many other respects deodorised. Yet, in spite of a five-penny income tax, of the School Boards, and the blessings of science, a steady increase in the mortality from suicide began to show itself even in '76. But, as all things must, the 'seventies came to an end. The penny-farthing bicycle and electric light its chief novelties and the fall of the Tay Bridge its final disaster, 1879 went out with the storm 'cones' up in most districts, and in worsening weather.

Last, but not least, all persons now between sixty and seventy years of age, who in our period helped to raise the population of England from twenty-three to twenty-six millions, were then engaged in being born. Providentially for many of them the average number of children in the families of the professional classes in the United Kingdom had not then sunk to what, I believe, the statistician has recently shown it to be—a figure in the neighbourhood of 0.9.

It is fortunate for a hazy and ill-informed historian that this paper is concerned not with life in the world of the real and actual during this decade, but with its reflection in the looking-glass of fiction. None the less, any attempt, and even one so superficial as this, to recall what those years 'looked like'—and to this end the trivial may afford even vivider and more telling glimpses than the important—may be of service in the company of that fiction. It vaguely presents the general scene; may give the reader a notion of his bearings. It may help to preclude prejudice.

'Some Women Novelists' of the 'Seventies—the phrase has at least the cadence of a lullaby. It conjures up in the fancy of those who were fated to share any fraction of that remote decade, of those who are not acutely (and also perhaps self-obliviously) hostile to everything tainted with the Victorian, a trim walled garden in June, bee and flaunting butterfly, pinks in bloom and tea roses, candytuft and mignonette. A closer view proves this to be a delusive picture. The walled garden leads out to where the vegetables grow; cherry trees and gooseberry bushes give place to the prickly briar and the grieving thorn, cypress and yew. And at length a waste appears, no rill of living water musical on the ear, bindweed and viper's bugloss its few clear flowers, bleached slender bones their only company in its sands. And of all things in this world, what is less easily retrievable than that which once breathed the breath of life and has now not only passed away but vanished out of remembrance?

In space our theme is confined to the British Isles, and that is fairly simple. It is in respect to the arbitrary division in time and still more to the division in kind imposed by it that difficulties abound. Even in history a decade is no more than a convenience, a fold whose hurdles prove extremely defective, and even when facts are its only sheep. But authors and books—it is impossible to segregate objects once so lively and sensitive as easily as that. Its date of publication is hardly even a book's birthday. That was when in one of the closest privacies known to man its first words appeared on paper. The seed of it, the animating nucleus, may have been germinating and quickening in timeless dreams for half a lifetime.

Ten years of childhood, too, and not in mere appearance of duration only, surpass a hundred of maturity. They have more influence on the mind and imagination than any that follow. Next in virtue of influence are the years of a man's youth. These are the well-spring of his after-life. 'By their fruits ye shall know them', but it was the season of blossoming that set those fruits to ripen. It is, too, what goes on in the world within rather than what goes on in the world without that makes our days valuable and significant to ourselves. Its near and dear, its deplored and detested, even its little things may affect us much more than its far, its multitudinous and its large. We buy newspapers, first to scan, and then to light our fires with.

The work of every writer therefore varies in quality and meaning and value at different times of his life; its last state may be (perhaps is bound to be in certain respects) worse than its first. But the finer and greater he is as an artist, so much the more signally, within certain limits, is that work the revelation of his own mind and spirit.

The creative impulse, the visiting spirit, is essential. His external surroundings, to whatever degree they may affect him, are by comparison of far less account. What curiously diverse and individual reflections of the 'seventies, for example, are *Literature and Dogma*, *The Unknown Eros*, and *Thrift*, *Character* and *Duty* by the author of *Self-Help*.

The civilised world may be pursuing the even tenor of its way across the flats of tradition while one man whose privy thoughts are fated to have the effects of an earthquake on that tradition may be living in complete obscurity. On the other hand, since great novelists occupy the world of their own day, the world of that day must in some degree occupy them. But they transmute it into their own terms. And so it comes about that the London of Dickens's era is for most of us Dickens's London; just as Chaucer, however close he may be to our hearts, humours and humanity, is largely our fourteenth century, and Malory, who flourished seventy years after Chaucer died, seems to have been his senior by centuries. Even although, too, a signally fine novel may have been markedly the product of its own age, it is apt to continue to live because it little seems to be so. Now a treasure for all time, it little matters that it is also a period piece. Conversely, a novel that continues to live and shed its influence, to interest, engross and amuse must in its own kind have something of greatness in it. It is no mere parasite of its age.

While, then, any particular decade can be said to illumine the annals of literature only with its best and brightest, its productions should modestly refrain from taking, on that score, too much unction to their souls. Apart from Thomas Hardy himself, to whom and to what do we owe *The Dynasts*? To Wellington, Nelson, Napoleon, and his satellites, and to the first ten years of their century, or to the first ten years of this? Or to the chance that introduced a child of eight gifted with genius to a cupboard containing a lavishly illustrated copy of *The History of the Wars*? Is *Arabia Deserta*—the author of which, when he was invited to contribute to a grace-offering to the poet of *The Dynasts* on his eightieth birthday, quite innocently enquired, 'And who is Thomas Hardy?'—is *Arabia Deserta* the patchoulied nosegay of artifice we associate however unfairly with the 'nineties'?

Novelists, too, tend probably to write of what they were familiar with when they were younger. However hospitable they may be to new ways, new ideas, new views, these are not their spiritual home. But to sort their achievements on this basis would be a feat for the kindly ants or ducks in a fairy tale.

If, then, any great novel had been written by a woman during the 'seventies it would not much concern us now. So far as I can discover none was. George Eliot's finest work had been done in the 'sixties, and only *Daniel Deronda* appeared during the next ten years. Of other than great—of sound, gifted, amusing and edifying fiction there was an abundant supply. How much of it is read nowadays, I cannot say; probably, little. For each generation in turn gracelessly and often unwisely discards the fiction of its immediate predecessor. We begin to read grown-up novels in our later 'teens, and then, apart from the old masters, those written by novelists many years our seniors, but hot from the press. A novel-reader upwards of forty, then, may be vividly familiar with the fiction current when he came of age, and yet have the vaguest acquaintance with that of his childhood. For this reason any little private excursion such a reader may nowadays make into the minor fiction of the 'seventies will largely be into almost virgin country. A variegated scene will spread itself around him, an adventure more curious perhaps than enriching may be his reward. If he is tempted to be condescending let him remind himself that current criticism cannot but be affected to some extent by current taste; that that veers with the wind; and that a personal judgment, also, is seldom innocent of prejudice, and may be as temporary as it is assured.

In 1897, for example, a large flat volume appeared entitled *Women Novelists of Queen Victoria's Reign.* It was written by a number of ladies 'who had been concerned for some years in the publication of works of fiction'; and it was intended as a loyal tribute to Queen Victoria on the celebration of her second Jubilee. It declined to 'assess the merit' of living 'lady fictionists' (its editor preferring this dreadful toast-and-water phrase to, let us say, *novelistesses*). Its hospitality was otherwise restricted to those women writers who had published their work after the Queen's accession.

While, then, such 'famous novelists' as Mrs. Gore, Mrs. Bray, Mrs. Hall and Mrs. Marsh were given no place in it, the works of Mrs. Archer Clive, of Anne Manning, and of Mrs. Stretton were duly appraised, and among its actual contributors were Mrs. MacQuoid and Mrs. Parr, whose pen-name was 'Holme Lee'. In spite of the fact that Queen Victoria's second Jubilee is so recent an event that all novelists now aged forty-three were born amid the rumour of its drums and tramplings, in how many minds, I wonder, will these names awake positively rousing echoes.

'Views' on fiction, we might assume, however, would not at that time differ very much from our own. Nevertheless we find so shrewd and vigorous a critic as Mrs. Oliphant asserting, first, that in 1897 homage to the Brontës exceeded that accorded to Dickens, Thackeray and George Eliot; next, that Charles Reade and Trollope were almost forgotten; and last, that the 'nobler arts' of fiction are all of them missing from the Brontë novels. When, however, in the course of her paper she refers to Charlotte as a demure little person, silent and shy, 'plain, even ugly—a small woman with a big nose, and no other noticeable feature—not even the bright eyes of genius', and when finally she expresses the hope that Miss Brontë's 'memory will be allowed to rest', we become conscious of a certain bias. Whether or not, straws like these show not only from what direction the critical breeze is blowing, but how the wild west wind of popular caprice may sweep a fiction once the joyous pabulum of millions into the all-but-lost, if not into the irrecoverable.

The distance that in fiction lends re-enchantment to the view, has indeed to be considerable. The once expensive furniture, glass and china of the late 'seventies must survive another thirty years before it safely attains the goal of what the American Customs Officers recognise as the 'antique'. First editions of its women novelists are in even worse case. As rank on rank, dwindling in perspective, they repose on their metallic shelves in the London Library and meet the faltering eye of the enquirer, they may shed a tranquillising calm—but they are unlikely to be collected. This is no proof however that they are unworthy of being *re*-collected.

'The demon of Chronology', in Mr. E. M. Forster's phrase, being in our midst, the driest statistics may be condoned if they suggest the positive situation. In the year 1875, then, when *Comin' thro' the Rye* appeared and Thomas Hardy had recently published *A Pair of Blue Eyes* and *Far from the Madding Crowd*, when Meredith was forty-seven and Henry James thirty-two, when Galsworthy, Bennett and Mr. Wells were not yet in their 'teens, no fewer than at least forty women were busily engaged and engrossed in the production of fiction: George Eliot (how futile is ink to blazon the colours these names deserve!),

Mrs. Henry Wood, Anne Manning, Mrs. Alexander, Mrs. Oliphant, Rhoda Broughton, Charlotte Yonge, Charlotte Tucker, Mrs. Lynn Linton, Jean Ingelow, Julia Kavanagh, Amelia Edwards, Mrs. Annie Edwardes, Miss Betham-Edwards, Mrs. Craik, Mrs. Marshall, Mrs. Hungerford, Mrs. Riddell, Elizabeth Charles, Harriet Parr, Hesba Stretton, Mrs. Archer Clive, 'Ouida', Mary Elizabeth Braddon, Rosa Carey, Charlotte Dempster, Rosa Kettle, Mrs. Linnaeus Banks, Florence Montgomery, Lady Augusta Noel, Mary Linskill, Eleanor Poynter, Florence Marryat, Mary Roberts, Mrs. Hibbert Ware, Mrs. Robert Stuart de Courcey Laffan, Anne Thackeray, Jessie Fothergill and 'Rita'. Adeline Sergeant was as yet only sharpening her quill. Of these novelists nine were responsible for some 554 publications, and these chiefly in three volumes. An average of sixty-one each, that is, with a remainder that would suffice in paper for the complete works of Flaubert.

This bare catalogue of names—a few of them famous, a few once notorious—naked and incomplete, may revive lively and halcyon memories in the minds of the elderly. But it has only a slender bearing on fiction as one of the fine arts or on books as literature, and it is no nearer a map of the long-past literary scene than is a mere collection of place names. It is also a confession of failure. For confronted with the vast reservoir of printer's ink thus conjured up, most of it, alas, completely stagnant (no ray of sun, no coursing swallow, no darting kingfisher, or mantling swan, but rank elder, sad sullen swamp and deadly hemlock) I must confess that I have merely dipped and dipped again. Its deeps and its shallows are all but inexhaustible. During the 'seventies alone 'that wicked Ouida' was responsible or irresponsible for no fewer than nine novels, including *Puck*; Mrs. Henry Wood for ten, including the tales in the *Johnny Ludlow* series, and Miss Braddon for sixteen, including *Vixen* and *Joshua Haggard's Daughter*.

A hardly less arid and harrowing means of hinting at the situation is to mention a few titles—a title being not less if no more an indication of the character of a novel than of a man. A large number of the novels of the nineteenth century written by women were called after their heroines—or their heroes. It matters little which, since both almost invariably imply a pursuer and the pursued; only a slight jar of the kaleidoscope, whatever the consequent form and 'pattern'. For the rest, *Miriam's Marriage*, *No Saint*, *Only a Woman*, *Two Little Wooden Shoes*, *A Rise in the World*, *Goodbye, Sweetheart! Can This be Love? The Doctor's Dilemma*, *Half a Million of Money*, *Wee Wifie*, *Her Dearest Foe*, *Pearl Powder*, *Above Suspicion*, *Ought We to Visit Her? The Beautiful Miss Barrington*, may surrender a glimpse of their general trend.

Compare them with *The Dove's Nest*, *To the Light House*, *Dangerous Ages*, *Told by an Idiot*, *Skin Deep*, *The Tramping Methodist*, *The Poor Man*, *Studies in Wives*, *Seducers in Ecuador*, *The Maternity of Harriett Wicken*, *Why They Married*, *Tents of Israel*, *A Pitiful Wife*, *Secret Bread*, *Precious Bane*, and, say, *The Sheikh*, and a difference in theme and aim, if not in quality, clearly discloses itself.

Seriousness whether it be a condition of the spirit or an attitude of the mind is closely akin to sincerity, and in some kind or degree, even if it may parch bad fiction like the sirocco, it is essential to fine fiction; although a novelist may smile and smile, and yet be frivolous neither in virtue nor in villainy. George Eliot was so serious as to be by conscious intention didactic, and to declare that her mission in life was that of 'an aesthetic teacher and an interpreter of philosophical ideas'. Yet her fiction seems to have survived the strain. Seriousness indeed (however airily variegated), prevailed in the minor novels of the 'seventies. It may be in part explained by the fact that women had been compelled to fight for the liberty of becoming novelists at all.

'Novel writing', said Mrs. Parr, writing in 1897, and she cannot have realised that less than half a century afterwards well over 300 women would be following her own precarious trade,—'Novel writing has now become an employment, a profession, distraction, I might almost say a curse.' 'The mania to see their names in print' had seized upon her sex. But when in 1833 Anne Manning burst into her father's study with the announcement that she had finished a tale entitled *Village Belles*, 'Papa,' said she, 'I don't know what you will say, but I have written a story!' 'Ho, ho, ho!' was what Mr. Manning said. He nevertheless read the tale, and afterwards remarked, 'My dear, I like your story very much.' But as he seems never to have referred to it again, and no Jane Austen was an observer of the little scene, the problem of what actually passed in Mr. Manning's mind is left insoluble.

It was still something of an event in literary annals so late as 1846 when, at the age of twenty, Mrs. Craik fled to London from Stoke, 'conscious of a literary vocation'. 'Women in her day', says Mrs. Parr, 'were in intellectual imprisonment.' Even in the later 'fifties, and in spite of the enthusiastic encouragement of John Keble, when Charlotte Yonge announced to her parents that she was about to publish a novel, a Family Council immediately followed, and its sanction to so daring a 'departure from the ladylike' was granted only on condition that Charlotte should not herself profit by any financial reward that might come of it. She agreed; and a large part of her ill-gotten gains enriched missionary work in Melanesia.

Not that such little hindrances as these were confined to one sex, for even in the 'seventies we find Amelia Edwards ironically enquiring, 'Can a painter by any possibility be a gentleman? Might a gentleman without loss of dignity write poetry, unless in Greek or Latin?' By that time, however, Women's challenge had been definitely issued, though quality in the ranks was still more conspicuous than numbers, and the battle was not yet to the strong.

Long before December 31, 1869, for example, the tint of the bluestocking, it might be supposed, had to be very dark to justify the ascription of the term. None the less in 1877 a novel of this title was published by Mrs. Annie Edwardes. Clementina Hardcastle, the bluestocking herself, had been brought up by her parents as most daughters in those days were. They hoped, that is, to see her well married. They were convinced too that 'under-educated men desire over-educated wives'. In consequence she writes to her long-absent lover a letter (beginning 'Dear Sir John'), which is restricted to enquiries relating to the geology of the Channel Islands. Bluestockings in those days, we are told also, wore a fringe and spelt humanity with a big H. Clementina's lively appearance, however, fails to suggest anything formidable. She has reddish brown eyes, reddish brown hair with a golden tint 'probably due to Auricomous Fluid at twenty-one shillings and sixpence a bottle', very black lashes and eyebrows, aided it may be by 'antimony and a pencil' (no reference to rouge or lipstick suggesting either that these were wanting or would be taken for granted), and she is wearing for a walk along the sea-shore 'a skirt, O, so narrow that it would take a year's study to learn to walk in it at all; a fan-shaped train carried over one arm', and a Mother Hubbard hat.

The New Woman, although, maybe, she was as yet unlabelled, was not unknown. In the guise of a 'writing woman' named Mattie Rivers, she appears in the same novel as 'the customary accessory' of a smart yachting cruise. She is described as 'an emancipated sister of twenty-nine, with a cavalier hat worn distinctly . . . over one ear, a rakish-looking double eye-glass, a cane . . . a palpable odour of Havana smoke clinging to her gentlemanly yachting-jacket, and short-clipped, gentlemanly hair.'

But even if the Havana smoke was of Mattie's own making, the heralds of the Keynote Series were in her day still in their nurseries, and it was not until the end of the century that the 'sex-problem'—dismallest, surely, of all drab and blighting phrases—had become, according to Mrs. Oliphant, 'the chief occupation of fiction', and that Mrs. Linton could refer to 'unveiled presentations of the sexual instincts which seem to make the world one large lupanar'—a term which I was relieved to find no trace of in *The (Concise) Oxford Dictionary*. However that may be, the novels written by women in the 'seventies were still for the most part either love stories, not very subtle, perhaps, but simple, and not usually sensuous, or passionate; or they were tales like *Bridget*, by Miss Betham-Edwards, or *Debenham's Vow*, or *The Mistress of Langdale Hall* by Rosa Kettle dealing with the domestic affections, and welcomed by the family circle, phrases both of them now as demoded as bent-iron- or poker-work. If, 'I don't *think* Papa would mind your being poor,' is one extreme of a delicate situation; 'I am quite sure Mamma wouldn't mind your being a marquis,' might well have been the other.

In *The Wooing O't* Mrs. Alexander tells us that Maggie, her chief character, a young woman (the daughter of a chemist), whose 'brave little heart' is not less endearing and delightful company than her sound little head, was guided in an amatory crisis by 'the fixed underlying feminine instinct which has probably kept more women straight than religion, morality and calculation put together, the true instinct that woman "should not unsought be won"'. A brilliant and charming man of the world, having rescued a titled cousin of his from marrying her, has himself gained her love—and she, though she doesn't know it, has his. 'She cried shame upon herself for thus casting her full heart before a man who didn't want it. . . .' 'To do that', Mrs. Oliphant agreed, 'is somehow against the instinct of primitive humanity.' So too would most of the heroines of the 'seventies. Nor did the women novelists who created them cast *all* that was in *their* full hearts or instincts before the public. The public had to wait awhile. Freud was not yet in the ascendant.

None the less, that public—an otherwise extremely hospitable one—had lately been presented, though only temporarily, with *Poems and Ballads*, and Rhoda Broughton had not only skimmed its pages, but had observed its influence on life itself. For Nell's sister, Dolly L'Estrange, in *Cometh up as a Flower* (Miss Broughton's first or second novel, with her 'passionate great velvet orbs', was, we are told, 'the sort of woman upon whom Mr. Algernon Swinburne would write pages of magnificent uncleanness.' She has a nefarious finger in the plot of the story—she forges a love-letter; but otherwise occupies little space in it; and I cannot recover what Mr. Swinburne thought of her. Even Nell, her Tennysonian sister, was probably in the nature of a bomb-shell for mothers with daughters. It is her own story, and she tells it in the first person, not always as the purist (in grammar) would approve—'every English gentleman or lady likes to have a room to themselves'. And Virginia Woolf, ignoring the un-roomed gentleman, has recently, but with a more delicate literary artifice, told us precisely why. The more dramatic episodes in this particular novel are narrated in the historic present, a device at times disconcerting: 'Great tears are standing in his honest tender agonised eyes—tears that do not disgrace his manhood much, I think . . . and as he so kisses and clasps me, a great blackness comes over my eyes, and I swoon away in his arms.'

Nell's pretty face varies in attractiveness according to her fickle moods. At one moment her 'curly red' hair falls in 'splendid ruddy billows' over the clasper's shoulder, and at the next, in her looking-glass, she scrutinises a 'wide mouth' in 'a potato face'. But even when that 'huge loose knot of hair' is 'crowned by a sevenpenny half-penny hat' she always 'looks a lady'; and when she enters a drawing-room, she is bound to confess, 'several people (men especially) looked at me.' What, I wonder, would be the precise equivalent of the quoted phrases in an 'advanced' novel of 1940?

Nell's seriousness, amply encouraged by her creator, takes the form of impassioned little discourses on such expansive themes as Death and Fate and Eternity. But simply because as a novelist Miss Broughton is so witty, high-spirited, generous and headlong, however serious she may be, she is seldom so sober, never so solid as most of her contemporaries.

If, indeed, kisses be the food of love, then Cupid is on famine commons in Jessie Fothergill's *Probation*. It is a tale—remarkably well told for a girl in her twenties—of life in Lancashire. The Civil War in America has converted the plenty of 1860 into the dearth of 1862. 'King Cotton' has for the time being abdicated. As in many of the novels of our period, and in few of our own, wedding-bells—a double peal—ring out its last chapter. None the less, only two kisses, so far as I can recall, are recorded in the complete three volumes, and one of them is the forlorn farewell of a rejected but still gallant admirer. In *Cometh up as a Flower*, which like many other novels of its day has a sad ending steadily foreseen, they are as multitudinous as dewdrops at daybreak on a briar rose. But both novels are 'love-stories', and both are representative of their time.

In general, perhaps, our novelists' heroines are left safe and sound on the outskirts of an 'untroubled future such as women ought to enjoy'—wedded bliss, that is, with a husband who usually has income enough to ensure comfort; although Leah in Mrs. Annie Edwardes' caustic, sharp-cut novel of that title, dies of heart disease half an hour after a wedding by which she renounces not only a nefarious peer but a substantial fortune. But Miss Fothergill, like Miss Rosa Carey, the author of *Robert Orde's Atonement*, would have agreed, I fancy, with Mrs. Humphry Ward's summary in *David Grieve* that, 'The most disappointing and hopeless marriage nobly borne is better worth having than what people call an ideal passion.' It is a choice between a grand slam and stalemate.

Nor was beauty in the heroine of the 'seventies indispensable. 'She was one of those women, who are not anything, neither ugly nor beautiful, until one knows them, and then they are lovely for ever.' That is a memorable thing to say of any woman, and is as true as it is well said.

All this is by no means to suggest that the fiction whose chief concern is with questions of sex, and whose first green leaf, it seems, was raised from a seed that may have escaped from Aphra Behn's pocket, but was assiduously watered by Charlotte Brontë, was not already in vogue. The intention was different. Love, as Miss Storm Jameson has declared, is an emotion that concerns not only the body, but the mind, the spirit and the imagination of man or woman. This seems to have been the view shared by most of the women novelists of the 'seventies, and it gives their treatment of the theme balance, proportion and depth. Women of the world they may have been, and women (as Rhoda Broughton puts it) 'too thorough . . . not to enjoy household work', but in their explorations of the House of Life they did not neglect the view afforded by its attics or lavish an unconscionably protracted scrutiny on its drains. Some of them were a little prudish; a few paddled in the shocking; but that, as yet, was not a difficult feat. Nowadays novelists bent on the same adventure and in search of low tide cannot but 'weep like anything to see Such quantities of sand'. Will that sun ever rise when the ultimate shores of the 'shocking' will loom into view and the artist be left to work in peace?

As for the 'free' woman in another sense, she was rather

frowned upon than otherwise. 'I thought', says Sebastian, one of the two heroes of *Probation*,

'I thought that if Miss Mereweather disapproves so strongly of men in general, it would annoy her to be mistaken for one of that odious and inferior sex; and, moreover, would only be a sign of how very different she must be from most women.'

'She is very superior to most women' [replies Helena, her devotee]. 'If that is what you mean, I concede the point willingly.'

'Well, if such a superior woman is often mistaken for a man, is not that a piece of negative evidence of the inferiority of women in general?' Sebastian asked politely.

Then, as now, we may assume, the majority of novel-addicts were women. None the less, note neither exclamatory nor interrogatory bedecked my library copy of *Probation* at this remark, and amateur annotators appear to have been grossly free with the pencil in those days.

Miss Mereweather finally marries a clergyman, the headmaster of 'a sort of college', and in face of this betrayal of her ideals, Helena refuses to regard her any longer as a friend. But by this time, bravely facing the grief and distress that have come into her life, she has realised what from the beginning has been clear to the reader—that she is in love with Sebastian, while his own love for her has convinced him that 'no man and no woman pitted each against the other could do any good, but that "the twain together well might change the world".'

Not all strife between the sexes in the fiction of the 'seventies ended as peacefully as this. Though the craving for a latchkey and similar emblems of emancipation was not yet vocal, though, as one female futurist puts it, 'the shriek of the Sapphos for love' seldom echoes in its courts, and even 'the longing', in Mrs. Oliphant's words, apropos of Mr. Joseph Taylor and Charlotte Brontë, 'for life and action, and the larger paths and the little Joes', is seldom vehemently expressed, there were other prevalent problems.

The monk from the monastery was still a romantic danger; the deceased wife's sister among the forbidden fruits (there are two such sisters in *Hannah*); and ritualism might wreck a home. *Under Which Lord*, by Mrs. Lynn Linton, is a lengthy and rather acid discourse on this theme. It tells of the conflict between the Hon. and Rev. Launcelot Lascelles and Richard Fullerton for parochial ascendancy and for the fealty of Richard's wife, Hermione. Richard has for many years of his married life devoted his leisure to the study of mythology and protoplasm. Too much science (or too little) has converted him to 'free thought'. Mr. Lascelles (having himself chosen the guests) boldly denounces him at Hermione's dinner-party as an atheist and an infidel. And Richard Fullerton, courageous and urbane opponent though he may be, is in a position which he realises too late is hideously weak. For owing to his father-in-law's sagacity in tying up Hermione's money, her worldly goods were only on sufferance his. For this reason, perhaps, he addresses her as 'My wife', or 'My Ladyhood'. When he wished to amuse her in the evenings, 'he told her some facts of natural history'. Robbed at length of his daughter, of his influence, of his agnostic working-men, and even his bank account, he bows his head and retires.

His enemy, Mr. Lascelles, is a sort of hieratic volcano, gaunt, frigid, capped with snow, yet menacingly eloquent of the suppressed and awful fires within. One of his flock, after an hysterical outburst at a harvest festival, dies of his dark influence. He secures most of Hermione's money, though she herself returns and is reconciled at last to poor Richard on his death-bed.

The effect of the story is oddly and garishly unreal; a bright hard theatrical daylight dwells on the scene; and both men are little more than waxworks. Yet its author's violent prejudices, though apparent, are ingeniously screened. Quite apart from Mr. Lascelles, she is no friend of man, as such; nor, though one herself, of strong-minded woman neither. The cleverest woman in her story is easily a match, in both senses, for the vicar, but even she has 'the curiosity of her sex'—in relation to octogenetic evolution. 'Men', we are told, 'never know anything of what goes on about them. It is only women who find the truth.' 'As if', again, 'the cleverest man in the world is not as helpless as a babe, when the right kind of woman, who knows how he ought to be managed, takes him in hand.'

A faint hope of refuge from this sad extremity springs up with Mr. Lascelles' tragic suggestion: ' "So few women understand the deeper thoughts of men. Some supplement us, but it is given to very few to really understand us." "I know that," murmurs Hermione, "being one of the few." ' But, alas, this is merely the old fable of the fox and the goose.

That Mrs. Linton was not only serious but intensely in earnest *The True History of Joshua Davidson, Christian Communist*, is overwhelming proof. What, perhaps, is more astonishing nowadays, this book had an immense popular success. In spite of its intention, it is not a winning tale, nor is *Under Which Lord*. Mrs. Linton's most impressive female characters combine the chill of the crocodile with the austerity of the priestess and the cunning of the fox. They suggest a sort of neuter sex, being at the same time queens of the hive and parish workers. Her intention is ardent, but her ink is icy, and at times corrosive, and her attitude towards man is shared by a lady in Mrs. Oliphant's *The Three Brothers*: she 'was endowed with that contempt for the masculine understanding that most women entertain'.

Such, so it seems, was the general reflex of life in the feminine fiction of the 'seventies. And this reflex concerns of course its kind, not its quality. When woman rules, her rod, then as always, is of solid cast iron. When she shares the throne, and takes her Queen for her model, or meekly submits to an autocrat, a little feminine tact or manageableness, or the love that finds out a way, or downright guile, or sly Lilith-like seducements, suffice for the day. Tears are still a resource, and not to one sex only; a good cry is still an anodyne and a tonic, although the swoon and the vapours are 'going out.' The women novelists themselves, if judged by their work, do not seem to have been made desperately unhappy because in Eden Adam needed a help meet for him. To read their fiction is to be refreshed by the courage, the fidelity, the wits, the loving insight, and above all the sovran good sense of the women depicted in it. Silliness, gush, sentimentality; the minx, the cat, the scold, the harpy, the gosling; the complete Grundy family may add their tang, but it takes all kinds of femininity not only to make the world as it is, but also even a faintly realistic fiction.

Yet, for the most part these novels seem soon to have faded out of remembrance. In 1904 W. L. Courtney published his *Feminine Note in Fiction*, a critical survey of eight women novelists of his day, John Oliver Hobbes, Mrs. Humphry Ward, Lucas Malet, Gertrude Atherton, Mrs. Margaret Woods, Mrs. Voynich, Miss Robins, and Miss Mary Wilkins. The abhorred shears had been busy, and the wind had changed since 1879. Of the twenty-three writers who wrote or were written about in *Women Novelists of Queen Victoria's Reign* his index mentions only four.

In his introduction he maintains that feminine fiction in general suffers from a passion for detail. It is 'close analytic, miniature work', usually limited to a narrow personal experience, with a tendency to the self-conscious and a limitation of ideals. 'Would it be wrong to say', he suggests, 'that a woman's heroine is always a glorified version of herself?' Her fiction is too strenuous, worn out with zeal, the labour of the half-educated. A woman is that kind of human being, he quotes, 'who thinks with her backbone and feels with her nose'. Her historical evolution may be summarised in a quintet of terms, three of which are derogatory, 'slave, hausfrau, madonna, witch, rival'.

This is a withering summary, though it is honey of Hymettus compared with the views of Mrs. Oliphant on the Brontës. Courtney's tests of the fiction of the 'nineties were severe; the great, and therefore, in his view, the man-made novel was his standard. We may if we please submit the fiction of the 'seventies to similar tests. Does it, in Mrs. Oliphant's own words, concerning its 'nobler arts', exhibit a masterly combination, construction, a humorous survey of life and a deep apprehension of its problems? Is it of imagination all compact, that imagination which, as Jean Ingelow said, is 'the crown of all thoughts and powers', though 'you cannot wear a crown becomingly if you have no head (worth mentioning) to put it on'? Is it the creative outcome of a central and comprehensive experience of life? Is it rich and vivid and truthful in characterisation? What ardour of mind went to its making, and what passion of heart? What kind and quality of philosophy underlies it? Are these novels mere puppet and spellican work, of an exquisite, or a variegated patchwork of cleverness, a relief to 'fine' and exclusive feelings, a rousing challenge or a deadly malediction? And last—the question that covers most ground—are they works of art?

A little quiet reading makes many of these questions look rather too solemn and superior. Few novels written by anybody will survive so exacting a catechism. High standards are essential; but what wilts beneath their test may still have a virtue and value of its own. And we can be most grateful for small mercies. In general the novels that enjoy a brief but vigorous heyday—the idolatry of the few, or the intoxication of the many—so succeed simply because they deal with current themes and theses, or are a lively and entertaining peepshow of their passing day's fads, fashions, fantasies and fatuities. Having served their purpose ill or well, they perish, or, rather, escape from view. And man has had as active a hand in this manufacture as woman. May to-morrow's brilliant masterpiece then be as modest as it can!

The rôle of the rival however, in literature as in life, is a restless and invidious one, and the mere steady approximation of the work of either sex to that of the other would be cumulatively distressing. As that astonishing and precocious young man, Otto Weininger, maintained, the sexes may be not simple but compounded, not two but many. If any particular human being, that is, may be said to consist of ten-tenths, some of the tenths may be masculine and some feminine, though it may be difficult in any particular case to fix the precise proportion. The man of genius is said to be compounded of himself, a woman and a child. It is the colourless *medium* that would be most deplorable. What was Emily Brontë or Christina Rossetti or Queen Elizabeth compounded of? Chromosomes and genes apart, we all have as many granddams as grandsires in our heredity. An Orlando may not be unknown to life, though he is at present unique in fiction.

None the less, 'man and woman created He them'. And a burning and secret hope may be forgiven that woman may yet discover in herself some inward faculty or power unpossessed by man, and one of which we as yet know little. Reality covers a large area. There may be complete provinces of it awaiting her exploration—a truth, a beauty, a 'meaning', as yet but faintly dreamed of.

There is little in the fiction of the 'seventies, one must hasten to add, to suggest this. Still, it nourishes a conviction, I once stumblingly confided to a masterful lady in the United States, whose gaze immediately froze it upon my lips! It was, merely, that Woman, apart from other graces, is gifted with her own fine faculty of divination; that she can flit like a fire-fly from A to F-F-F-*Fool*—as Whistler once reiterated—without bothering about B, C, D and E; and that her common sense, in the old meaning of the phrase, is peculiarly her own. For which reasons perhaps she tends to be a persistently practical idealist. Of all the divinities made in man's or her own image, none that I am aware of has been the creative imagining of a woman. An assertion a little less sweeping might be made in respect of domestic inventions, those labour-saving devices which are sometimes the joy but usually the secret scorn of the modern housewife. In this fiction, at any rate, ardour for science, pure or applied, is as little manifest as the transcendental. If *The Time Machine* had been written in the 'seventies, its author would still, I think, have been a man. So also with *The Return of the Native*. On the other hand, neither Thomas Hardy nor Mr. Wells was the author of *Sense and Sensibility*, *Villette*, or *Wuthering Heights*.

Voteless, 'unskilled', man-dependent though most of the women of the 'seventies were, there is surprisingly little of *Lamentations* and of *Ecclesiastes* in their fiction. Even although its liveliest interest is in human beings as social creatures rather than as pilgrims of eternity. Revolt was in the air—if a very partial and unmethodical survey be a safe guide. But extraneous 'purpose' seems to have been rare, and still more rare, challenge and battle-cry. For the most part these novelists were eager, absorbed, diligent recorders. They were assured of what they believed in. They were happy in the company of their characters and delighted in merely telling a story, though even that simple, ancient, now rather unusual, and priceless achievement cannot but involve a good deal of 'life' in solution.

The ghost drifts or shambles in; the psychic intrudes. But

the effect of the spectral in Rhoda Broughton's *Twilight Stories* is a little deadened by the terse postscript, 'This is a fact.' Mrs. Oliphant's solemn and memorable *A Beleaguered City* was of 1880. But nowhere apparent in this fiction is man's peculiar inclination to regard an infinite (or finite) universe as though it were a concatenation of miracles, or an over-populated mousetrap, or an 'unweeting' machine, or an excruciating jest. One becomes conscious of a vague difference in intention, in the views given of life, and in what one most wants in it. There is more wit and irony than humour. Fantasy finds small place in it, and there is nothing —unless unintentionally—grotesque. The smart, the self-conscious, the too clever is uncommon, and where it is found it is, like old rubber, desperately perished in appearance and effect. Even the sentimental seems to outlast the meretricious; and the faded, old-fashioned, commonplace love story, quietly and serenely told, and even the mildest record of the domesticated, may keep enough of their interestingness to make them still readable by the not too fastidious.

In matter, many of these novels are singularly substantial; in style, sound, workmanlike, practised, and tending to the formal. If anything, their authors appear to be a little over- rather than under-educated; or, rather, somewhat too well-informed. For the fine novelist is in most (that he needs most) self-schooled, self-taught. As a child, with his hornbook, Nature stood him, not always very kindly, at her knee. For the rest he went, mind and heart, to the world at large. Its gallery is enormous and open to all. *Knowledge*, however valuable it may be, may prove imaginatively indigestible.

Of the men-characters in the 'seventies the *paterfamilias* and his generation are usually natural and vigorous enough. The romantic hero, the Lothario, the daredevil, the man of fashion or about town, the Bohemian, is apt to be less so.

These novelists are seldom completely at home in their younger men. They are making them up; the creative breath is faint that should free them into life. Even a hero, who is 'good, rich, handsome, clever, and kind'—and nowadays these epithets would appear in a different order—may remain inadequately vitalised. We watch him, but remain uneasy and incompletely transported. It must be remembered, however, that fiction consists solely of words, more or less evocatory, and that it rests in great part with the reader to decide on the more and the less.

There may be artificial hindrances. Richard Harold M'Gregor, for example—with his dark grey eyes and great yellow or 'heavy tawny' moustache, his head of curly yellow hair, a sabre cut on his cheek, a meerschaum pipe between his lips, his severe Greek beauty gilded by vespertinal carriage lamps, or starlit as he sits with his sweetheart, 'each on their several tombstone'—is it credible that if this ravishing young man were yet alive he would still be only in his later 'nineties? Others of his contemporaries too, with their arch or sprightly or solemn conversation, their elegance, or their boisterousness or their boorishness or their artisticalness, or the exquisite aroma (or stifling reek) of the tobacco that clings about them—all this suggests tapers at a shrine, or a sensitive shrinking from the embraces of a bear. Because our novelist is obviously a little self-conscious in their company, so are we. We must strip off this mask of the period and evade this trepidation before we can use what else we are given, and out of these fragments and what they imply make of such characters explorable wholes.

But although even the finest fiction consists solely of words, every such word may have been the outcome of an impassioned choice. Its maker himself, therefore, cannot but be immanent in it, though usually he is not at hand. He influences the scene as may the intangible presence of a divinity, whose all it is, and whose presence is everywhere, even though it remain unheeded. In fiction which falls short of this standard, but not too far, that presence is more obvious and externalised. The reader is on private property, and evidences of its owner are everywhere conspicuous. At an extreme, such a story becomes a mere essay with illustrative puppets. And what if the lord of the manor be a lady?

Whatever the converse may be, I am inclined to think that when a man is reading a novel written by a woman, he is more or less pervasively aware that he is in feminine company. This awareness cannot depend on any lack of artistry since, surely, it is never absent when Jane Austen is delighting us with her company. It has a subtle and pervasive effect extremely difficult to define. Rhoda Broughton—vivid, impulsive, romantic, satirical; Mrs. Oliphant—cultured, fervent yet amused, courageous and austere; Mrs. Lynn Linton—mordant, daunting, cold; Mrs. Alexander—sympathetic, equable, just, tender-hearted; Jessie Fothergill—earnest, reserved, aspiring, a little stilted; Mrs. Annie Edwardes—bold, acute, worldly; Ouida—witty, cynical, flighty, odd; Rosa Carey—observant, sentimental, scrupulous, lover of scene and season; Jean Ingelow—oddly unreal, meandering, but with occasional glints of penetrating imagination: mere glimpses all of them, and of but a few of many, and on how slender a foundation! But how in a few words convey the phantom of personality, which in every one of us has so many strands, as it disengages itself from a piece of pure invention concerned with imaginary scenes and characters, and whose influence when it is entirely unpremeditated is only the more effective?

But apart from this various and often engrossing companionship and apart from all pleasures and interests of a literary kind that await the reader of this bygone fiction, it affords another diversion—and one which was certainly not aimed at by its writers. At the mere thought of it, indeed, the busy pen might at once have fallen idle from the nerveless fingers. None the less, alas, it may possibly prove the most entertaining—the charm, that is, and the illumination afforded by the antiquated, the demoded, the out of date. Here it is the realist, the copyist, who suffers most, or, at any rate, who suffers most for the time being. Centuries hence the antiquarian may fall upon her work as if it were the funeral memorials of a Tutankhamen. After an interval of seventy years its appearance is merely odd and queer and pacifying and, if one was then a child in these matters, a little pathetic. Manners, habits, hobbies, dress, furniture, food, frivolities—how swiftly the insidious and fatal charge of *quaintness* can be brought against them!

Here, for example, is an interior, admirably informed, but closely resembling the pell-mell of an auction-room, yet still as inhabitable as a dream. We have mounted the steps into a prosperous city man's London mansion, in the days when dozens of young stockbrokers, 'more or less jewelled, white-hatted and blue-cravatted, were to be seen flitting to and from about Mark Lane . . . any sunshiny morning between March and October'.

'There was the suite of reception rooms, three in number —the yellow damask room, the blue satin room, and the crimson velvet room—all panelled with enormous looking-glasses, lit by chandeliers like pendent fountains, and crowded with gilded furniture, pictures in heavy Italian frames, tables of Florentine mosaic, cabinets in buhl and marqueterie, ormolu clocks, and expensive trifles from all quarters of the globe. Here was nothing antique—nothing rare, save for its costliness. Here were no old masters, no priceless pieces of majolica, no Cellini caskets, no enamels, no intagli, no Etruscan tazza, no Pompeian relics; but in their place great vases of the finest modern Sèvres; paintings by Frith, Maclise, Stanfield, Meissonier, and David Roberts; bronzes by Barbedienne; Chinese ivory carvings, and wonderful clockwork toys from Geneva. The malachite table in the boudoir from the International Exhibition of 1851; the marble group in the alcove at the end of the third drawing-room was by Marochetti; the Gobelin tapestries were among the latest products of the Imperial looms. Money, in short, was there omnipresent—money in abundance; and even taste. But not taste of the highest order. Not that highly trained taste which seems to "run" in certain classes of society, like handsome hands or fine complexions.'

It is an amusingly ostentatious museum piece, after Edward Gibbon; but, alas, the intervening years seem to have put it under glass.

A dining-room, on the other hand, from *The Wooing O't* exhibits taste of an order high enough at least to satisfy the first-cousin of an earl, and a fastidious cousin at that:

'. . . A most dainty apartment it was: the walls a pale grey, richly but lightly decorated in the Pompeian style; the hangings of soft amber, fringed and relieved with borders of red-brown velvet.

'The dinner was perfection. The poetically-arranged dessert, with its delicate service of engraved glass and silver, the profusion of flowers, the noiseless attendance which seemed to anticipate every want, the easy elegance, the quiet simplicity, made one forget, by the absence of effort, the immense cost at which this completeness was attained.'

But Maggie, one of the guests at this feast, is not quite at her ease, for her rival shares its perfection, and this is her *demi-toilette*:

'. . . rich, dull, thick silk, of the most delicate spring-like green, with quantities of priceless white lace, and emeralds sparkling at ears and throat—a sort of half-subdued sparkle in her great eyes, and a rich colour in her clear brunette cheek.

' "Can the force of civilisation further go?" thought Trafford, as he unfolded his napkin and prepared to enjoy his *potage à la printanier*. . . .'

And here is Mr. Lascelles' drawing-room, the Mecca of his 'spiritual harem':

'The table was deal, with heavy, plainly-squared legs and a plain, unornamented "autumn-leaf" table cover; the old oak chairs were stiff, hard, and straight-backed, and there was not an arm-chair, nor a lounge, nor a sofa anywhere. The cold grey walls were hung with a few pictures—all sacred subjects; some in oils, copies from the Old Masters, and some of the Arundel Society set in plain white frames, without even a gilded edge. A few flowers in *grès de Flandres* vases gave the sole signs of living life there were; but these were only on two brackets which flanked the feet of a large carved ivory crucifix—an antique—that hung against the wall. . . . It was a room that suggested more than it expressed. . . .' And it continues to do so.

And last, here is Lady Lanchester's country-house dining-room bedecked for an improvised 'hop'.

'I don't wish to see a more cheery scene than the Wentworth dining-room—transmogrified with pink calico and Union Jacks and wreaths of evergreens and flowers, it hardly knew itself, the band consisting of a big fiddle, a little fiddle, harp and bones.'

As for dress, an old lady in *Poor Pretty Bobbie* by Rhoda Broughton tells how in her day young people damped their clothes, 'to make them define more distinctly the outline of form and limbs'. 'One's waist was under one's arms, the sole object of which seemed to be to outrage nature by pushing one's bust up into one's chin, and one's legs were revealed through one's scanty drapery with startling candour as one walked or sat.' Not quite so in the 'seventies:

'How lovely she was! None but a very lovely woman

could have stood the dull ivory satin dress she wore, fitting tight, without a fold or a crease in the waist . . . trailing straight and long behind her. She wore a black lace fichu, and elbow-sleeves with black lace ruffles falling from them. The fichu was fastened with a golden brooch; beyond that was not a ribbon, not a frill, not a jewel or a flower about her. And her beauty came triumphant through the ordeal.'

And here is Hermione; at the dinner party when her husband, the atheist, is unmasked:

'She had never looked so well and had never been dressed with such a prodigality of wealth and luxury. Her dress was "moonlight"-coloured satin . . . with a good deal of fine white lace and silver embroidery about it. She wore diamonds in her hair and round her neck. . . . She didn't look more than twenty-five years of age with her fair innocent face, crowned with the curly golden hair. . . . Her beautiful arms with one diamond band on each; her softly moulded figure which had bloomed into generosity without losing its grace.'

If the 'seventies be any guide, then, the novelist who falls short of the best and brightest must beware of a too-precise descriptiveness. 'Art is coy and loves a secret.' And Time caricatures the lately past in precisely the same fashion as Mr. Punch may scoff at the just-arrived.

No longer—in fiction—does a young married woman flush with timidity at meeting a strange young man in a field of barley, or steal out for a 'dawdle and scramble' into her kindly, detested, land-owner husband's park in the dowdiest cloak and hat she can find—having first removed her wedding-ring. And as for the Dolly who reminded Miss Broughton of *Poems and Ballads*, she reappeared not very long ago (though in a different walk of life) as the heroine of *Gentlemen Prefer Blondes*, and there was fully explored. Yet even she might have been a little scandalised at the notion of reading *Humphrey Clinker* (or, let us say, *Ulysses*, or its equivalent) to her father in her 'teens, as did the old lady of 1820 in *Twilight Stories*.

For the not insensitive sexagenarian there is a plangent flavour of pathos as well as irony in the passing references in this faded fiction to what was then 'the latest thing out' and to the sprightly taken-for-granted in that remote, smaller, darker, gayer, unevener, homelier London: to the innovating pre-Raphaelites, for example; to Wagner, to Mr. Tennyson, to the current craze for Bach, Botticelli and blue china; to gas that mortified the atmosphere and blackened the ceiling; to tea at ten o'clock; to defunct card games, Commerce, Chow-chow; to old-fashioned criminals —Palmer, the poisoner, Rush—who on the day before he was hanged sent an urgent note to his gaoler, 'Pig to-day, and plenty of plum sauce'; to bonnet and shawl (a combination which poor man has never forgotten having succumbed to); to the learned lingo of the latest science; to a gentleman's sunshade, to the hansom cabman 'in his Sunday black'; to the new-fangled mowing machine, to old-fangled opiates and cosmetics; to Solitaire, to waltz and galop and mazurka, to 'pipesticks' and silk slipper tobacco-pouches; to Martinis (the rifle); to personal letters from Worth to his choicest clients; to neuralgia—the 'malady in vogue', and finally, to children who 'feared' their parents, and to servants who refused to stay in service more than the 'conventional year'.

We gaze wistfully on these fading memoranda of a vanished scene. We are surveying the waxen effigies, horrors of two distinct orders, of an old Madame Tussaud's; we are perambulating the courts and draughty galleries of a Crystal Palace whose final conflagration was a beacon betokening the demise of a complete and now derided era. We are amused. But now and then we may surprise ourselves smiling a little gingerly and wryly at the discovery that many of the novelties of which we are most aware in our own disillusioned age are not quite so dewy and verdant as we may suppose. One of our departed novelists assures us that, 'No young gentleman who is a gentleman ever *is* eager about anything now-a-days.' Another that, 'It was not that he felt at all happier or satisfied or contented—not that life appeared much brighter to him, only *it had to be lived.*' These are hardly sentiments alien to our time. The objection of the dowager of the 'seventies 'to the newest kind of dancing', may be no surprise, but it is something of a shock to chance in *Probation* on such a passage as, 'I fancy the children are as good as their parents would like them to be. . . . The new education theory is that when children are allowed their own way they always do right, or if they do wrong someone else is to blame for it.' And we are by no means in strange surroundings when we read:

'Hugo and his companion left the mill-yard, and paced down the street in the bitter cold of the March twilight, now rapidly becoming darkness. The lamps were being lighted; some shops were open; the passengers along the streets were not many; the great factories were silent, there was no cloud of smoke to obscure the frostily twinkling stars.'

These and many similar curiosities will be the unforeseen reward of an adventure into the novels of the women of the 'seventies. If the reader disdain them and their like, he will be so much the worse off. All fiction, however little its artificers may have intended it, becomes at last a picturesque and easily digestible annotation of history. The very prejudices displayed in it are revealing. But as with much else in life, what may appear to be an advance is not necessarily progress. Time puts things into proportion, or at any rate into a clearer relation one with another. The novelists attempt a similar feat, but Time has his way with them too.

For which reason, and apart from the work of the masters and mistresses of the art, there must be of fiction, as of most things civilised, a constant supply laid on, like gas, like water, like beauties and celebrities, *cause célèbres*, leading articles, politics, propaganda, and panaceas. Yet although the fashion changes, in essence fiction changes little. And, alas, even although any particular specimen and species of it may flourish as briefly as a poppy in the wheat, it may have consumed the very soul of its maker. The press rings and rings again with carillons of congratulation and flattery, bawls 'This will never do', or damns with faint praise. The critic gently or severely displaces the reviewer. A hurricane may sweep across the insular scene from France, from Russia (or from Germany, it may be). A Henry James may widen the range, refine the technique, and multiply the difficulties; and the censor may add to the price and increase the sale of some forbidden and even possibly purging dainty which he intended to destroy.

But when all is said, to share, eager or yawning, for hours at a stretch, the intimate company of these once living and ardent and now all-but-forgotten 'lady fictionists'—and even of the less endearing of them—is a rather tragic experience.

Blow, blow, thou winter wind,
Thou art not so unkind
As man's ingratitude. . . .

A dead book is a more pathetic, a more forlorn object than a tombstone. It strikes nearer home. In the reading of many such books, even although in the process life may stir in them again, one's mind, if it is capable of sentiment, becomes haunted at last. These authors are ghosts. A clumsy interloper has pushed open a door only just ajar, and his heavy tread resounds in the still, abandoned rooms. The phantom tenants, once earnest, eager, ambitious and warm-blooded, would, I believe, gladly keep him out. They are less alien to him than he to them. But the wan dismantled house—the wind in its willows, the owl in its cold chimney, night-skies of the nowhere overhead—remains defenceless. It cowers in silence, it cannot eject the trespasser.

And the distant rumour that thrills the air is not only that of the tumult of Time's dark waters but is mingled with the roar of our own insatiable printing presses. 'As we are, so you shall be!' runs the trite and hoary adjuration. Dead novelists tell no tales. The very years we ourselves so actively occupy will presently be packed up hugger-mugger in the Zany's old satchel and labelled 'the 'Forties'. And our own particular little hot, cold, violent, affected, fresh or stale, brand-new or ages-old modes and manners, preferences and prejudices, ideas and ideals, hobbies, obsessions, causes, conventions, customs will have had their heyday, have faded, all but evaporated, leaving for record of *our* best and brightest only a frigid deposit of 'history', a few treasurable buildings, some pictures, some music, a few books—and an immense mass of printed matter, little of it ever to be disturbed, or by eager living eye even glanced at again.

Authorship—any art—as a profession, involves problems and difficulties which continually confront the mind, the heart, the conscience, the spirit, and of course the pocket. There is only one discharge in that war. In the heat and mellay of the conflict it is perhaps inadvisable and indiscreet to meditate too long on the serene moonlit indifference of the night that will follow. A legacy amassed with much hope, thought and anxiety which nobody will deign to accept—a pork butcher can manage better than that. And even if—for writer, Don Juan, and tyrant alike—there are worse things than to be forgotten, and even although no book is assured of oblivion until every copy and memory of it has been destroyed, one can hardly but regret that frigid indifference as one reconnoitres, rummages, grubs and burrows among these old novels, and in the spectral company of those who were responsible for them—reanimating moribund heroes and heroines, not so much dead and buried as in the coldest storage. The curious, the theme- or thesis-hunter, and the venturesome may occasionally visit the derelict scene, leaving perhaps the tribute of a few immortelles behind them.

Lay a garland on my herse
Of the dismal yew;
Maidens, willow branches bear;
Say, I died true:

And perhaps, at length, just perhaps, the dying 'strain of strutting Chanticleer.' For the rest, it is silence.

Such is the fate of the vast majority of writers. And in fiction, if to be not forgotten and revivable is one's faint hope, it appears to be wiser to aim at the imaginatively real than at the realistically exact or over-earnest. Walter Savage Landor was confident that his work would be remembered. 'I shall dine late; but the dining-room will be well-lighted, the guests few and select.' That too may be the postponed joy of some of our novelists. But Landor knew also that such a destiny is unusual:

'... Laodameia died; Helen died; Leda, the beloved of Jupiter, went before. It is better to repose in the earth betimes than to sit up late; better, than to cling pertinaciously to what we feel crumbling under us, and to protract an inevitable fall. We may enjoy the present while we are insensible of infirmity and decay: but the present, like a note in music, is nothing but as it appertains to what is past and what is to come. There are no fields of amaranth on this side of the grave; there are no voices, O Rhodope, that are not soon mute, however tuneful; there is no name, with whatever emphasis of passionate love repeated, of which the echo is not faint at last.'

The *Dream**

The unfailing delight of *A Midsummer-Night's Dream* is its gaiety and inconsequence, its music, its magic, and its poetry. With *The Tempest* the most lyrical, it is also perhaps the least intellectual of the Plays and the most curiously intermingled. Its wooded borderland is overlooked from afar by the upper windows of Olivia's house; and from those of its own palace on a clear day may be descried the far-stretching archipelago of the sea of Romance, and there, in a remote haze of summer blue, the island of Prospero and Miranda. It is called a dream, it is in the nature of a dream, and, as if in a dream, we may submit ourselves to its sweet influences and fantastic enchantments. Unlike a dream contrived by the wizardry of sleep, however, we can at any moment recapture it, since here we have 'the book of the play'. We have but to open its pages again to fall immediately under its spell.

Moreover, even while we bear in mind that the play was intended for the Elizabethan stage and to be acted, not merely the easiest but perhaps also the happiest and most profitable way of enjoying it is to read that book intently page by page, listening to its verbal music, pausing perhaps to mark, but not bothering much to remove any transitory difficulty, and ignoring every will-of-the-wisp that may entice the attention out of the text. For the most part the sheer interest in what is happening under the gaze of the inward eye will carry us on over every momentary hindrance, and this as

* From the Scholar's Library Edition of *A Midsummer-Night's Dream.*

lightly and easily as the music-lulling water of a brook a mirrored leaf upon its surface.

On the other hand, as soon as one has been infected with what may be called a detective interest in this occupation, then any vitally annotated edition of the play, let alone Furness's *New Variorum* Edition, may prove one of the most alluring, exciting, and amusing adventures the world of books has to offer. The *Dream* alone, indeed, offers as many problems and clues, and is redolent of as many 'scents' as the wizard of Baker Street was fated to follow and elucidate during the whole course of his working life. Better yet, it is no grisly corpse, nothing dead or desiccated that is the crux of our dilemmas, but a mind in its heyday, as rich as it was subtle; an imagination of unbounded range and variety; and a living soul, Shakespeare's.

Not that there is obvious reason to believe that he himself took particular pains over mere trifles. 'I see him', says Sir Arthur Quiller Couch, 'as a magnificently indolent man, not agonising to invent new plots, taking old ones as clay to his hands, breathing new life into that clay; anon unmaking, remoulding, reinspiring it.' Given the renewed impulse, then, he could engross himself in bettering his work; but not necessarily in any conscious endeavour to perfect it. That he was aware of the supremacy of his indefatigable genius, who could doubt? But far from attempting to explain or to originate his Plays, he made no effort apparently even to ensure their being printed. His chief interest was in the theatre. He had watched his comedies and tragedies acted and re-acted; the playhouse copies had sufficed for all their needs. Hence the prodigious labours of his editors and commentators in refining his text, removing obscurities, tracking down his allusions, and tracing his sources.*

* As to his 'learning', in a scholarly sense, 'Now, I appeal to you, Sir,' wrote John Dennis, 'what time he had between his

Still, the crucial question, as has been so frequently repeated, is not what silver or gold he borrowed, but how he laid it out; what flowers, of his own seed only, sprang up in the footprints he left behind him in other men's snow; what delicate and elaborate silk purses he alone could fashion out of any old sow's ear that came his way. Revelation of that is richly welcome; and the *Dream* is packed with it. Here, the novice can but cautiously and diffidently follow the experts, keeping as closely as he can to the ground-plan they have laid down of the play—on a scale, let us say, of half a line of verse to a paragraph of dissertation.

The forbearance of the reader being taken for granted then, three distinct aspects of the *Dream* at once present themselves: first, the story, including the plot, related *in* the play, as it is unfolded scene by scene by means of its characters and episodes; next, the history *of* the play as a dramatic composition—its origin, borrowings, intention, and date;* and last, an account of its text. In all three respects, the *Dream* bristles with beguiling riddles, many of which have not been finally solved. And one at least of these is of sovereign interest.

Even the history of the *Dream* as a specimen of printing has a peculiar feature. One of the four shortest plays in the Shakespearean Canon, it twice appeared as a Quarto before

Writing and his Acting, to read anything that could not be read with Ease and Pleasure. . . . Therefore he who allows that Shakespear had Learning and a familiar Acquaintance with the Ancients, ought to be look'd upon as a Detractor from his extraordinary Merit, and from the Glory of *Great Britain*.' On the other hand and even more concisely, Maurice Morgann: 'There is . . . nothing perishable about him, except that very learning which he is said so much to want.'

* 'The dates of the plays', says Sir Arthur Quiller Couch, 'have for me as much relevancy to the plays themselves as has a chemical analysis of the Paper of the Folio or the ink of the Quartos.' Relevancy apart, however, even this question may be a rewarding one.

its inclusion in the first Folio. The two Quartos differ from one another only in detail, but occasionally in illuminating detail. The accepted *editio princeps*, the Quarto published in 1600 by Thomas Fisher, a draper, was, in Professor Dover Wilson's view (and as Pope surmised), set up, by a printer unknown, from a theatrical prompt copy of the play, just as Shakespeare himself had left it—a manuscript that may have been wholly or in part in his own handwriting. The second Quarto, ostensibly printed by James Roberts, bears the same date, 1600. Yet, in spite of the light that has beaten more fiercely and persistently on the minutest particulars in the history of the author of the *Dream* than on any throne of gold and ivory in the whole history of the world, it was not until the year 1909, and 'by what ranks as the most brilliant and convincing feat of modern bibliography', that Professor A. W. Pollard and Dr. W. W. Greg were able to prove that this Quarto, together with eight other Shakespearean or pseudo-Shakespearean texts, was actually printed by William Jaggard in 1619. In a word—a word in very frequent use nowadays—the 'Roberts' Quarto was 'a fake'.

Nor, as we shall see, need a close scrutiny of the text of the *Dream* be confined to matters of detail—misreadings, misprints, punctuation, and so forth. Indeed it has recently resulted in certain discoveries which, if they are accepted, reveal not only when the play was written, and possibly with what occasion in view, but also shed a light on the art and craft and practice of the dramatist. Had the *Dream* been a play unique and anonymous, it would, I imagine, far beyond any of the apocryphal or unfathered plays of its period, not excepting even *Arden of Feversham*, have excited the abstrusest speculations of the experts.

As for the incidental plot in the *Dream*, it is as a device simplicity itself, and is yet almost absurdly bewildering. To the onlooker, his eyes fixed on the stage, all may be clear; the actors and the action are self-explanatory. The reader, on the other hand, who has not their voices, mannerisms, and dresses to help him, may find it almost past solution. I confess that hitherto, before, that is, I had seen the admirable diagram on page 114 of the Scholar's Library Edition of the play, I had cheerfully given it up.

No trivial difficulty connected with the plot, however, need detract from the lively interest of the *story* in the *Dream*. And a good story in its own nature is likely to be of more intrinsic value and significance than any plot, however ingenious that plot may be. Its last word said, it may still continue to interest us, may live on in our minds, a delight and a touchstone, a personal imaginative experience and an active memory. Whereas, however skilful and engrossing a plot may be, it is little better than a maze, a riddle. As soon as the riddle is answered, and we have emerged from the maze, they cease to interest us. Even an excellent plot confines its characters in a cage, whereas a well-told story gives them their utmost ease and freedom. A good story, too, may be told again and again, with differing detail, a wider scope, and a greater mastery, and still retain its freshness. Originality lies in the handling of it, in the intelligence and imagination it displays. A plot once used has lost its capital virtue, its novelty; a virtue redeemable only by combining it with a new setting, another story.

A brief synopsis, though much must be forgiven it, will perhaps best reveal how straightforward yet how fantastic and original a story the *Dream* has to tell. Since too, whatever use he made of them, Shakespeare appears to have derived many of its details and most of its chief characters from literary sources. Brief references may be made to them as we proceed. There are also several sign-posts, pointing beyond the confines of the play not only to authors whom he read, and made his eternal debtors by borrowing from them, but also to the world at large of his own time. Whether or not we conclude that they point in the direction claimed for them, we can take account of these also. The story in the *Dream* and also the history of the play can thus be combined.

Let us first remind ourselves, however, that, apart from a few scanty stage directions, our complete knowledge of what is happening in the play, all that we see and hear and delight in as we *read*, depends solely on what its characters are saying. Their vivid phantasms are in process of being built up in our minds out of their words and out of nothing but their words. We can hardly, then, attend too closely to their speeches. As Shakespeare himself wrote rapidly on, he was dramatising each one of his imaginary creatures and creations in turn, and each character in accordance with his own species—his thoughts, feelings, fancies, fantasies, and imaginations: evolving them, that is, out of his mind and memory. One and all, if we accept them as his, they are 'modifications of his thought'. They reflect then himself in a score of disguises, and would still so reflect him even if he had taken them direct from life. At that, even the best of them are but 'shadows'; but how wondrous a sun shines down upon them out of his heavens.

To return, then, to the story. In spite of the title of the play—which, *pace* the German critics, may be due either to the fact that he borrowed it from a play already in being; or that of 'midsummer madness' the *Dream* is far from innocent; or that it was intended to be acted on the night of June 24th; or that 'on such a night' the happy notion of it stole into Shakespeare's mind; or that, as with *As You Like It* and the sub-title of *Twelfth Night*, no better or more charming one occurred to him—it opens on the eve of May Day. Both in place and time it is a remote May Day. The general scene, which *might*, as in *Pericles*, be described as 'dispersedly in various Countries', is 'Athens, and a wood hard by'; and when our curtain rises (let us continually, if we can, keep the stage in inward view), we find ourselves in contemplation of a hall in the palace of the Duke Theseus, King of Athens and founder of the Attic state.

Apart from a few occasional references—to the battle with the Centaurs, for example, and the murderous riot of the tipsy Bacchanals when Orpheus was torn to pieces, which are curiously accompanied by an allusion to the recent death of an ill-fated friend of the Muses—very little ancient history is enshrined in the *Dream*. Theseus's chief adventures, at any rate, amorous and otherwise, are of the past. Aided by Ariadne's artful thread, he has long since slain the Minotaur and fought against the Amazons. Indeed, their Queen, Hippolyta, now shares with him his Athenian palace. And Shakespeare, it seems, discovered them both—with much other treasure—in North's translation of Plutarch's *Lives*, the first edition of which appeared in 1579, the second in 1585. A few scattered memories of Chaucer's Knight's Tale, in the *Canterbury Tales*, seem also to have recurred to him.

In four happy days' time, we read, 'with pomp, with triumph and with revellings' is to be celebrated Theseus's and Hippolyta's nuptial hour. 'Attendants' they must have, but, unlike Cleopatra's, they have been given no speaking parts. At once there enters an old man, Egeus. He shares only his name with one of the two fathers attributed to Theseus, and we are told nothing of his rank, station, or office. (In the Folio he reappears in Act V; but not so in the Quartos, where the *whole* of his part is given to Philostrate). At the moment, he is merely that depressing spectacle, an outraged parent, and is haling along his daughter Hermia, followed by Lysander and Demetrius, two 'young gentlemen' who are both of them impassionedly in love with her.

Demetrius is the suitor chosen by Egeus; but Lysander has won what Hermia has of a heart. Unless, Theseus declares, she consents to wed Demetrius, although apparently no penalty will attach to Lysander, she will be condemned under the Athenian Law either to die the death, 'or on Diana's altar to protest For aye austerity and single life'. In spite of Hermia's entreaties, in spite of Lysander's ardent arguments, Theseus consents to give her only four days' grace. By the next new moon*—whose sickle is due to appear in the sunset of his own wedding day—she must decide. Somewhat imprudently in the circumstances, Egeus, Theseus, and the rest here make their exit, leaving the afflicted lovers to their own devices. Lysander then confides to Hermia that by the grace of Olympus he has a childless 'widow aunt, a dowager, Of great revénue,' who 'respects' him as her 'only son'. 'From Athens is her house remote seven leagues.' There they will be exempt from the sharp Athenian law. They vow to meet again on the following night in a wood lying one of those seven leagues beyond the city, a wood where once with Helena they had gone a-maying. Helena, the daughter of 'old Nedar'—one of only two references to him—now enters. In a ding-dong dialogue of rhymed couplets she implores Hermia to divulge the art by which she has enslaved Demetrius, whom she herself loves wildly but in vain. She is told by Lysander of the next night's assignation, 'when Phoebe doth behold Her silver visage in the wat'ry glass' (a name for the moon, and for Diana, that occurs only once elsewhere in the Plays); and, after a monologue of twenty-six lines curiously unequal in poetic quality, she departs to betray to Demetrius his rival's trysting-place:

I will go tell him of fair Hermia's flight:
Then to the wood will he to-morrow night

* The conduct of the moon throughout the *Dream* is fickle to the last degree. *If* this mention of her has any bearing on the date when it was written, it may be noted here that the moon was 'new' on April 24, 1590; and again on May 1, 1592.

Pursue her: and for this intelligence
If I have thanks, it is a dear expense:
But herein mean I to enrich my pain,
To have his sight thither and back again.

There follows, instanter, an abrupt, complete and blissful break in scene, company, and kind. We are transported into the cottage of one Peter Quince, a carpenter. He and his neighbours, a weaver, a bellows-mender, a tinker, a tailor, and a joiner (positively gaping to be enshrined in a nursery rhyme, and named, as Dr. Dover Wilson declares, according to their trades), are discussing the script of a play which is to serve as an interlude in the revelries on the Duke's nuptial night. To all appearance they have none of them either mother, sister, sweetheart, wean, or wife.

Peter Quince forthwith explains that his play is 'a most lamentable comedy and most cruel death of Pyramus and Thisbe.' He is the author of its prologue, if not of the play itself; and this is based of course on the lovelorn and hapless tale of two sweethearts, as guileless, tender, and devoted as Daphnis and Chloe; which is as old as Babylon; is to be found in Greek, Latin and all the chief European languages; was allegorised by the monks in the Middle Ages and retold by Chaucer; and whose honey, although he put it to very odd uses, Shakespeare has abstracted, for Quince's purposes, it seems, from Golding's translation of Ovid's *Metamorphoses*. This was published in London in 1567. Quince also ventures, it is said, in the lines referring to the desperate risks involved in Bottom's conception of the part of a roaring lion, to remind his audience of recent revelries at the court of James VI of Scotland; when, as the king and queen sat dining after the baptism of Prince Henry, and were being entertained, a blackamoor at the last moment was substituted for a lion as steed to a triumphal car, in case the shag-haired king of beasts should scare the Scots ladies. The incident had been the laugh of London in 1594. This, then, is a 'topical' joke.

From these 'mechanicals' and their confabulations—they are to meet again for a rehearsal at 'the Duke's oak' the following night—we are wafted as gently as if on the wings of a sucking dove to the *moonlit* wood and trysting place appointed by Lysander. Here Robin Goodfellow, the Puck, bent on a nocturnal errand with which as jester he will later entertain his master Oberon, has encountered a wandering fairy, 'a spirit', who is gathering dewdrops to hang for pearls in the ears of the freckled gold-coated cowslips. At first onset the spirit is uncertain who Puck is, though she knows him well by repute. As too did Shakespeare, for though he may also have encountered him in books and print, he must have been familiar with him since his childhood. Mingling two beings of one kind, he gives him an *alias*, Hobgoblin. But Puck, Robin, or Hobgoblin, whatever his name may be and whatever the remotest origin of his faunlike nature, with his restless vagabond mischief and scorn of clodhopper man, came clean out of the old wives' repertory, and—like Quince and his company—was already English of the English; though it is Shakespeare who for ever commandeered him and made him his own.*

* Having failed in her début as the Spirit of the Mustard Pot in a pantomime Ellen Terry took the part of Puck when she was a child in a revival of the *Dream* by Charles Kean. She was then, says Th. Fontane in *Aus England*, 'a blond, roguish girl, about ten years old . . . a downright intolerable, precocious, genuine English ill-bred, unchildlike child. Never the less the impression of her mere appearance is so deep that I cannot now imagine a grown up Puck, with a full neck and round arms.' When she twice vanished from the stage, it was 'by machinery'. Most of the epithets in this passage sound like abject nonsense based on unaccountable prejudice; but there it is; and as Furness well remarks, 'No one can bear an allusion to her salad days, her extremely salad days, with better grace than she who has been ever since those days so hung upon with admiration and applause.'

Puck tells the fairy that in jealousy of a sweet and lovely boy whom Titania, the queen of the fairies, has stolen from an Indian king, she has quarrelled with King Oberon. And Titania is the name not only of Diana in particular but of the nymphs and sylphs also who were the descendants of the Titans. With the oreades and naiades and dryades, these nymphs, lovely denizens of man's imagination, dwell in the golden haze of that region of romance which is beyond earthly time and space. And from them has come down to us, unless we have wholly banished them not only from our credence but also from our imaginative conception, the whole host of 'Phairie' or Faërie, the Silent Folk. It is likely, we are told, that Shakespeare took the name Titania direct from Ovid's Latin. However that may be, she is *his* elfin queen.

Even while Puck and the 'spirit' are talking, lo, the clearing in the woods—hoary now with the flooding light of the moon, and fresh and lustrous with distilling dew—is suddenly thronged with fairies, Oberon's and his queen's. Thus unexpectedly confronted, they continue their quarrel.

And whence came the seed in Shakespeare's mind for Oberon?—a seed that, like Titania's, must have instantly germinated into the complete presence we see before us? Perhaps from the old romance entitled *Duke Huon of Burdeaux*, though an Oberon may have appeared on the English stage, between this and Shakespeare's. The romance, at any rate, refers to Titania's mysterious changeling. The kingdom of this Oberon (whose father was Julius Caesar, and whose mother, by a previous marriage, was the grandmother of Alexander the Great!) was situated, it relates, in India, the India which in mediaeval times was believed to lie somewhere to the East of Jerusalem. He himself has 'an aungelyke vysage', and in stature is 'but of iii. fote, and crokyd shulderyd.'

'The dwarfe of the fayre, kynge Oberon,' continues

Furness's quotation, 'came rydynge by, and had on a gowne so ryche that it were meruayll to recount the ryches and fayssyon thereof and it was so garnyshyd with precyous stones that the clerenes of them shone lyke the sone. Also he had a goodly bow in hys hande so ryche that it coude not be esteemyde, and hys arrous after the same sort and they had suche proparte that any beest in the worlde that he wolde wyshe for, the arow sholde areste hym. Also he hade about hys necke a ryche horne hangying by two lases of golde, the horne was so ryche and fayre, that there was neuer sene none suche.'

'Rich' indeed he looks—in an English prose of which we seem to have forgotten the recipe. Shakespeare *may* also have chanced on this dwarf's crook-backed master in a play by Greene, also cited by Furness. This was in manuscript about 1590. It is entitled *The Scottish History of James IV*, and 'intermixed' with it is 'a pleasant Comedie' presented by the 'King of Fayeries'; spelt thus.

'What were those puppets that hopped and skipped about me year whayle?' inquires Bohan, a Scot, attired like a ridstall man, who has leapt out of a tomb, the tomb of Ninus, founder of Nineveh (Flute's 'Ninny's tomb'), placed conveniently on the stage.

'My subjects,' retorts Oberon.

'Thay subjects! whay, art thou a king? . . .

'The deil thou art! whay, thou lookest not so big as the king of clubs, nor so sharp as the king of spades, nor so fain as the king a' daymonds: be the mass, ay take thee to be the king of false hearts; therefore . . . away!'

Titania, to return to the *Dream*, scorns these 'forgeries of jealousy', and arraigns Oberon for the brawls he has caused between them, ruining the delicate sports of her followers to such a degree that, as if in revenge, the early summer has been a misery of sunless floods and frosts, with all their attendant evils.

And here again, according to the commentators, a sign-post points not to Ovid and literature, but to just such untimely weather as afflicted England in 1594, precisely as Titania describes it in such vivid and lovely detail. If then, Shakespeare had in mind this notoriously malign season, the writing of Titania's speech, even if of that speech alone, cannot have been of an earlier year.

Oberon pleads again for the surrender of her idolised changeling, the son of a 'votaress' of the Faëry order, to whom Shakespeare, alas, has vouchsafed no speaking part, and whom, though he is actually with Titania in the woods, we never (at least in the reading) *see*. It is a fact that admits, perhaps, of a whispered, Why? The elfin king then inquires how long his queen intends to harbour in the woods; and, at her reply, 'Perchance until after Theseus' wedding day', and at her disdainful refusal to give up the changeling—'Not for thy fairy kingdom' is her challenge—he both vows revenge and instantly conceives how to effect it.

He forthwith bids his henchman Puck fetch him a certain little western flower called Love-in-idleness—the pansy, the herb trinity, the cull-me-or-cuddle-me, the pink of my John, being other country names for it. He reminds Puck of how, once, Cupid, 'armed' cap-à-pie with quiver, bow and arrows, took aim 'at a fair Vestal, thronèd by the west,' but missed her; the first time surely that bright and burning blue eye had ever failed of its mark. His fiery love-shaft, 'Quenched in the chaste beams of the watery moon,' had fallen instead on this selfsame western flower, while she, the Vestal,

the imperial Vot'ress passèd on,
In maiden meditation, fancy-free.

Now in this single page of the *Dream* we are confronted with one of the most famous and controversial allusions in the whole of the Plays. By the Vestal, says Warburton, everyone knows is meant Queen Elizabeth—an assertion that has never been contested. It may be mentioned nevertheless that the word 'imperial', usually reserved in the Plays for royalty and its kin, is given to Love himself in *All's Well that Ends Well* (II. iii. 81): 'Now Dian, from thy altar do I fly And to imperial Love'; while 'votaress', a word used by Shakespeare only in the *Dream*, occurs in the Prologue to Act IV in *Pericles*; and there again in reference to Diana, who haunts the *Dream*: 'His woeful queen we leave at Ephesus, Unto Diana there a votaress.' A little later in the Prologue is a reference to Marina's friend in girlhood, Philoten, who, like Helena and Hermia was skilful with her sharp 'neeld' (spelt thus, as in the *Dream*, in the Folio), 'weav'd the sleided silk With fingers, long, small, white as milk,' would sing also, to the lute, and 'with rich and constant pen' would 'vail', do homage, to (yet again) 'her mistress Dian'. The lines following this particular passage are dull and clumsy by comparison.

By 'the mermaid on the dolphin's back', in Oberon's speech, Warburton proved with the utmost ingenuity, but this time solely to his own satisfaction, that Mary Queen of Scots was intended, and her husband the Dauphin of France, son of Henry II. An alternative suggestion is that in these allusions Shakespeare had Kenilworth Castle in mind, and 'the Princelie Pleasures' wherewith Leicester, in 1575, entertained Elizabeth; when he himself, then a boy eleven years old, *may* have been smuggled in by a Stratford friend or kinsman to watch the revels and the Masque, and actually to listen himself to 'the dulcet and harmonious' Meare-maide'.

The guileless 'little western flower' has also provided the thorniest of problems. Even Amy Robsart has been selected as its original, but she, unfortunately, was murdered in 1560. One of several other conjectures is Frances Lady Sidney, who married Robert Earl of Essex in April or May 1590—when the Queen was fifty-seven—and afterwards Leicester. It may again, and in spite of certain difficulties which are yet, says Dr. Dover Wilson, 'not fatal to the possibility', have been intended for Elizabeth, the daughter of Sir John Vernon of Hodnet in Shropshire, who married the Earl of Southampton, Shakespeare's friend and patron, in 1598, when the Queen was sixty-five, and was still 'in maiden meditation, fancy-free.' Twenty-three years, it will be noted, separate the revelries at Kenilworth and Elizabeth Vernon's wedding; origins of this allusion none the less, so far sundered in time even as these, have satisfied the several commentators concerned. The problem is set forth in full in Mr. E. K. Chambers' *William Shakespeare*.

Clearly, the honey-laden lines are as resonant with contemporary allusions to actualities as a hive is resonant with bees. No less clearly, Shakespeare must have had his own good reason for despatching Puck so far afield in search of one of the commonest of English wild flowers, a reason, presumably, that the initiated in his audience would be certain to divine. 'Fetch me this herb', says Oberon, 'and be thou here again ere the Leviathan can swim a league.' In 'the third part of a minute' the poet could have explained why he had chosen it; but since he refrained, sixteen complete and ample pages in the minute print of Furness's *Variorum* Edition of the *Dream*, representing numberless months of devoted research, are occupied with the scrutiny of this one passage!

Nor are we yet out of this wood either. To what dramatic purpose is Puck's errand? Why does Oberon need the flower? To extract from it a magic juice, a charm, a philtre. 'Having once secured this juice', he declares:

I'll watch Titania when she is asleep,
And drop the liquor of it in her eyes;
The next thing then she waking looks upon—
Be it on lion, bear, or wolf, or bull,
On meddling monkey, or on busy ape—
She shall pursue it with the soul of love.

Whence then came Shakespeare's first acquaintance with any such wizardry? From Young's translation, it has been suggested, of Montemayor's romance entitled *Diana*, which did not actually appear in print until 1598. This is concerned with another 'lamentable Comedy', the grievous loves of a shepherd, Syrenus, a shepherdess, Silvagia, and Sylvanus. They have sought out the lady Felicia for aid and counsel. She retires into an inner chamber and returns with two 'cruets of fine cristall in either hande, the feete of them being beaten golde, and curiously wrought and enameled'. They contain a sovereign remedy, she assures them, for all the ills and sorrows that even Dan Cupid can inflict. Having sipped of the goblet, they fall immediately into a deep untroubled sleep. The magic potion having thus prevailed, the lady Felicia presently after smites each of her visitors in turn upon the head with a book which she has taken out of her bosom. On their awakening, every heart is in that place where it should have been; excepting only Syrenus's. His is afterwards adjusted by an antidote—yet another herb, which Oberon also will presently put to sovereign use, and which he calls 'Dian's bud'. And did not Lady Felicia herself, exclaims Furness, dwell in Diana's temple! And is not Diana (when she is not called Phoebe) the regnant goddess of the *Dream*?

Puck having departed swift as Ariel, Demetrius, followed hotfoot, not by Hermia whom he loves, but by Helena who loves him, appears upon the woodland stage. Having remarked, doubtless on behalf of the groundlings in the audience, that he is invisible, Oberon stays to listen to the griefs of the contrary lovers. Puck returns with his Love-in-idleness. The two humans having departed, Oberon bids him seek out the disdainful Athenian youth, and, having discovered him, anoint his eyes with drops of the magic juice. With the rest he himself hastens away to seek Titania in the haunts where she is accustomed to sleep, lulled 'with dances and delight', the bank 'where', or as Pope preferred, 'whereon' 'the wild thyme grows'. Puck chooses the wrong Athenian. Peter Quince and his company come to rehearse their interlude under the Duke's oak, this green plot their stage, a hawthorn-brake their tiring-house. Puck, out of his own mischief and not at Oberon's direction, adjusts an ass's head (referred to in one of the Quartos as *the* ass's head, thus suggesting that Shakespeare's company had only one of these properties) on the shoulders of Bottom the weaver, on whom will open Titania's drowsy eyes; and the 'plot' of the play—the bemusement of the victims concerned—as distinct from its story, is now in full career; an intricate situation that can be remedied only by Oberon with the juice of 'Dian's bud'.

And anon, in the first sweetness of the morning, the dawn of May Day, to the clamour of horns, enter Theseus, Hippolyta, and their attendants 'arrayed for the hunt'. They too have come a-maying. There follows the famous speech of Theseus, as richly packed with poetry of one kind as the enchanting and enchanted songs of the fairies are with another, that describing the musical discord, the sweet thunder of the voices of his hounds, which though they be of Sparta, every English gentleman of the play's day would recognise as of a familiar breed and breeding. Theseus discovers the four lovers laid asleep, and bids his huntsmen rouse them with their horns. They perplexedly awake, entreat his grace, confess their previous folly; and he declares that, 'by and by', sharing the ceremony in the temple with himself and his Hippolyta, they shall eternally be knit in wedlock. Meanwhile, 'Away with us, to Athens! three and three. . . .'

And what of poor ass-headed Bully Bottom and his fairy retinue? Our next scene is Quince's cottage again. Here the rest of the company are assembled in despair, bemoaning the absence of their transfigured weaver, their 'best person too', 'a very paramour for a sweet voice'. '"Paramour!" Paragon!' exclaims the scandalised bellows-mender; 'a paramour is, God bless us! a thing of naught.' With a cheery 'Where are these lads? where are these hearts?' Nick himself suddenly enters, as large as life and wholly natural again. Not a word of (undramatic) explanation will he utter. On with the play; the duke has already dined; 'let every man look o'er his part.' 'And, most dear actors, eat no onions, nor garlic; for we are to utter sweet breath; and I do not doubt but to hear them say, it is a sweet comedy.'

At length it is midnight in the royal palace. The 'sweet comedy', the interlude, is over; and all the merry company, with a promised fortnight's revels still before them for renewed jollity, have retired to bed. In the sombre light of the dead and drowsy fire Puck appears, broom in hand, and is followed by the whole starry shining fairy host. They sing and dance, and so disperse, to bless every chamber of the palace with their 'field-dew consecrate', and bring it peace. Thus—with an epilogue spoken by Puck, and echoed long afterwards in graver language by Prospero himself,

If we shadows have offended,
Think but this, and all is mended,
That you have but slumbered here,
While these visions did appear—

thus ends *A Midsummer-Night's Dream.*

A marvellous rich dream it is, maugre this clumsy rendering of it; a most rare vision, a discoursing of wonders, and one almost past the wit of man to describe. Still, while keeping steadfastly in mind what follows these words in Nick Bottom's speech in his first awakening moments, we can now examine it from another angle; in relation, that is, to its theme and its characters.

What is the underlying *idea* of the play, and what was the attitude of the young dramatist towards that idea? It is a comedy, radiant with imagination, gaping with rustic farce, and was almost certainly written for an occasion—to entertain the company and guests after a noble marriage. Its last scene indeed rounds off the celebration of no fewer than three marriages. And apart from Theseus and his placid Amazonian queen, Hippolyta, never surely did the course of love run less smooth. The four young Grecian lovers have been continually at odds. Oberon, after a rancorous quarrel, so humiliates his Queen that she is compelled to surrender her beloved changeling. And although Peter Quince and his cronies themselves appear to be one and all unblessed with women-folk and unvictimised by Cupid, their only object in the play is the production of an interlude which in effect is a mockery of one of the world's most famous love-tales.

It is then a *love*-play, that love being chiefly an infatuation induced by the magic properties of a herb. A minim or two of sorcerous juice gently dripped between the eyelids, whether the victim be Titania—next to Ariel, Shakespeare's divinest creation in the praeternatural—or that fickle and fatuous 'young gentleman', Demetrius, still under its influence when the curtain descends, the effect is the same. He or she who had fallen in love, as incontinently falls out of love, and then, it may be, falls in again. So delicate and illusioning are the veils of fantasy which enchant the mind as we read, that we may fail to realise to what a futility has fallen this all-necessary, all-transmuting, extreme and delicious malady and madness of the heart and head that men call love. Here it has no more substance, sweet reasonableness, or finality than the tricks and airy nothings of the lunatic and the poet. The mighty Theseus, who certainly speaks out of a wide experience of its ravages, tells us so.

Indeed *this* poet's earlier plays, those prior to 1594, with the doubtful exception of *Romeo and Juliet* (since even Romeo has but lately jilted his Rosaline), are mainly concerned with the accidents, artifices and pranks of love. Love, moreover, but love in other aspects, is the mainspring of the Sonnets, the *Venus and Adonis*, and *The Rape of Lucrece*.

Though then it might be an exaggeration to assert that the *Dream* is little more than a parody on the theme of love between the sexes, it keeps consistently to the surface and is in a vein of banter, levity, if not of downright disrespect. Its snow, in Theseus's words, is 'wondrous strange', and there is little heat in its ice.

Next, there are three groups of characters—the Greeks, the 'mechanicals', and the fairies. On the stage they are one and all embodied; visible and audible. What of the reader, who has nothing for their scenic setting but the little theatre of his mind? Are they equally realisable there *as* characters, or do they vary in this crucial respect one from another as, let us say, our realisation of Henry VIII differs from that of Mr. Rochester or of an absent friend? If we *can* thus distinguish between their effects on us, in their degrees of 'reality', we should expect, surely, that the Fairies, with their king and queen, would be the least real, since, at any rate to the mortals in the play, they are invisible—airy 'spirits', changeless, ethereal, following and transfiguring the darkness like a dream. In actual fact they are not a whit less 'real' in imagination than are mortal and gross Nick Bottom and his cronies.

Silent Folk they may be, but their songs and voices are as small and wildly sweet as that of the wind in seeding grasses or of water chiming in a well. Tom Snout the sooty tinker we can all but taste, and can certainly smell. And the very breath of the south wind over Titania's woodland thyme and violets, one of Shakespeare's favourite flowers, is sweet with her presence. Even in *their* reality, moreover, these four elfins differ one from another. Puck has an inward being that is not precisely Oberon's. And as for Peaseblossom and Mustardseed, told we may be that the cowslips tall their pensioners be—an allusion to Queen Elizabeth's gilt-halberded bodyguard of fifty of the tallest, handsomest and noblest young men in her realm—and that they can creep into the cups of acorns. Nevertheless, it is a little difficult to visualise them in this infinitesimal fairy guise! They are, rather, just English children wondrously metamorphosized, and, if it had been feasible, could have been lent for the occasion of the play, naked as Nature made them, by Flute or Starveling or Snug. The woods, the flowers, and Theseus's hunting dogs, these (even though Dr. Bradley has demonstrated that the poet was no dog-*lover*), these also are English, and we pay far less heed to Athens in the play than to the Bermudas in *The Tempest.* Why indeed, we may speculate, did the dramatist hie back two thousand years or more for his chief characters, yet never in actual imagination stray very far from his beloved Warwickshire?

What then of the young amorous Greeks? Are *they* equally real in effect? If they are not, then in what degree are they *un*real? Hippolyta, though 'large and bland' to fancy's eye, is but a shadowy figure compared with Theseus, who is vividly individualised. He speaks for the most part with his own voice, utters his own mind, both of them being virgin Shakespeare, and he is far less rhetorical than are many other royal personages in the Plays. But is he always wholly in keeping with this conception? The quartette of young lovers, on the other hand, have the misfortune to be more or less at the mercy of the plot, and that is always apt to be a devitalising ordeal. But even if full allowance is made for this, there is still, as Malone pointed out, a pronounced 'want of discrimination' among them. In what other play of Shakespeare's shall we find four characters so vague and baffling? Their parts are ample, their actions lively, their opportunities rich. Nevertheless, from first to last, and Hermia and Helena utter not a syllable in the last long scene, one may remain very tepidly affected by their joys and griefs, their follies and misfortunes. They have a full share of Nick Bottom's density in one sense, but few blessed traces of it in another. Can it be that on the evening of September 22, 1662, Samuel Pepys nodded off in his seat at the King's Theatre in the fairy scenes, and so, with little of Shakespeare's *Dream* but these lovers in mind, dismissed it in his diary as 'the most insipid ridiculous play' that ever he saw in his life?

We certainly derive from what we *read* of them only the haziest conception of their appearance, and hardly less hazy a conception of themselves. And yet 'we cannot . . . do otherwise than admit that there must be distinct principles of character in every distinct individual. The manifest variety even in the minds of infants will oblige us to this.' Still, if by a printer's error some of Lysander's rhyming lines had been given to Demetrius, and *vice versa*, should we have the faintest misgiving that anything was wrong? Here and there Helena actualises herself. When, for example, she tells of her own and Hermia's childhood and of the sampler they shared together, sitting close on one cushion—two lovely berries moulded on one stem—we see her clearly; but even the cherry metaphor is slightly disordered in the text. 110 lines later, she is denouncing Hermia as having been a vixen even in her schooldays, and all is vague again. Helena is tall and fair, Hermia is short and dark—Shakespeare's company, it appears, included two young men apt for women's parts of this description—and bitter jests are made about it. They quarrel like cantankerous prefects in an academy for young ladies. Young ladies indeed they are; and numberless leagues more distant than

Athens is from Lysander's aunt from certain women in the plays—lewd-tongued, pitiless, proud, vile, and heartless. And their lovers, in spite of their highly uncivil revilings, are 'young gentlemen'. But not surely in the precise shade of meaning of these slippery words that we usually associate either with Athens or with Shakespeare.

All four of them may be described then as only intermittently real; and few critics of the *Dream* have disagreed with this general verdict, though it has been variously expressed; in such phrases, for example, as 'intellectual weakness', 'crude' psychology, 'little vitality', 'a cramped, gritty, discontinuous quality'. Whole scenes in the play, says R. H. White, are hardly worthy of Shakespeare's 'prentice' hand, 'yet seem to bear the unmistakeable mark of his unmistakeable pen.' But do they *consistently* bear this mark?

When Quince, having looked up moonshine in the almanac which he keeps in his bag, declares that 'on the night' she will be at full, Bottom chimes in with, 'Why, then may you leave a casement of the great chamber window, where we play, open; and the moon may shine in at the casement.' 'Ay,' says Quince, 'or else one must come in with a bush of thorns and a lanthorn, and say he comes to disfigure, or to present, the person of Moonshine.' Now this, pure prose though it is, is faintly suffused with poetry. One has only to listen to the rhythm and matching assonances of the sentences to discover that. 'He must be a very ignorant Player who knows not there is a Musical Cadence in speaking; and that a man may as well speak out of Tune as sing out of Tune.' It is too Shakespeare's moon that is shining, and it is his lanthorn. Compare this prose with such verses as,

'*Do not say so, Lysander, say not so.*
What though he love your Hermia? Lord! what though?
Yet Hermia still loves you; then be content.'
'*Content with Hermia? No: I do repent . . .*'

or with

'Lysander, keep thy Hermia: I will none.
If e'er I loved her, all that love is gone.
My heart to her but as guest-wise sojourned,
And now to Helen is it home returned'—

or with

'Nor is he dead, for aught that I can tell.'
'I pray thee, tell me then that he is well.'
'An if I could, what should I get therefore?'
'A privilege, never to see me more,
And from thy hated presence part I so:
See me no more, whether he be dead or no.'

Far from there being any hint of poetry in lines such as these, they are unburdened with much sense. What order of bright wits and tender feelings indeed ever expressed itself in strains so jejune? Of whom and of what by their aid do we catch the least lively glimpse?

Now Quince and his friends are not of course radiantly intelligent human beings. Their interlude is no more a work of fine art than its 'presenter' is a master of artifice; and these cultured Greeks, including the insipid Demetrius, make hay of their buffoonery in a sense that not even braying, swaggering Nick Bottom could approve. But there's no mistaking *their* individual actuality. Stupid they may be, but they are consistently and distinctly stupid. From the little they say, a few hundred words between them, how much we divine. Why? Because that stupidity is a gift from Shakespeare. He knows these mechanicals through and through, and sharing his understanding and hospitality, we take them to our bosoms. We love, while we laugh at, them. Contempt of them is itself contemptible, as Theseus, in his wisdom, intimates. They are minute planets circling around the sun named Falstaff (soon to rise in the dramatist's heavens); humble cousins, however far removed, of Sir

Toby Belch, Malvolio, Slender and Touchstone; and their voices are clamorous in every mob that surged and brawled on Shakespeare's stage. 'Shakespeare's Clowns and Fops', as Theobald says, 'come all of a different House; they are no further allied to one another than as Man to Man, Members of the same Species: but as different in Features and Lineaments of Character, as we are from one another in Face and Complexion.' And 'in great art, as in life, character makes the bed it lies on, or dies on'.

What then is the cause of this strange state of affairs in this particular play—the real, the so little real, and the unreal sharing even adjacent sentences? And this from a dramatist whose employment 'as a *Player*', in Theobald's words, 'gave him an advantage and Habit of fancying himself the very Character he meant to delineate'.

Now, since, as we read the *Dream*, we realise its characters solely through their speeches, if this criticism of the lovers is justified, something must be amiss with their speeches. Indeed this is so. The more closely we examine them and compare them with Oberon's and Titania's and the best of Theseus's, the more conspicuous become the radical differences between them, not only in rhythm, colour, and verbal melody, but also in pace and pressure of meaning, in 'syntactic rush'. Titania's speeches are poetry in essence, 'potable moonlight'; the lovers', though not invariably, are 'poetical' merely in tincture. The former are compact with beauty and meaning; the latter are shallow, stumbling, bald, and vacant. The stubborn words quoted above are being compelled to fit the metre, to occupy the lines—that 'Lord! what though!' that 'as guest-wise sojòurned', that 'part I so' —as the feet of the Ugly Sisters were made to fit Cinderella's glass slipper. So we have the truly-Shakespearean in

Fair Helena! who more engilds the night
Than all yon fiery oes and eyes of light,

and it is followed immediately by lines so faintly Shakespearean as

> *Why seek'st thou me? could not this make thee know*
> *The hate I bear thee made me leave thee so?*

Can we recall any other play written at one time and by one author that reveals discords in style and inequalities of mere intelligence so extreme? Did ever a fine poet indeed—let alone that pre-eminent prince of poets, Shakespeare—when once his imagination and his gift of expression had come of age, thus indulge, now in excellent, and now in dull and characterless verse? Except perhaps deliberately and of set purpose?

Can he then never have intended to individualise these Greeks, to seal them with that stamp of the unique which may make even his second murderers, his servants, and his tapsters emphatically his own? Not that his lovers in the *Dream* are by any means secondary characters. The story, the plot, the play itself are centred upon them. Even if he had so intended, and it seems a somewhat wanton if, his unsurpassed gift for the creation of character, surely, would make such a feat impracticable. He could hardly help himself; what he but touches with his finger comes alive. Besides he did make Shallow and Aguecheek and Audrey and Quince stupid on purpose; and we see with how vitalising and original a result.

Another just conceivable explanation, perhaps, is that although he triumphs with his Venus and Adonis, with his Tarquin, and his Romans, his Egyptians, Venetians, ancient Britons, Scots, and Welsh, he found these antique Greeks a trifle beyond his genius; that, in spite of every effort, and unlike Ariel, Richard II, Mercutio, Duncan, Lear, Perdita, Iago, they proved a failure. Can we credit *that*?

Or yet again; can it be that the doggerel Interlude is itself a skit on the love-talk of the very Greeks who are ridiculing it? 'When', says Schöll, 'these gentlemen consider Pyramus a bad lover, they forget that they had obviously been no better themselves; they had then declaimed about love as unreasonably as here Pyramus and Thisbe. . . . In fact, the whole play is a bantering game, in which all parties are quizzed in turn, and which, at the same time, makes game of the audience as well.' It is an amusing notion but hardly solves our dilemma, since only some of this love-talk is inane, and it is but a minute fraction of the play.

Yet another explanation, accepted by some of Shakespeare's editors, is that the *Dream* is *early* work. How early? One editor, Furnivall, suggests about 1590 as the date when it was written. Shakespeare was then twenty-six. Others, either ignoring or taking into account the various allusions in it which have been already referred to, have ranged from 1592 to 1598. The most obvious escape from this conflict of opinion, and one widely accepted, lies in the suggestion that the *Dream*, as we have it now, was composed at different times, laid aside and taken up again; or that, having been completed, it was redrafted and revised.

Before expert evidence of this is cited let us glance at yet another of the Greeks, the old, permanently indignant, and minor character, Egeus. He is given one long speech in the first scene. It is a speech, like many of those bestowed on the young lovers, that resembles a duet between two distinguishable voices. 'Thou hast,' he charges Lysander,

Thou hast by moonlight at her window sung,
With feigning voice, verses of feigning love;
And stol'n the impression of her fantasy
With bracelets of thy hair, rings, gauds, conceits,
Knacks, trifles, nosegays, sweetmeats—messengers
Of strong prevailment in unhardened youth . . .
With cunning hast thou filched my daughter's heart . . .

So far, so good. We recognise whose mind it is that can thus squander its wealth in verbal music. But suddenly, and almost in the same breath, this tiresome old man is babbling lines as rudimentary as those which a mere schoolboy might thump out upon his desk, lines 'pretty much like a child's finger playing on two notes alternately on the piano':

> *I beg the ancient privilege of Athens;*
> *As she is mine, I may dispose of her;*
> *Which shall be either to this gentleman,*
> *Or to her death, according to our law,*
> *Immediately provided in that case.*

'In that case'! It is little better than mere sampler work, and its plainness is oddly out of keeping with the skilful embroidery of the conceits above. What can be the reason for this abrupt change both in form and content? Was the poet, perhaps, at rather frequent intervals, merely 'bored, or in haste, or . . . careless'?

Now, in his criticism of the *Dream* in the new Cambridge edition, with engrossing skill and insight, and in an argument which the novice will attempt to condense at his peril, Dr. Dover Wilson maintains that even externally, the text of the play (as it appears in the Quartos and in the Folio) reveals three distinguishable layers or levels. He begins by analysing Theseus's first speeches in the Fifth Act. These consist, as was perceived by Shakespeare's earliest editors, of passages of regular blank verse, interspersed with passages wherein the printer has failed to divide the lines as the writer of the play clearly intended them to be divided. Lines 5 to 8, for example, were originally printed as three lines instead of four; lines 33 to 35 and others are similarly disarranged. Hitherto, I believe, this mistake has been merely attributed to an indifferent printer's setting up of his copy. But what caused him to go astray?

When, with Dr. Dover Wilson's help,* we observe, first that the disarranged lines in these speeches are their best and most pregnant and mature; and next that omission of them leaves the sequence of the story and of the action unimpaired, what is the inference? Simply this, that the disarranged lines have probably been written in on the margin of a play-house copy not wide enough to admit of the proper spacing of the lines. Continuing his textual dissection, Dr. Dover Wilson suggests also that complete pages of new manuscript have been on some occasion inserted into the original text, that passages in it have been deleted, and that there have been many minor alterations.

His general conclusion from these hints is that the first draft of the *Dream*—'represented chiefly by the dialogue of the lovers'—was early work, perhaps of 1592, and that the play was afterwards twice revised, recast and enriched, once in 1594, and again in 1598, and on both occasions for the celebration of a marriage. If this be so, and the evidence is as intricate as it is cumulatively convincing, we have here an almost unique opportunity not only of watching Shakespeare at work, but of comparing states, as it were, of his poetic and dramatic genius at intervals of a few years.

But even this solution of the problem would still leave him responsible for the peculiarly tongue-tied and tedious Greeks, and for verse all but denuded of every sovereign quality that delights ear and eye in the *Venus and Adonis*, which was published, but assuredly not written, in the April of 1593. Can we be content with it? Is there any other play of the period, in large part unquestionably Shakespeare's, that contains verse resembling the speeches of the Greeks, or sharply dissimilar from that of his usual level, which is yet interwoven with verse worthy of him in 1594, the year of *Richard II*?

* And to him I owe the great kindness of having read the proofs of these pages.

We shall find both in *The Book of Sir Thomas More*, a play which certain evidence suggests was written either late in 1593 or early in the next year. It is concerned with another May Day, not in ancient Greece, but the 'ill' May Day in England in 1517; and it was censored. 147 lines in the Third Scene of this play are in manuscript still extant. On the evidence afforded by the handwriting, by the idiosyncrasies of its text, and by the subject matter, it has been unqualifiedly accepted as Shakespeare's, and as his work. 'In these three pages', says Professor A. W. Pollard, 'we have the tone or temper of Shakespeare, and of no other Elizabethan dramatist I have read.'

Faced by a mob who are clamouring to have the foreigners—the French Flemings and the Fleming French—banished out of England, Sir Thomas More is speaking:

> '*Grant them removed, and grant that this your noise*
> *Hath chid down all the majesty of England;*
> *Imagine that you see the wretched strangers,*
> *Their babies at their backs with their poor luggage*
> *Plodding to the ports and coasts for transportation,*
> *And that you sit as kings in your desires,*
> *Authority quite silenced by your brawl*
> *And you in ruff of your opinions clothed;*
> *What have you got? I'll tell you: you had taught*
> *How insolence and strong hand should prevail,*
> *How order should be quelled; and by this pattern*
> *Not one of you should live an agèd man,*
> *For other ruffians, as their fancies wrought,*
> *With selfsame hand, self reasons, and self right,*
> *Would shark on you, and men like ravenous fishes*
> *Would feed on one another. . . .*'

This vigorous, concentrated, pell-mell speech is preceded by lines similar to these:

> '*I, being then employed by your honors*
> *To stay the broil that fell about the same,*

Where by persuasion I enforced the wrongs,
And urged the grief of the displeasèd city,
He answered me, and with a solemn oath,
That, if he had the Mayor of London's wife,
He'd keep her in despite of any English.
'Tis good, Sir Thomas, then, for you and me;
Your wife is dead, and I a bachelor:
If no man can possess his wife alone,
I am glad, Sir Thomas Palmer, I have none . . .'

By comparison, not only is this latter speech more compact in meaning, and, as to technique, in better verse than many that could be quoted from the *Dream*, but there is fully as striking a contrast between it and the Shakespearean lines that precede it as there is between the worst verse and the best in the *Dream*. Might not it too have been accepted as early or 'prentice work' of Shakespeare's if we had not ample proof that it was in fact written by Anthony Munday, and is in his script?

The *Dream* is scattered also with odd little errors, distinct from mere misprints. The part, for example, of Thisbe's mother in the mechanicals' play, at the debate in Quince's cottage, is given to Starveling; that of her father to Quince; and Pyramus's father's to Snout. No such characters appear 'on the night'. The nuptial new moon referred to by Theseus in the first scene as due in four days' time is actually flooding with her copious reflected lustre the midnight woods on the very next night. She obeys either the whims or the fickle memory of the enchanter who bade her shine thus anomalously, or Quince's almanac, and not the Duke's bidding. Bottom forgets that Mounsieur Cobweb has been despatched to fetch a humble-bee's honey-bag, and entreats him help Peaseblossom scratch his head. Poor Moth, who in a previous scene hailed his new master so heartily, is given not a single further recorded word to utter.* There are broken lines and conspicuous repetitions both of phrases and ideas; and rhymed verse for no perceptible reason is frequently interlaced with blank. All this clearly reveals a play that has passed through inconsequent adventures and suggests that its reviser worked hastily and not with extreme care. That being so, which is the likelier, that when, as artist and craftsman, Shakespeare came to revise the *Dream*, he should have spared so frequently his own early endeavours and retained his own less valuable shreds and patches, or those of another and inferior hand?

What is also apposite to this question is the fact that the speech-heading, 'Puck', in the printed play has been usually but not invariably substituted for that of 'Robin'; and that, in Dr. Dover Wilson's view, the failure so to do is an unfailing symptom of revision. It is Robin for example who fleets away to fetch the little western flower, but it is Puck who returns with it. *Robin's* speeches, that is, are chiefly in accordance with the earliest draft of the *Dream*. Can we detect in them, then, any trace of what we should not expect to find there if they were *not* solely of Shakespeare's handiwork?

Well, perhaps the best-known of these speeches—one in much superior to the doggerel of the Greeks, but none the less, as it seems to me, vaguely out of harmony with the usual vein and grain of Shakespeare's many-sided and inexhaustible humour—is that beginning,

Thou speak'st aright;
I am that merry wanderer of the night.
I jest to Oberon, and make him smile . . .

* His namesake in *Love's Labour's Lost*, on the other hand, 'tender juvenal', 'well-educated infant' that he is, has many witty, impudent, worldly-wise and knowledgeable *sentences* to utter, and might be a darling nephew of Sir John Falstaff himself.

To smile at what, indeed, prove to be rather primitive and un-Oberonian schoolboy practical jokes. It consists of only seventeen lines; and it contains no fewer than eleven words that either do not occur, or do not occur in this sense, or as these parts of speech, in any other of his plays: bean-fed, filly, foal (substantive), bob, dewlap, aunt, tailor (a debated word), quire, loff for laugh, waxen (verb), neeze. Words in the speech used only once in the other plays are three-foot (adjective), and cough (substantive). Again, the phrase 'hold the hips' appears to be a unique usage, and the word 'Faery', thus spelt in the Quarto, and thus, apparently, trisyllabically pronounced, is also used only once in the whole of the Plays, whereas 'fairy' occurs in the *Dream* some nine times in a few pages.

Is it probable, is it possible, that the poet when he was twenty-eight (in 1592) can have lavished on lines so few so many words that he was never to use again in writing in the following eighteen years of his working life?* What, then, of Oberon's speeches, which for the most part, it is said, are later additions? If we take seventeen lines of Oberon's no less familiar speech, that referring to Cupid all-armed and the fair Vestal, only *one* single word, 'smartly', in its signification of *briskly*, is not to be found in the other Plays, and two phrases—'love-shaft' and 'fancy-free', though we find bow-shaft and shot-free. This peculiar discrepancy may of course be due solely to mere chance and coincidence; it would require laborious investigation to make certain. Meanwhile, may it not hint at the activities of quite another mind, provided, naturally, in some respects, with a different vocabulary?

* As evidence in his disproof that Shakespeare was the author of *A Lover's Complaint* Dr. Mackail has pointed out that there are 46 words in its 329 lines which in their precise usage in this poem do not occur elsewhere in Shakespeare—a far smaller proportion; while, on the other hand, there are in *Lucrece* only some five words not used elsewhere, a poem of nearly two thousand lines.

Shakespeare, says Maurice Morgann, 'scatters the seeds of things, the principles of character and action, with so cunning a hand, yet with so careless an air, and, master of our feelings, submits himself so little to our judgment, that everything seems superior. . . . Action produces one mode of excellence, and inaction another. . . . The Chronicle, the Novel, or the Ballad; the king, or the beggar, the hero, the madman, the sot, or the fool; it is all one; nothing is worse, nothing is better; the same genius pervades and is equally admirable in all.' Again: 'I should conceive it would not be very difficult to feel one's way thro' these Plays,'—he is speaking of the English Chronicle plays—'and distinguish every where the metal from the clay.' 'I object, and strenuously too, even to *The Taming of the Shrew*; not that it wants merit, but that it does not bear the peculiar features and stamp of Shakespeare.' Can we in the *Dream*, then, distinguish between its metal and its clay?

And Pope: 'His genius in these low parts is like some Prince of Romance in the disguise of a Shepherd or Peasant. A certain Greatness and Spirit now and then breaks out, which manifest his higher extraction and qualities.' He 'is not so much an Imitator, as an Instrument, of Nature; and 'tis not so just to say that he speaks from her, as that she speaks thro' him'. And again: 'Had all the Speeches been printed without the very names of the Persons, I believe one might have apply'd them with certainty to every speaker. . . . He seems to have known the world by Intuition, to have look'd thro' Humane Nature at one glance.' Admiration is apt to gild its praises; but could we conceivably so apply many of the speeches uttered by the infatuated young Greeks?

Surely, to accept as Shakespeare's, at any age, what is provably not merely scamped or heedless but poverty-stricken verse—verse that advertises a dull and stubborn pen—is more extravagant than to discredit its being his at all? The former forces us to believe that a hand capable in 1592 of—

> *No? then I well perceive you are not nigh:*
> *Either death or you I'll find immediately* . . .

and an abysmal *descent* to—

> *Or in the night imagining some fear,*
> *How easy is a bush supposed a bear!*

could in 1594, by some astonishing legerdemain, be faintly but perceptibly pre-echoing, so to speak, the grand-mannered Milton's characteristic accent and cadence:

> *How canst thou thus for shame, Titania,*
> *Glance at my credit with Hippolyta,*
> *Knowing I know thy love to Theseus?*
> Didst thou not lead him through the glimmering night
> From Perigouna, whom he ravished?
> And make him with fair Aegles break his faith,
> With Ariadne, and Antiopa? . . . *

The one theory forces us to credit that an almost miraculous improvement in Shakespeare's imaginative power and gift for expression took place in a bare two or three—or, at most, four—years. The other theory, namely, that the earliest draft of the *Dream* was not of his own workmanship, leads merely to the supposition that (Johannes Factotum, Jack of all Trades, for his company, as in his younger days he certainly was, and 'employed by the players only to re-fit and repair') he either borrowed or was given a play—

* His eye might there command wherever stood
City of old or modern fame, the seat
Of mightiest empire, from the destined walls
Of Cambalu, seat of Cathaian Can,
And Samarchand by Oxus, Temir's throne. . . .

Milton, we know, was familiar with the *Dream*; have we here then faint traces of *his* footprints in its snow?

'as they give Strays to the Lord of the Manor'—written by some more or less artless scribe, and that, according to his wont, he set to work to transmute and amend it. And thus, at last, his *Dream* concluded but still unfinished, he made of it the lovely, visionary, entrancing, helter-skelter and oddly-fashioned masterpiece we have before us. The suggestion may be a piece of flagrant heresy of which only the merest tiro could be capable. So great an authority as Mr. E. K. Chambers, indeed, is content with a far more simple explanation: 'The differences of style between the lover scenes and the fairy scenes . . . seem . . . sufficiently explained by the difference of subject matter.' And again, 'I am prepared to accept some very poor work as Shakespeare's.'

Still, even a fine poet's worst work, like a hastily scribbled signature, must wear, however faintly, his characteristics. The seal is his even if the impression is blurred; his failures are failures in kind. We know well, moreover, and the sources of the *Dream* bear witness, that what at any time Shakespeare borrowed, by comparison with the use he made of it, usually resembles a cocooned caterpillar by comparison with the butterfly-to-be. By a secret process of the mind he often instilled into it a ravishing form, colour and grace, gave it wings; and skies also worthy of its living beauty. To accept the complete *Dream* as his, then, is to charge him not merely with having supplied, but with having been content to leave but partially animated, his own caterpillar.

However that may be, the *Dream* remains in much a fascinating mystery, and, in spite of the commentators who have gone about to expound it, it is still as richly tinged with midsummer madness as are most such phantasms of sleep and of the night.

A Book of Words*

There are lovers of books—undeserving perhaps of the more elegant term bibliophile—who confess to an almost panic dread of libraries. It is a strange imbecility of mind, though perhaps the fumes of perishing calf and morocco, the hue of fading gilt, the inaudible channerin' of the worm in the folio, or the spectral lamentations of forgotten authors aid in their undoing. Repetition of the experience seems only to intensify their unease. What to the elect is an earthly paradise is for these simpletons a form of purgatory both of the body and the spirit. Their only tolerable excuse is a sort of modesty. Are they not, they may plead, in the presence of that with which not even the diuturnity of an Old Parr would suffice to familiarize them? How can they, then, but be conscious that nine-tenths at least of the living waters in reservoir around them must, so far as their own thirsty souls are concerned, remain for ever stagnant?

For such poor shrinking creatures a multitude of books is no company. They would far rather share the tittle-tattle of the loved-one in the wilderness, sans even verses, jug and bread. And yet every volume, even the dingiest pamphlet in those lifeless vaults, once held the attention of a living eye and brain. It must, it surely must, contain humanity in some detectable degree of solution? It fulfilled an obligation or an office, an ambition or an ideal. It was well-intended—maybe

* *A Glossary of Words, Phrases, Names, and Allusions in the Works of English Authors, particularly of Shakespeare and his Contemporaries*, by Robert Nares.

to instruct, to edify, to proselytize, or to explain; honourable privileges all. It may even have supplied a long-felt want. But alas, it is books of this very kind that are apt to wear so badly. Likely enough, it is their mute presence in congregation that so afflicts the over-sensitive. Their existence is little but a perennial mouldering. They are fated to serve no posterity however patiently upon their shelves they stand and wait.

With this in mind, one is tempted—though it might be dangerous—to maintain that the best books in the world were written chiefly for pleasure and with an after-hope to please. For if, in the words of the *Familiar Letters*, love not only sets the imagination in a strange fit of working, but also 'amuses the understanding', so too should a labour of love. Its incitement comes from within; its source is in the hidden uplands of the heart. Not that it can be a labour without effort. The cost of it may be extreme. For it is nothing but a fallacy to suppose that what men do of their own choice and affection is less exhausting than a task against the grain. Self-imposed burdens are burdens none the less; but we carry them with a serener spirit, and with an inward happiness which shows itself in a grace and persuasiveness otherwise all but unattainable.

Better yet, what in the making—given the material, means and craftsmanship—pleases the maker of a thing has pleasure in its gift. It will charm as well as interest; may in proving useful prove delightful. How this mere state of mind and mood reveals itself in a book it may be extemely difficult to detect and to specify. The influence is as elusive as the dream in happy eyes, or playing rainbows on the sea. But nothing by comparison, no motive, no zeal, no skill is so effective, or so stealthy. For it may haunt the most unlikely places, and may play the oddest antics. It grimaces at us from the corbels and gargoyles of an old church, dances in a picture of the stillest life, calls beauty into the darkest of Thomas Hardy's lyrics, bandies snatches of song under the thunders of *Lear*, and *may* even peep out of the crannies of a *Critique of Pure Reason*.

Probably the last personage and place in which we should expect to discover this incentive, this reward, are a lexicographer and his dictionary. When Walter Pater prescribed the literary novice a daily dose of Johnson, he certainly intended it rather as a tonic than as a cordial. Under *flea*, it is true, under *patriot*, under *lexicographer* itself, the Great Bear deposited a rare honey. Doubtless the tomes of the *New English Dictionary* secretly scintillate with intellectual gaiety and glee and verve. But who, at the name of Richardson, happily recalls, not Samuel, but Charles? The vision of what kind of Ark arises in the fancy at mention of Noah Webster? What porridge had Dr. Peter Mark Roget? The term dictionary remains austere, and, no more than either lexicon, concordance, or thesaurus, suggests a paradise of dainty delights.

For this reason, his own work in this kind completed, Robert Nares avoided the title. He preferred the more modest 'glossary'. For his book, his preface tells us, represents not 'the labours of the anvil or the mine', but the avocation of a studious leisure. He confesses without shame or caution that its compilation 'amused' him; and he gave it to the world in the hope it would entertain its 'readers'. In a similar happy condition of mind Bunyan began and finished his *Progress*: setting 'pen to paper with delight'. So, too, Montaigne:

'Reader, loe here a well-meaning Booke. It dothe at the first entrance forewarne thee, that in contriving the same I have proposed unto myselfe no other than a familiar and private end: I have no respect or consideration at all, either to thy service, or to my glory: my forces are not capable of any such desseigne.'

Not that Nares, any more than Bunyan or Montaigne, slighted anvil and mine. His life was a full and various one.

Son (as a lexicographer should be) of a celebrated musician, he was born in 1753, and attained the satisfactory age of seventy-five. Apart from his *Elements in Orthoëpy* (a not ingratiating title), he wrote 'light pieces', essays, and pamphlets. In 1782 he was presented with the small living of Easton Maudit, and in 1800 became archdeacon of Stafford. He earned respect, we are told, not only as a gentleman and scholar, but as a sound divine. He launched the *British Critic* and steered it in triumph to its forty-second volume. For twelve years he was librarian in the Manuscript Department of the British Museum. He helped to found the Royal Society of Literature. He was thrice married.

Such industry and enterprise might well have satisfied an ordinary man. But these activities were his occupations, his 'more serious occupations'. His *Glossary* illustrates the scholarly joys in between. It grew and spread slowly in the interstices of his workaday life, like a blossoming vine on the walls of an old house. Take an instance:

'WOODBINE, or WOODBIND. The common name, ancient and modern, for the wild honeysuckle.

'See Johnson's Gerard, p. 891, etc.; but there is reason to think that Shakesepare employed it instead of *bindweed* for the convulvulus, in the following lines:

> So does the woodbine the sweet honeysuckle
> Gently entwine; the female ivy so
> Enrings the barky fingers of the elm.
>
> *Mid. N. Dr.*, IV, i.

'Two parallel similes must be here intended, or we lose the best effect of the poetry; and the former comparison seems quite parallel to one of Ben Jonson:

> Behold,
> How the blue *bind-weed* doth itself infold
> With honey-suckle.
>
> *Masq.*, *Vision of Delight*.

'Now the blue *bind-weed* is the blue convulvulus (Gerard, 864), but the calling it *wood-bine* has naturally puzzled both readers and commentators; as it seems to say that the honeysuckle entwines the honeysuckle. Supposing convulvulus to be meant, all is easy, and a beautiful passage preserved. Another mode of construction makes. . . .'

This is a fragment representative of Nares's method and his style. Let the blue bindweed be his scholarly interest, the honeysuckle his mind's delight, and we realize what keeps his *Glossary* sweet. As occasion allowed, he took it up; as duty dictated, he set it aside. The slightest acquaintance with its pages reveals both the range and the felicity of the literary journeyings it represents. Not only are its contents honey in the hive, but they admit us, if only in glimpses, to the wild stretches of valley, wood, and meadow whence their nectar was gathered.

The *Glossary*, moreover, was not only the reward of a peculiar species of delectation; its incentive was one of the best man can have, either in this world or in view of the next—admiration. Nares's primary aim was to enable every reader of 'our admirable Shakespeare' 'to enjoy the unencumbered productions of the poet'. He found his idol—above a century ago!—almost overwhelmed by his commentators. Armed with the sharp billhook of erudition and good sense, he attacked their female ivies. All his long life he had played Tom Tiddler, his 'ground' the Elizabethan playbooks and the like, and the specimens in his *Glossary*—obsolete even in his own day—are his shining 'gold and silver'.

At need and with justice he can rebuke and correct even his master Shakespeare. Far oftener he sighs his 'exquisite' and 'beautiful'. His unwearying joy both as a man and as a lexicographer is in the creative literature of his chosen period. He entranced his eye with its poetry, bringing to its illustration a mind and memory filled full of 'life'. He etymologized, if ever man did, with his eye not only on the word but on the object.

In general his criticism of a commentator is as urbane as it appears to be final: 'Spital or Spittle. An abbreviation or corruption of hospital. . . . Mr. Gifford has attempted to establish a distinction between *spital* and *spittle*; thus giving our ancestors credit for a nicety they never reached or intended.' And so on for a full column of instances. Or again, respecting *bases* and petticoats: 'Thus it will be seen that Mr. Gifford's conjecture on the subject (Massinger, vol. iii, p. 141) was nearly right.'

His common sense is twice blest:

'To *draw dryfoot* was, according to Dr. Johnson, to trace the marks of the *dry foot*, without the scent. Dr. Grey would have it to follow by the scent; but a dry foot can have no scent. Who shall decide when doctors disagree? In this case, perhaps, sportsmen, to whom I refer it. A *drawn fox* is a hunted fox: "When we beat the bushes, etc., after the fox we call it *drawing*."—*Gent. Recr.*, *Hunting*, p. 17, 8vo.'

Again:

'Eyes, kissing of. The commentators on Shakespeare have very sagaciously told us that: "It was formerly *the fashion to kiss the eyes*, as a mark of extraordinary tenderness." . . . Say rather, that it was the natural impulse of affection in all ages. . . .'

On occasion, Nares will draw even more openly on his personal experience:

'Tuttle, the maze in: that is, the maze in Tothill Fields. Of these fields, let me speak with the respect which Dr. Johnson, in the first edition of his Dictionary, paid to Grub Street. They were the Gymnasium of my youth. . . .'

But—and 'commentators' are not a timid or over-sensitive folk—Nares can also be pungent and severe: 'A droil . . . Mr. Lemon deduces it from τρίβω, tero, but his etymologies are often made as if for sport, to try the patience of his readers.' 'This is mere stuff' is another tartish reference to Mr. Lemon. 'How rash conjectural criticism is, when the language of the author criticized is very imperfectly understood.'

But such little tournaments as these are only a subsidiary form of entertainment. To the expert they no doubt prove as provocative as was a fanfare of distant trumpets to the war-horse in the Book of Job. The novice may enjoy them in the same way as any amateur of a game of skill enjoys the practice of a professional. For Nares is always easy, never specialistic or dry. His desire is not to humiliate an adversary, never merely to exhibit his own erudition or ingenuity, but to elucidate, retrieve, disencumber. As criticism of his fellow-craftsmen, therefore, his *Glossary* is not only a lesson in method but also in manners. A drawn donkey is doubtless a hunted donkey. But Nares is out not to bait, but for sport, to entertain himself and his reader. His aim is to free his beloved originals from mere artificial difficulties. He believes that what they wrote they wrote with deliberation and intention. He simplifies.

The chief use of Nares, then, is as an occasional aid to lovers of the literature of the sixteenth and seventeenth centuries. He illustrates what is obsolete, not only in the language, but in the manners and customs of that period. It was not his aim to venture beyond Elizabeth, and he left the compilation of similar dictionaries for the works of Chaucer's age, and for what preceded it, to his successors. For this reason his *Glossary* is usually to be found, concealing its gems of purest ray serene, among 'works of reference'. It is a sad reflection on our own times that the 1905 reprint of his book, edited by J. O. Halliwell and Thomas Wright, has lately been 'remaindered'—though this may bring it within easier reach of the true enthusiast.

Merely to visit it is to make a sad waste of its abundant

hospitality, to ignore the very virtues that differentiate it from its fellows. For Nares not only gives information, he gives himself. His book is reading in the real sense, not for the snatched minute but for the solid hour; and reading so various and condensed that even a repeated exploration of any one page fails to exhaust it. Such is the natural resilience of the ordinary mind that certain sorts of information slip as easily out of it as they slip into it; but not without friction, it may be hoped, and not without the vestiges of a deposit.

The book is instantly entertaining. What decent curiosity could resist, say, such a succession of enigmas as *pes*, *pestle* (*not* the mortar variety), *peter-man*, *peter-sa-meene*, *petrel* (not the 'stormy'), *pew-fellow*, *to pheeze*, *pheuterer*, *Philip*? Because it is instantaneously entertaining, while not exciting, it is an excellent bed-book; heavy only in a material sense. What more dream-exciting lullaby for an adult head could be found than such citations as 'You shall (in this *New World*) as commonly see legges of men hang up, as here with us you shall find *pestels* of porke, or legges of veale'; or, 'Being one day at church she made mone to her *pew-fellow*'; or:

> *Peter-see-me* shall wash thy nowl
> And Malligo glasses fox thee.

or:

> To whit, to whoo, the owle does cry,
> *Phip*, *phip*, the sparrowes as they fly.

The unconscious, surely, whatever and wherever it be, requires constant nourishment. A weekly platter of *hors d'œuvre* should not come amiss. And Nares is crammed from cover to cover with these seductions. Yet it is no mere collection of gauds, toys, trinkets, gewgaws, pieces of festive finery. Its aggregate is the mirror of a time, of a state of the imagination, of a complete continent of human interest. It is English in bouquet to the minutest bubble of its foam. It is the work of a man's mind, masculine, substantial, sound, various. One may speculate whether in the natural order of things it could ever be even the delectation of a woman's.

Its one requisite in a reader is simply a delight in words—words as words, and for their own sweet sake: the words beloved by Edward Thomas:

Out of us all
That make rhymes,
Will you choose
Sometimes—
As the winds use
A crack in the wall
Or a drain,
Their joy or their pain
To whistle through—
Choose me,
You English words?
I know you:
You are light as dreams,
Tough as oak,
Precious as gold,
As poppies and corn,
Or an old cloak;
Sweet as our birds
To the ear,
As the burnet rose. . . .
But though older far
Than oldest yew,—
As our hills are, old,—
Worn new
Again and again:
Young as our streams
After rain:
And as dear
As the earth which you prove
That we love. . . .

Such delight is not perhaps the plant of a season's raising. Yet its seed seems to be innate in the human mind. While facts to the youthful digestion may prove as distasteful to it as fats, from his first birthday onwards a child hungers for words almost as instinctively at least as he pines for sweetmeats. His mother tongue is as natural a nutriment as his mother's milk. And a lively interest and joy in a word as often as not precede the acquisition of its exact meaning.

Indeed the finer shades of signification in the larger part of a mature vocabulary—woefully limited as such a vocabulary usually is—have rather been divined from a series of contexts than ascertained from a precise definition. For the lasting vivification of a word, the presence of the object to which it applies is of course indispensable. Yet word may come first, its object later. The virgin senses, the quick apprehension, and the tenacious memory of childhood and youth alone perhaps are capable of their indissoluble welding together. Of name and thing our most valuable knowledge consists. In later life, thank heaven, the desire for knowledge may sharpen; but our powers of assimilation are then desperately poorer. The prevalent weakness, too, of many minds—the radical deficiency of mediocre books—is not only the possession of a scanty vocabulary, but also of a vocabulary nebulous, unattached, inexact, inert. On the other hand, the weakness of a copious over-latinized vocabulary usually consists in its feeble relationship to the senses, to actuality. Thomas Brownes are few. A *little* intellect adrift amid abstractions is a spectacle far less entertaining than a balloon. If as fully as possible we animated in our minds all that we attempt to express, how much we should be expressing!

Alas, then, Robert Nares's *Glossary*, since it is not a child's book, and treats of the obsolete, can only indirectly enrich one's verbal treasury. To put his treasures to actual use to any pronounced extent would be but to parley euphuism. Perhaps even the notion that a word which has once fallen into disuse can be reinsinuated into the common speech is nothing but a mumpsimus. Certainly to patch and purfle out a style even with the Philip and Cheyney once the common wear would make it conspicuous, but scarcely admirable.

None the less our modern English, whether in speech or in writing, needs renovations of the kind that farces this old *Glossary*. A language stales. Not only new terms for new-found needs—and the imagination to coin them—are required to give it freshness, colour, and vivacity, but an abundance of approximate synonyms. The tendency to make one word enough when two or more would be a feast is a curmudgeonly one when carried to an extreme. Writers nowadays are apt to lead rather sequestered lives—a little vacant of event, out of the world's pomp and pride and vehemence. Between the classes and between the professions gulfs are fixed that in Shakespeare's day were easily bridged. And though thoughts and ideas are excellent company, they are the wholesomer and much the happier for a close alliance with the seven senses. Unless the memory is stored with easily retrieved words and phrases, sure, resonant and idiomatic, and, above all, with such as instantly evoke objects and qualities, and set echoing near and far the secret heights and recesses of the imagination, the mind starves, and the tongue falters for the means to express itself. Nares is a museum of words that once so served our animated forbears; and even if they have earned, as now they possess, a lasting privacy, they and their illustrations will dance the eye, titillate nose and ear, and strengthen the wits.

After all, whatever its chances and changes, however mummified and fossilized it may appear to be, a word is never dead. Like its maker, it awaits reanimation. Ours the trump. Isolated, it may be a meaningless (though according to some philosophers it can never be an impotent) symbol. In the company of a few of its kin and kind its rediscovery may be as exciting an experience as that of finding a strange animal taking its ease in one's bedroom. A racy pleasant-sounding old word even in isolation may act on the fancy like a charm. In conference with its fellows it resembles an incantation. Up and down the pages of every dictionary, these strange decoys are sounding—if only we will give ear to them.

Language is one of the few things of priceless value and little cost which every human being of any intelligence acquires by a natural impulse. In all essentials we teach ourselves our mother tongue. In 1842, of the 264 convicts condemned to transportation on the *Earl Gray*, 53 could read and write, 23 could only read, 188 could do neither. All could talk. On debarkation one only could do neither. In 1850, 152,744 marriages were solemnized in the United Kingdom; rather under one third of the bridegrooms and and one half of the brides could not write. There may have been one or two mutes among them, but otherwise all could talk. Illiterates are few in this enlightened age, and these statistics may be shocking. But what is of vital importance is not literacy but the use that is made of it. Illiteracy is a mild disadvantage indeed compared with languagelessness. To listen may be more valuable than to talk; and silence can be golden. 'If onyman gessith himselff to be religious, and refreyneth not his tunge . . . the religion of him is veyn.'

How far, on the other hand, an acquired language is adequate to our inmost needs, what alternative could better it, to what extent it is made use of by the mind and feelings in solitude, and how far it is then a help and a hindrance are questions not easily answered. Nothing here however affects the fact that reverence for one's mother tongue, an interest in its history, and the forlorn hope after a lifetime's usage to have refrained from contaminating its purity (and even perhaps to have infinitesimally enriched its treasury), are incentives that may even claim to be philanthropic.

If all human societies had bees in their bonnets as harmless as that 'for Pure English' their honey would not be the less sweet and wholesome. To incite men to take action may be well or ill; to persuade them actively to take thought can hardly be ill. Thus the mind comes into its own. Indeed, the longer we patiently practise ourselves in thinking, imagining, speaking and writing, the clearer becomes the evidence not only that it is immeasurably difficult to express ourselves in truth, but that it is ultimately impossible to express anything else of so much value. Nevertheless our words in some degree delimit as well as free mind and heart.

A supreme treasure-house and museum like the New English Dictionary is not merely a verbal reservoir, but a narrative in symbols of the bodily, mental and spiritual pilgrimage of the English race. The Dictionary of National Biography recounts for the most part the exploits, achievements, enterprise, heroism of rarely endowed and signally fortuned individuals. That of our words recounts the creative exploits not only of the cultured and erudite, the man of knowledge, and the catacombed bookworm, but of the people, the man in the street—and elsewhere. The hospitality of a dictionary, moreover, embraces not only the dead, the archaic, the moribund, the current and the brand-new, but it awaits the as yet unborn. Here in indescribable medley are the complete manifestations of a certain racial order of human consciousness, revealing the actual and potential scope of its freedom of thought, the degrees of its sensibilities, its powers of discrimination, its forlorn and lost, its vivified and vivifying causes. To find its equal, even for mere conciseness, in the revelation of human enterprize, not only physical but imaginative, one must open an atlas.

And many of us are singularly insensitive to the rewards of either.

Even a cursory scrutiny of the objects which a personal experience has collected for us—either in themselves or as mental imagery—instantly proves that they are almost inextricably bound up with their names. There are interesting, beautiful, significant objects cursed with bad names. There are unworthy objects blessed with good ones. However that may be, the sensuous or intellectual appropriation of anything is but partially attainable without the appropriation of its name. Any attempt, for example, to recall the birds or wild flowers seen in a hedgerow in a summer morning's walk, or the listeners to a lecture on a winter's afternoon, will usually retrieve with positive definiteness only those we can *name*. It is not only the savage who finds it difficult to discriminate between object and word for it. If we but breathe the words, thyme, hawthorn, crowsfoot, willowherb; skylark, wagtail, kingfisher; Vega, Orion, Capella, the Chair, are they not instantly ours again in sense and spirit? Rather than debase a secret coinage, are we not betrayed at times into calling a Mr. Jones Mr. Robinson? Why should Mr. Jones be so much affronted? Does he wish to look like one? 'With a name like that. . . .'

Not many years ago a London child, nine years old, gently shook her head when as gently asked if she could point out the palm of her hand and the sole of her foot. In Glasgow, it has been whispered, the children have to be taught the meaning of the word 'sky'. Sterility of terms entails sterility of mind. The mere learning of them by rote resembles the ploughing-up of a field. It will afford an irresistible welcome to whatever seeds the winds and bees and Providence may bring. Words have their dangers; and an otiose, even a copious vocabulary—just as may a meagre one—entails the risk of becoming word-ridden. For to have constantly at the very tip of one's tongue the name of an object, an abstraction or a sentiment, *may* eventuate in the partial loss of any due response to it, or in the failure to perceive that any such object or sentiment is most valuable when it is unique. If a close and vigilant eye and attention be kept on both name and thing, then all is well.

A man, of course, may express himself in other things than words: in facial expression and gesture; in manners and dress; with needle, saucepan, spade and axe; with sword and gun; in paint, in metal, in wood and stone. The merest nincompoop realizes at sight of activities of this order—a farm, for instance, with its barns and byres, its crops and furrows, the vermin dangling on its shed, its plough and wains, its furniture, the pictures on its walls, its ploughman's smock, its goodwife's cradle, cider, and needlework—that they are one and all the expressive outcome of taking thought, that skill in their accomplishment cannot be attained without long and traditional practice, that they represent the result of an arduous and prolonged process. Chiefly perhaps because we acquire our liveliest vocabulary in the nursery, we may fail to realize that words are also the most delicate and most easily blunted tools of any we possess, that endless toil and effort and circumspection went to their naturalisation, and are needed for their efficient use.

By and large, it is true, words are common property, they thus tend to become more or less stereotyped and inert. None the less in individual use and exercise and effect they are as fluent and chameleonic as the dyes on a humming-bird. Practice in them is not only audible. We partially muse in them, can dream in them. We make magic with them, may comfort and solace with them beyond belief, or injure and wound irrevocably. We pray in them, and we die with a poor last few of them on our lips. Should we not then be a little bolder, more human, humorous, and original in our efforts to acquire them, to become fully articulate?

There are families who enjoy private countersigns. We all of us value the names of our private belongings. Beyond this few of us venture. But invite, yet again, an imaginative child (if the phrase be not tautological) not to answer 'M or N?', or repeat To-be-or-not-to-be, but out of the livingness and innate abundance of his eye and mind to invent a name for toy, doll, flower, insect, room, place, sensation, or acquaintance—and be astounded at the result. It is, alas, the grown-ups who are *not* children in these matters. None the less, might we not in the silence of our hearts compile a small choice private vocabulary, 'a little language' of our own, if but for a purely personal use and pleasure, and for the sharing of it with the deserving? This indeed is the achievement of every poet; and he keeps it private by publishing it for the few that can translate it.

To state that every word in our language was once used for the first time by a single human being and that some other human being was the first to pass it on is no less animating a commonplace than the reminder that *somewhere* throughout the day the sun is rising (and setting) may be a curiously quickening or disconcerting one. But the mimicry, the sensitiveness, the apprehension, the creativeness it implies! To inquire how a word—lighter than thistledown, secret as the odour of violets—spreads and speeds from tongue to tongue, from sense to sense, from mind to mind, is almost as idle as to inquire what song the Sirens sang—even although every time we do so inquire we hear from afar off those secret strains again. To debate which of them one would most gladly have fathered is amusing: degladiation, terminological, as, slug, quodlibetically, heterogeneity, soul, flea, kamptulicon, omniscience, slops, cuspidor, pink, heartsease, comfrey, rhinoceros, skunk, ant, weevil, hyssop, Aldebaran, meu, rue, syzygy, or baldmoney? On the one side the needs and adventurings of the scholar, the philologist, the Groves of

Academos; on the other those of the shepherd, the sailor, the 'illiterate', the farmhand, the craftsman, the housewife, the 'people', youth with eyes in its head and a tip to its tongue.

We began to listen to words a long time ago; for childhood in retrospect from any adult age *is* a long time ago—however instantaneous may be the transport of oneself in imagination thither. We listened to, attached to their 'meanings' and hoarded up words that were occasionally bestowed on us or spoken in our presence months before we ventured to try our tongues on them, and then boldly proved ourselves ardent, enterprising, but erratic novices. I once knew a child less than three years old, for example, whose f's were all s's. 'Oh, Mummy,' he cried one fine morning on seeing some dead rabbits hanging up in a fishmonger's shop, 'look at those *sunny surry sish*!' Later, when we have learned to read, we again prefer or are decoyed by our blessedly fantastic English spelling into our own private methods of pronouncing what we have to that degree made our own.

I can myself recall a few of the words which 'mizzled' me when I was young. Giant Golathy, Fōb for Phoebe, epitōm, ingrediments. I remember too how arch and charming a face I saw in fancy when an Irish friend of my mother's once remarked in my hearing that he would do something 'Connie Mory'. Confessions concerning a more recent past are embarrassing. But there must be many people too modest to venture on using a valuable fraction of their available vocabulary owing merely to a doubt of the best way of pronouncing it. But why this sensitiveness? So prodigious is the hoard (let alone horde) of current human knowledge and of outlandish terms incident to it that a little more daredeviltry is desirable. One's bold virgin use of some new scientific verbal abortion should be welcomed with mirth, amenity and camaraderie rather than be left to wither in a morbid silence. At present there is as dreadful a danger in referring, if refer one must, to the esoteric, to ideologies and so forth, as there is in eating peas with a knife, calling fox-hounds dogs, or passing the port wine against the sun.

Words, however, may die on us not because we cannot pronounce them but because they have fallen into bad company, have become defaced and ostracised—'genteel,' 'couch,' 'frantic,' 'limbs,' 'sedate,' 'demure,' 'dignified,' even 'pious'. They are of service only as ghosts, as it were, of their own misusage; for purposes of irony or of unashamed jocosity. As for that ass-of-all-work, 'psychology', what now should we do without it? 'Amiable' again, once a word of price is now no more 'likeable' than it is 'lovable', and must be retained on sufferance; while as for 'naïve'—if only we might once and for all de-diærisize and de-alienize it and add it to our homonyms by calling it 'nave'! It is not a mere substitute for artless or ingenious.

There are rows and rows of other words shivering on the brink: superior, respectful, elegant, the adjectives choice and fancy, modish, ascertain, inebriated, felicitous and felicitations, marriageable (husbandable and wifeable?), objurgation, hymeeneal, conjoogal, those old horrors, fiancé and parti, those fetiches, transpire and strenuous. Nobody nowadays, according to the birth-announcements, seems to know for certain whether a woman is delivered of, by, with or from an infant, and resort is had even to '—a lady baby'. And what about stipend, remuneration, emolument, honorarium, salary, even fee? Why not the plain, calm, equalizing, honest old M.E. 'wages'? The wages of sin is death—in spite of its emoluments. The labourer after all is worthy of his 'salt', even if it be only a penny a day. If one had the courage and the incaution one might perhaps venture on a word with the poets, too, who ride a stableful of knackery such as 'pale' so cruelly, although they may have banished grove and swain and zephyr. Then, again, what of the saw-dust words which express real and active and often quite respectable things so lifelessly—nonconformist, dogma, exegesis, democracy, company-promoter, district visitor, litigation, bishop, infant mortality, co-respondent? Blurred, blunted, flaccid terms damn a good cause, screen a bad. Why endure them? Good margarine is streets better than rancid butter.

But we must enrich if we are not intending to impoverish. Here Elizabeth the Only could lend a willing hand to King George the Sixth. For, Heaven be praised! there are, once more, always children in the world eager to try—and even to try out—their tongues. 'Not help *myself*, Mother! That *would* be dishomely!' 'Better (or bet I) eat the core?' Surely we should deliberately and heedfully pack these bright young minds with as many good words as possible—as many and as sesquipedalian, if vital, as they can digest. They will venture, will 'elect', and will transform what they use as gaily as the supreme master of words himself, with his mere 16,000. And let us listen to them and mark, and overhear. If, too, such liberty and enfranchisement is good for the little, why mayn't we poor old habituated grown-ups occasionally scare the family circle, the bench, the shop, and the counting-house (a triple nosegay beloved of the pulpit), with occasional bold little 'neologisms' of our own?

Given a wary eye and a sensitive tongue, impulsive, easy-going, venturous writing does no more harm to a language in the long run than headlong talk. The stylist, the scholar, the general good sense of mankind see to that. And the lexicographer is never a blind shepherd. Words so soon grow lazy, inept and unapt, and the longest are usually the laziest. We want to live, body and soul, and that we can't do unless our words come seemingly mint-new from our under-minds, ashine with our meaningfulness, vivid with our truth, burning-hot from the fire of our reality.

And if there is any amiable terminologist, lapping his

soul in the main current, *tirelessly* respectful to our 'grand old mother tongue', and pooh-poohing all need or hope of advance, let him read an oldish but excellent book, Lady Welby's *What is Meaning?*, or Mr. Alan Gardiner's *The Theory of Speech and Language*, and then go on perhaps to Mr. Ogden and Professor Richards. And my 'perhaps' is only intended to hint that, as Bacon said, and as certain frail digestions will attest, some books are to be tasted, some few are to be chewed, even though we take only that much advantage of them at our own risk and to our own cost. Adventurers we might all be in the witching forest of thought. But we must first secure a nice sharp axe.

Incidentally, the English language has borrowed freely, if not always well, and in times past tried to make the alien feel, and look, at home. To refuse this process, as Robert Bridges maintained, is not merely to be reactionary but too, too superior. It is to insist on the naturalized dressing up as foreigners. As there are lazy talkers who reduce many of their vowels to a general *er—ter* for to, *frerm* for from, *ern* for on, *erv* for of—so there are amateur pedants who write and possibly say *impasse* or *cul-de-sac* for blind alley, *résumé* for summary, synopsis, or abstract, who prefer *mêlée* to (or before) mellay, *naïf* to naïve, *suave* to suave, and possibly *clinique* to clinic (not to mention technic, trai*t*, canoozer, garridge, barridge, and Defoe's Pirates' rendy-vouzes). They may soon be imposing italics on vogue, crisis, bouquet, baton, refugee, wig, mob, and cab, not excluding ignorami and omnibi. A little learning (and I am of necessity referring to not much) is merely making faces when it indulges in rhododendra, narcissi, momenta, miasmata, lexica, indices, apices, pantechnica, linolea, let alone gerania, ideae, chori, asyla. Thus to treat what is now friendly and familiar is like coming out in Piccadilly weepers or introducing a friend of Huguenot or Norman descent with: 'Thees ees Meestaire ——.' Seemingly 'good old' English words are almost as likely to be loanwords—never paid back—as to be hidden metaphors. It is pardonable to cock a snook at 'foreword', and 'Englished' (or Frenched) by, and all similar affectations, and head to head and dancing tea have less to say for themselves than face to face, or possibly allymode. But even although mutton, beef, veal and pork refuse to be Anglo-Saxon, it would spare many condonable blushes if a bill of fare ceased to be a mennoo, and 'eats' were written in the common, even if it be also the vulgar, tongue.

Then again, it would be a sorry state of affairs to dismiss as heinous any delving in old books in blithe and eager quest of verbal pelf. Quite the contrary—and even although in this brief sentence there are half-a-dozen words now out of work for which Mr. Pearsall Smith entreats a little friendly exercise. Not that one should fash oneself in search of such foison. There are writers too nice and nesh in these matters. On the other hand, as Standard English tells us, 'the hog and sow still have their pigs, and are all of them swine'.

There are also little niceties in English syntax and grammar over which even practised hands in the disposal of suspended relatives, in the use of compound passives, of wills and shoulds, of peculiar, and whether, and party, and perspicuous, and unique, who are ready, if need be, to neatly split an infinitive rather than to for mere propriety's sake or with a futile craving for impeccability leave it uncloven may have their moments of torturing hesitation. And after all the worst possible grammar is that which proclaims itself the best. Only the dead languages, subsequent to dissection, can be reduced to an absolute grammar. The living defy the process. And it is well to realize that verbal problems exist, trivial and vexatious, it may be, but still problems. The use of the hyphen, for example:—In these little matters, self appointed specialists, Literary Society professors, grammarians, so called ex English assistant masters, and such like, who have a *bona fide* passion not merely for the ship shape but for perfection made perfect, tend to be over severe on their fellow writers; but their cause, however purely self less their good will, is ill served when, ardently inclined to further the 'Pure English' campaign, they have the ill grace to scold the easy going business man for falling short of self improving his home made style into the man of letters's. Hyphenate according to rule, then taste.

Every living language, like everything else endued with life, is in a state of unceasing change, growth and decay; it is rich in some respects, less rich in others, and has certain defects and deficiencies. The first edition of Noah Webster's Dictionary appeared in 1840. It contained a vocabulary of 74,000 words. That of 1864 was 114,000; of 1890, 175,000; and the current edition of this noble emporium displays a vocabulary of over 400,000. Only Mr. J. D. Beresford's 'Hampdenshire Wonder' who, well before his teens, had amassed by heart the complete current *Encyclopaedia Britannica* would be cramped and hampered by so few. There they are. Yet Webster has no one word signifying he-or-she, or his-or-her, at one extreme; and none for the antithesis of 'poetry', or 'poem', at another.

Again and again a writer of experience discovers to his chagrin that his pen is in the middle of a sentence which has no grammatical exit. He finds himself in a blind alley, and to get out must turn back. The amateur composer even of a Collins or bread-and-butter letter realizes that his mother tongue is a stubborn means for the communication of gratitude, either real or feigned. Collinses apart, Words fail me; No words could say; I could never tell you; are confessions that even the élite of the intellect and of the heart cannot disdain. Only by the flame of the taper somehow kept burning within us can we (with the utmost feebleness) discern what children, lovers, the poets, the saints, the mystics cannot say. As for the generality of us weavers of words, Bottom, with the help of Shakespeare and St. Paul, only just achieved the full expression of our inexpressibility: 'I have had a dream, past the wit of man to say what dream it was. . . . The eye of man hath not heard, the ear of man hath not seen, man's hand is not able to taste, his tongue to conceive, nor his heart to report, what my dream was.'

The only language that would suffice even for our own complete self-expression would be a language entirely of our own creation. If no one else's smile will serve our facial needs, no second- (or thousandth-) hand word will fully and precisely serve our tongue's, our mind's and our heart's. The style is the man, not the words made use of in it, although it consists solely of words; since he can give them a flavour and savour of himself chiefly by means only of their context. None the less, every man's *star*—and his eye welcomes rays of it all to himself—is *his* 'star' only. That corruscating, remote and unimaginable marvel may be anyone's for the gazing; his setting of it is none the less unique.

Most doers, makers, inventors, game-players, tool-users, technicians, men of knowledge and of science, are frequently in need of verbal innovations—some they find are apt, racy, vivid, and serve; others are awkward, dead-alive, clumsy, pedantic; and many are ephemeral.

Slang, colloquialisms, solecisms, vulgarisms are determined gate-crashers. Most of them, like their American posterity of our own day, enjoy an existence wild, wanton, circumscribed and brief. A certain number at length become not only recognized but paying guests. They go up in the world; are received—into Standard English. In a Slang Dictionary of 1874, I came at random on such acclimatized riffraff as crows-feet (of the brow), crusty (morose), cupboard-love, cure and curio (both from curiosity, as fan and vamp with nuances of their own are from fanatic and vampire), house-warming, horsey, big-wig, bilk, blackguard, carpet-knight, capers (frolicsome), chum, claptrap, yokel, weather-eye, tub-thumping, topsy-turvy, tiff, snobbish, slick, and skinflint. A few of these words still wear cotton stockings, so to speak; and the stockings are not blue. The rest are now—if not exactly high hats at a wedding—respectable enough. But the fastidious must use caution. Lord Chesterfield, who extorted one of the most exquisite rebukes in English from the author of its most famous Dictionary, and to whose mind nothing was so ill-bred as audible laughter, warned his natural son against false English, bad pronunciation, old sayings and common proverbs; which, he said, are so many proofs of having kept bad and low company. He saw no need even so much as to mention cant and slang. None the less, even the writer who plays for safety, and trusts in the pure and simple, may also be permitted an occasional fling—some little innovation in word or phrase, even if only to prove that he has kept his own company. Otherwise he may stereotype what he wishes to vivify. Valour is at times the better part of discretion.

Incomparably the richest of all mines of excellent but obsolescent or obsolete English stagnates is Dr. Wright's great work, *The Dialect Dictionary*. In this, in lush and lovely abundance, are the wild flowers of our peerless language; and it is doomed to become all but a *hortus siccus* until some enthusiast compiles a Standard-English—Dialect glossary; and other enthusiasts make a lively and sagacious use of it.

' "De Quincey once said that authors are a dangerous class for any language." And Ascham: "He that will wryte well in any tongue must folowe this council of Aristotle, to speak as the common people do, to think as wise men do." ' The wise men, having thought, should know what words they need and where to seek them. But as yet there is no compendium of the wanted. It would be extremely entertaining and informative and could not fail to prove useful.

Since, again, English (with the help of its supremely ingenious handmaid 'Basic') bids fair to become the dominant language of civilization, it must be continually flexible, adaptive, catholic, hospitable. There is America—a very large and highly vocal country; and there are the Dominions, the Colonies and the Dependencies. They are all of them rapidly moulding an inherited language into their own idiosyncratic forms. Progress must be by little and little. Personal impulse and insight are fully as necessary as scholarly care. To love a thing is to treat it well and to wish it to be itself as much as possible. It is to be zealous for its powers and privileges, its being and its life. That is why the reading of grammars or treatises on style may be far from a stuffy occupation. Nevertheless it is prudent to be frugal in the use even of a grammar. There are certain writers—excellent in many respects—whose works for obscure reasons have a peculiarly sterilizing effect on the minds of their readers. Unlike the books that set free the fancy, exercise the wits, excite the imagination, trouble the heart and cry on us, *Go thou, and do likewise!* these whisper, *Thus far, but no farther*. We rise from them grateful and edified perhaps, but sated, aridified, depressed. Theirs is the peculiar secret of turning off the fountain of life. Treatises on composition and even such invaluable counsellors as *The King's English* and *Modern English Usage* may prove to be of this company. Only an expert is competent to acclaim their merits. They are pillories which incite even the tiro to excellent intentions But he has to wait until their influence has subsided and his habitual immodesty has been restored for an opportunity to profit by their counsel. Undigested gobbets of them will risk his becoming grammar-conscious and word-bound.

For although some exact knowledge of the laws of syntax is desirable, example remains better than precept. To have read the excellent is probably the best means of learning to write well. It is unfortunate that grammarians and specialists can hardly avoid exemplifying their rules with infectious infringements of them. It is unfortunate also that they are compelled to submit to reason what is largely a matter of intuition and taste. Merely to be presented with a table of commandments may put the breaking of them into our heads, and make the keeping of them more difficult. We become aware of the delicate nuances of signification in words all but synonymous almost as naturally as we become aware of the differences between the leaves of trees, of tints, of human faces, of the meaning of speech-tones. Style can no more be taught than euphony. Attention to rules—to be simple, lucid, concise, unaffected—will help a man to write decently; it will not teach him to write. And even if it would, *what* to say—unless, like Rousseau, he has been fated to be oppressively fecund in thought and feeling—he will discover, is a more exhausting and exacting problem than how to say it. He is faced with a curious and exquisite difficulty—that of achieving coincidence and accordancy of content and form, of matter and manner. And at long last the acquisition of a technical mastery in any art—too rare a feat perhaps to cause anxiety—is by no means nothing but gain.

This may in part be the reason why writers in general are a peevish and ungrateful folk. They are apt at length, while continuing to use it, to be as shy in the use of ink as a cat is shy of water. Flaubert is their high priest, and the Commination Service their daily fare, and it was hardly the craftsman in Stevenson that pooh-poohed them as *filles de joie.* Having imprudently contracted a habit, as inescapable as the Old Man of the Sea, they take pains to add to their burden. Yet they may win their reward. The longest of books comes to an end. How rarely refreshing an experience is that told of by Gibbon in his Autobiography—after a prolonged and feverish spell of reading and writing

—to run back from these phantasmal haunts, to shake free of words and to discover the world of the real patiently awaiting a long-deferred tryst. And lo, there, the dark ample sky, powdered with its stars! An air sweet with the immortal springtime of the spirit moves in space. And to see again the face of the constant moon is to see again the face of one loved, and even the more lovely for having been for a while unremembered.

If, and (at last) finally, we indulge a personal taste for antiquated words, as we may for old porcelain, furniture, curios, or postage stamps, Nares again will prove a priceless repository. For like all such objects, words gather with age a curious flavour, look, mien, and reference. The bloom —if at times only a mildew—of sentiment creeps over them. The process is obvious. The neologism subsides into the colloquial, the colloquial may attain to the literary (the Promised Land), or to the poetic (a sort of Nirvana), or it may lapse into disuse. In the last resort it becomes, first *passé*, then old-fashioned, then antique, then archaic, then a mere relic. But even if, unlike flowers and insects, words are man-made, a certain respect for them should be theirs even when they are in the sere, and a more curious appearance of hidden energy may be manifest the older they grow. There the old thing lies in its shroud—a verbal Methuselah: yet but one instant's imaginative use of it may restore its voice, its character, its energy, and its personality. It is, too, seldom the words of infrequent and fastidious usage that utterly perish; only the miserably and heedlessly overworked. For antique words, on which Time has scattered her poppy, lulling them to an agelong but terminable sleep, awaiting only their Prince Charming, Nares again is the lively hostel.

Or if, once more, stray fragmentary remembrances and mementoes of a wild and copious and full-charged day, that long since rang to its evensong, attract and entice us, then

Nares yet again is our lure. Share his comments on *mandrake* or *iniquity*; *owle-glass*, *gorbellied*, *Pimlico*, or *ivy-bush*; *elements* and *humour*; *gib-cat* and *Judas-coloured*; *knives*, *neck-verse*, *starch*, *primavista*, *Nicholas*, or *kneeling*; *muck*, *hell*, *gloves*, *cock-shut*, or *golden plaister*—by so doing you may not thereby become a full man, you may not even join the ranks of the well-informed, but you may deserve to be his grateful devotee. If—and in these slippery times it may any day prove a serviceable one—if the faculty is ours to enjoy a dainty, obsolete or obsolescent, even though its ingredients consist solely of inscrutable reactions excited by the alphabet, then *jumball*, *manchet*, *marchpane*, *Florentine*, and *lumber pie* are ours for the calling—and *lambswool* and like potations wherewith to wash them down. Otherwise:

'Let the cooke bee thy physition, and the shambles thy apothecaries shop: hee that for every qualme will take a receipt, and cannot make two meales, unless Galen bee his Gods good, shall bee sure to make the physition rich and himselfe a begger: his bodie will never bee without diseases, and his purse ever without money.'

Nares was a man of taste, and a scholar; he was also quite evidently a man of wholesome and full-blooded appetites. His book radiates the zeal and zest of his literary coursings and questings and lyings-in-wait. Games of all kinds—parlour, grass, and otherwise, fabrics and clothes, 'characters', actors, streets, taverns, and the more romantic type of rogue are all after his fancy.

The mere suggestion that his *Glossary* may feast the idle and ignorant, given only a liking for the Elizabethan vernacular and habits, may appear to cast a shadow on its learning and scholarship, its seriousness. Far from it: his book is a godsend to the dunce. He leaves the obscure illuminated. He thoroughly knows, and can hospitably share, his knowledge. Guide he set out to be; philosopher he proves himself to be—a critic of mankind neither harsh, nor fastidious, nor aloof, yet, one we feel, with unflinching principles and standards. And at last and at best, Nares becomes a friend, pleased with and modestly proud of his collection, and anxious only to share it with a fellow fanatic.

To abandon one's age and environment, even when it wears so callous an exterior as for the time being does to-day's—to flee away into the past and be at rest—is not only an impracticable feat. It would be a poor show of insight and courage. Contrariwise, to live only in to-day is to be the slave of the clock, let alone the newspapers. An occasional rapid and light-hearted excursion into the imaginable regions of another century, the century of England's greatest literature, of her loveliest music, her most romantic enterprize, to which mere distance no doubt lends a large and deceptive fraction of its enchantment—this surely is the pleasantest of mental stimulants. As a cursory reading book, Nares's *Glossary* consists, it may be granted, of titbits and snippets. As a whole, it is a gallimaufry, though one neither confused nor heterogeneous. It may be reserved, and no doubt the undeserving will continue to reserve it, for the noonday's need, not for the midnight's luxury. Still, first and foremost, its amused author hoped and intended to 'entertain' his reader. He succeeds in so doing, with *words*; and what better claim on our attention can novelist, historian, or poet prefer?

Maps Actual and Imaginary

It is a mournful thought that every explorer, since Adam was exiled from the Garden of Eden and the brighter stars were called by name, has ultimately only succeeded in contracting the human conception of the universe. The world as conceived by Homer was but a small blot on the world known to Ptolemy and the world of Ptolemy merely a fraction in area of that mapped out by Martin Behaim. And yet the centuries in driving back the frontiers of *terra incognita* only finally succeed in cramping the fancy. For it is in the vaguely dreamed of and in the wholly unknown that the imagination takes its ease and delight. The present generation has experienced the treacherous novelty of having, first, the North Pole and then the South served up with its breakfast. It danced round them for a while as eagerly as children used to dance round a Jack-in-the-Green.

But these May Days will never dawn again. Does any unknown sea remain into which a yet-to-be-astonished mariner shall be the first to burst? Ought not the civilized world to have saved a few such, as children save a *bonne bouche* or sweethearts the last page of a love-letter? To muse indeed on a piece of water or mountains never seen by mortal eye, blind, can we say, even to its own being, and known only by an inconceivable Creator to be good, is to muse on a mystery past divining.

For use and wont, as well as a rather abject adoration of the practical, make maps of things-as-they-are dullish documents. Nimble spirits may, of course, entertain themselves no less pleasantly with a minute Mercator's Projection as with an Ordnance Survey imprint of twenty inches to the mile, in which one's neighbour's haystacks and duckpond make as fair a show as Baghdad and the Amazons. But the spectacular pens and vivid surmises of the past are also things of the past. Utterly out of fashion now are the beautiful roses, the brilliant banners above the tiny miniature cities, the winds and half winds and quarter winds, in black and green and carmine, of the portolan skin charts of the fifteenth and sixteenth centuries, with their seas of generous blue and emerald, lavishly edged with gold. And we should hardly even ourselves venture to huddle into the uppermost corner of Europe, as once the map-maker did, an amateur representation of the earthly paradise.

Few latter-day travellers, perhaps, would envy Scylax of Caryanda, the author of the oldest known Greek periplus, his coastwise voyage of 153 days in circuit of the Mediterranean; but the most prosaic grown-up would rub his eyes, for pleasure (mingled with scorn) at a geography chequered with such dream-wide suggestions of infinity as, 'Beyond the Pillars of Hercules, which are in Europe, there are many trading stations of the Carthaginians, also mud, and tides, and open seas.'

One of the saddest reflections which can accompany the thought that we are hastening to decay is that our earthly journey has been in all but a bee-line. How blissfully circuitous might have been the route even if we had merely groomed a little more assiduously Shanks's mare. Stuck for the most part like a limpet to our local rock, we many of us forget even to keep count of the tides. We may even be, poor souls, almost impeccably moral, fearless of the tax-collector, punctual at Sunday matins, and well on our way to a golden wedding surrounded by hostages to the *n*th generation. Nevertheless, life proffers duties that are in fact a pure pleasure; and to have left the world without seeing and praising more than a meagre fraction of it will make a melancholy and shamefaced cargo of some of us when we sit, glancing dumbly and apprehensively this way and that, amidst the night-hung waters of the Styx.

A little volume by Mr. W. P. James, which is as densely crammed with meat as an egg, exacerbates this prospect. Leave it for a moment in the draught of an open window, and the zephyrs will flap over its hundred pages to the enticing tune of *Thalassa, Thalassa*. It is as resonant with place-names as a gazetteer, as noisy with pilgrims as Mecca, and as quiet with books as was old Holywell-street. Like Satan in the first chapter of Job, but wholly unlike Satan for the innocent enthusiasm on his countenance, its author came from going to and fro in the earth, and from walking up and down in it. And his sole theme is the joy of perpetual motion. Come indeed to his chapter on the three-volumed novel, we speculate for an instant as to what conceivable purpose it can serve in a book that is else an uninterrupted pæan on Mr. Bartholomew, local colourists, Odysseys, mountaineers, sentimental travellers, pirates, and merchant adventurers. Then we realize that it was its title that beguiled him—i.e. *The Old Three-Decker*; and the fact that, after sailing the high seas of literature for over a century, thanks to Walter Besant, this pompous old craft was wrecked at last on the shoals of Six Shillings and the rocks of Democracy.

Otherwise how could he have forgiven Thackeray, even when prostrated with an ague, for glorying at the prospect of a whole day in bed with no other company than merely *The Woman in White*, when he might have been perambulating the cosmos with Cobbett or Marco Polo, Humboldt, Coryat or Gesner, or slipping from dream to dream under the spell of *Hajji Baba*, *The Golden Ass*, or the map of China made for Hang Ki by the Jesuit? Not that Mr. James disparages the novel or agrees with Sir Anthony Absolute that it is 'the fruit of an evergreen tree of diabolical knowledge', and 'such common cant'. On the contrary, while he acknowledges that this Lady Paramount of Literature, with rather too many didactical and problematical fish to fry, is apt to forget that she came into the world to be 'interesting and pleasing', this particular chapter proves that he has read (and, better still, remembered) as many masterpieces of fiction as he has of travel and pilgrimage.

It is none the less a fact that we many of us tend to neglect living for reading, and that we fly to other men's romances when we might be busy harvesting our own. If Keats, as Mr. James reminds us, had 'many reasons for going wonderways' to make his 'winter chair free from the spleen', we, surely, have no fewer. The afflicting thought may at times chill the imagination that every day of terrestrial discovery cannot but restrict the amateur vagrant's opportunities. One glance at Mr. Bartholomew's white and fawn presentment of the Sahara, or of the blue and still bluer acreage of his Pacific, will remedy so natural an apprehension. Not only is it still possible for a child to survey the familiar with eyes as renewed and surmiseful as Cortes's when he stared at that ocean in the real, but it is unlikely that there lives a man in Peckham so diligent as absolutely to have exhausted the solemn and vivid mysteries (as G. K. Chesterton might have put it) even of his own back yard.

That is what every map-explorer is 'telling' us. The one danger of any such book is its chief virtue. The very abundance of its references may end in the confusion and disheartening of the novice. May he be well shaken when every dose of it is taken. It should be read slowly. Its clues should be pertinaciously followed up; the books recommended sought out; an ample atlas should lie agape on the table; or the Ordnance Survey (a mile, if possible, to the inch) burden the thyme on the hillside. How indeed Mr.

James has managed to read, mark, and learn so many rich, rare, crusted and obscure books, and has yet apparently tramped England from end to end (his only, but certainly not his only justifiable, boast), we cannot conceive. Probably, unlike those who have their literature thrust on them—schoolboys, would-be bachelors of arts, subscribers to lending libraries, tea-table men and reviewers—he has followed his fine fancy:

Tell me where is Fancy bred,
Or in the heart, or in the head?
How begot, how nourished?
Reply, reply.
It is engendered in the eyes
With gazing fed....

Heaven grant that we ourselves shall have followed an iota or two of his example ere the last cradle receive us and the little steeple begin again its habitual 'Ding, dong, bell'!

It is the generous credulity, the childlike wonder, the independence of spirit (all excellently disguised as a passion for accuracy) in the ancient cartographers that are the fascination of their work. One can pore over the Catalan Map, for instance, for hours together, and rise refreshed as with the waters of Hippocrene. Why does the City of Lop, leagues south of the route of the caravans which pass 'from Sarra to Catayo across a great desert', so intrigue the fancy? And the Island of Chis? Has perchance Lord Dunsany trodden the echoing courts of the one, the yellow sands of the other? Why, for quite other than obvious reasons, does Regio Feminarum, tucked securely away in the remote, clear-cut oblong of the Island of Jaua, so cordially 'invite the soul'? Names as outlandish and bizarre throng every gazetteer, but the effect is comparatively sterile.

Whither is fled the visionary gleam?
Where is it now, the glory and the dream?

There are, of course, more succulent sops to the imagination even than these: 'Here reigns K. Stephen, a Christian. In this land lies St. Thomas. Look for the City Butifilis.' We look for the City Butifilis; and there it is. Cook be our guide; we will pack up to-morrow! Up in the N.E. corner, again, sprawls the princedom of Gog and Magog, securely confined amid delicious mountains as well as 'shut up by Alexander of Macedon'. Gog must have yearned northward over those impregnable hills for the islands where abound 'many good Gerfalcons which are taken for the Great Can', and Magog must have turned yearning hungry eyes due south towards the '7,548 Islands' in the seas of the Indies 'where grow the spices', where dwell 'naked savages', and southwards still, towards Taprobana, 'last in the East', called by the Tartars Great Cantij, wherein flourish not only cannibals, negroes, etc., but wherein also unceasingly decays and falls into ruin a nameless 'City destroyed by serpents'.

But the Catalan Map is of A.D. 1375. Gog and Magog have now been reduced to a tavern sign, and the Great Khan's immortality is inextricably bound up with Samuel Taylor Coleridge's.

Mr. James's earthly novelties are drying up; the desert of Gobi has been ravished; the Great Wall laments; travellers' tales must grow ever leaner and leaner. But since there are vagabond ghosts in men's bodies, the desire for adventure will never perish. We shall seek other means for travel, dare land beyond land's end, and Thules still more ultimate. Our Moon awaits us. Mars shines for conquest. And, who knows? the gradual awakening of a sixth sense might renew and transmogrify the whole habitable globe? Let (is it not so?) our eyes—which are gifted only with *sight*—shift an octave in vibrations upwards in their sensitiveness to light, then although our glass windows would be darkened, we should see through our walls.

Meanwhile there remains a way out of possible stagnation and ennui that has as yet attracted few adventurers. Neither Columbus nor Cabot, Vasco da Gama nor Vespucci ever set sail bound solely for the regions of Romance. Yet romance has always edged into, only to be as pertinaciously banished from, man's record of his earthly voyagings. Castles in Spain may have a poor reputation; yet even their relics, viewed through the perspective of time, continue to wear a winning aspect. And to give to airy nothing a habitation and a name is the office not only of the lover and the poet but also of fiction. The song the sirens sang everybody knows the tune of, although nobody may remember the words. But we can only guess at the sandy trysting-place of Man Friday and Robinson Crusoe, and we are unlikely to explore on our own legs the fabulous island of Monte Cristo. The whole problem, indeed, of the where, the how, and the when of the imaginative novelist is still obscure. Modern story-tellers for the most part lap their creatures in the luxuries of a real Mayfair, or people with phantasms the streets-in-being of an actual Wigan. They only thinly disguise their Wessex, their Dartmoor. Chaucer's substantial yet imaginary pilgrims trod a tangible Watling Street. Scott was a microcosm of his native wilds. George Eliot was a *genius loci*, the stones even of *Wuthering Heights* may be viewed from a motor-coach. The journey of Little Nell and her grandfather may be traced from London up to Tong. Borrow, Kingsley, and Dumas moreover could swear pretty straitly by the map.

Houses however are not quite the same matter. And, although by some elusive wizardry we realize that in *that* particular corner of her boudoir our heroine flung herself upon a prie-dieu to weep, that her lover, finger on lip, stole in to comfort her through a french window on the left, and that his miserly old uncle died at last in his fourposter with his face to the ivied window, it would often puzzle us to fit in the unspecified floors and storeys of an otherwise admirable mansion of the fancy; while to descend from attic to cellar in certain imaginary edifices—the House of Usher, for example—would be an experience of the purest nightmare. It is no layman's question whether a novelist should actually call in an architect before he sets to work, or should preface his story with a detailed plan—hall, 'lounge', reception rooms, bedrooms, garage, and the usual offices. The thriller adds a twinge of horror to crime by indicating the locale of its corpse with a cross. These little conscientiousnesses are now far from unusual—whatever practical use a less conscientious reader may make of them. Mr. Conrad has told how a fair, inquisitive, gushing visitor one working day morning shattered in his imagination for the time being the complete universe of *Nostromo*. Every rumour of her stilled at last, he built it up again, but had no need to map it out with compasses and Indian ink. We can watch a Robert Burton absorbedly recording every gulf, morass, creek, reef, and quicksand in the sad and mighty realms of Melancholy; but hardly a Milton, quill in hand, tracing out the frontiers of Paradise. And what of the itinerary of Dante's pilgrimage? What of Prospero's and Ariel's place of exile; of Endymion's wanderings; and—to come earthwards again, Jules Verne's prodigious underworld? Any romantic tale of high adventure, of course, may be pleasingly enriched by a clear and precise all-round-the-compass sketch to scale of some region of the purest fantasy. It may be a rather juvenile fancy, but it is none the less precious for that.

Precious now and then, at any rate, and even to the tune of £44. For this was the sum squandered some twenty-five years ago on the original of the chart prefixed to *Treasure Island*. It represented the stockinged hoardings of a lifetime, but the buyer made a good bargain. The map is a little masterpiece. The story goes that it was designed to beguile a youthful stepson. For youth's sake alone the thumbed and perishing chart was sewn up in a packet with Billy Bones's nefarious ledger and this was sealed with a thimble. So be it, but we know our Stevenson. 'It is about nine miles long and five across, shaped, you might say, like a fat dragon standing up, and had two fine land-locked harbours, and a hill in the centre part marked "The Spy Glass."' 'Methinks it is like a weasel'—but fat dragon will serve. No fancy-itching detail has been overlooked in that 'facsimile struck out by J. Hawkins', and the original of that is probably in the possession of the heirs of Flint's quarter-master, 'along with his timber leg'. It has been lovingly done—the rayed compass, the ships in bellying sail, solemn dolphin, spouting whale, and somewhat lamentable sea-nymph, swamp and spring, tide and cove and sounding, and above all in bright red, in dingy red, in greeny-blue, the scripts of 'J.F.' of 'W.B.' ('this twenty July 1754') and—of Jim.

'We had run up the trades to get the wind of the island we were after—I am not allowed to be more plain'; for there is still 'treasure' there—silver—not yet lifted! It is odd that, in spite of so definite a description—'. . . General colouring uniform and sad . . . grey melancholy woods and wild stone spires . . . odd outlandish swampy trees . . . the fog had now buried all heaven . . .'—that this island remains, in one faraway vision of it at least, ablaze with emerald green, sea-blue and sunshine. Was it 'the nutmeg and azalea', 'the poisonous brightness' of the foliage that led fancy astray, or did the brass buttons *thick* on the unctuous, the sly, the murderous and impossible John Silver's coat cast a reflected and unfading glamour of light upon that 'sweet pretty place'? Jim may write, with artful understatement, of 'our dark and bloody sojourn', but his memories of that dark must have been richly gilded by the doubloons, double guineas, moidores and sequins, stamped with the pictures of a whole century's kings of Europe which came afterwards. And the shores of Treasure Island (except where the victim of chuck-farthen and of his brass-hearted shipmates, Ben Gunn, ran doubled-up down the hill) remains radiant with gold and coral, lit not only by a tropical sun, but also by the lamp which Israel Hands left burning in broad daylight in the cabin of the Hispaniola, and the incontinent fires of the mutineers. Forty-four pounds! It was a mere bagatelle for so lively a keepsake of a genius that enchanted us when we were young and that kept the austere Dean Church for half a night out of his bed.

Then again, a chart designed by an evil Chinese is mentioned, though it is not represented in Mr. Wells's *Treasure in the Forest.* Poe reproduces Captain Kidd's cryptogram (written probably in a solution of regulus of cobalt in spirit of nitre), but, alas! he supplies no chart washed in with tints of Legrand's heaven-sent scarabaeus. *King Solomon's Mines*, however, is handsomely prefaced by the old Dom José de Silvestra's map, scratched down on a fragment of linen with his last trickle of blood (before he was frozen cold as mutton) 'in the little cave on the north side of the nipple of the southernmost of the two mountains I have named Sheba's Breasts'. Its language is Portuguese, and the bare route stretches from the River Lukanga to the mountains at the end of King Solomon's Road. 'I know not', writes Allan Quatermain, 'how to describe the glorious panorama which unfolded itself to our enraptured gaze.' So we must take his word for it and condone his modesty. But he makes reiterated play with Sheba's Breasts and refers to a scene 'like Paradise'. This is vague, but there is beauty other than that of landscape in his record, that of 'the young ladies', 'like arum lilies', for instance, who danced the dance of death before the one-eyed Twala, and 'the snowy loveliness' of Good's bare legs. Detail would not have come amiss regarding 'the five miles round of fertile ground' of the palace at Loo—'unlimited Loo', according to the facetious owner of the legs. But Allan makes up with thrills what he lacks in the picturesque and (with *Treasure Island* in mind) in style.

William Morris's chart, showing the course of the Sundering Flood, is a very different thing. It is the work of an artist—not apparently of Osberne himself—and so outside the story. And the decorative rather than the truly romantic was its inspiration. It is, if anything, too definite, and perhaps a little literary and artificially elaborate. We read of dromonds and round-ships, but the salt sea wind of the Hispaniola does not pluck at their shrouds. We read of far countries and outlandish folk, of dread and unknown tongues, of dwarfs and land-wights, of 'a little cot somewhat kenspeckle'. But Morris is not bent on congealing our blood or even trying our nerves, the cot remains somewhat 'kenspeckle'. And *The Wood Masterless* is somehow less woody than poetical. In one thing, too, narrative and chart are at quarrel. So long as in a series of pictures serene and pure the little carle, Osberne, meets and talks with Elfhild on the Bight of the Cloven Knoll, with fifty feet of roaring water sundering each from each, the romantic dream remains unstirred, unbroken. The shooting of the boy's gifts across the gulf, those two loving faces whose nearest approach is in a steadfast gaze—all this is gay and tender and charming. And Elfhild's 'O thou beauteous creature, what art thou?' is no less tender an impulse than her 'But what else canst thou do, Champion?' is an arch and womanly piece of naivety. But chance and circumstance separate the children. The supernatural machinery creaks a little. Steelhead is a hard nut to crack. And then, disappointment of disappointments, when the lovers meet again, Elfhild has long since crossed the magic waters of Sundering Flood, but by a ferry! The idea, the symbol has been betrayed. The very essence of the romance has fainted into thin air.

Inspired schoolmasters there may be who set their scholars not the vast cutlet of Africa, sea-fretted Scotland, or the hundreds-and-thousands of the Grecian Archipelago to map out on paper, but a fantastic country of their own contriving, crammed with strange beasts and wildernesses and precipices and virgin streams and valleys. One such contraption was devised far too many years ago by a certain small boy now small no longer. Outlined in cloudy blue, hedged about with tottering, ungainly print the shores of his isles—of *Goats*, of *Ba* and *Be*, of *Rags* and *Riggerbar*—are washed by the tides of the *Graca Ocean* and the *Sea of Rega*—its capital S back side before. 'Here is a Forest' (green as green), 'Here is the Rem Mountains', 'Here is a great Castle', run his legends. And an indulged and indulgent uncle ventured on the letterpress:

'. . . Now to speak of the Islands that we went in rowboats to visit before our ship set sail thither (a N.W. point near the River Dum), the weather remaining calm and fair for three days and till the fourth morning, first we landed on the *Isle of Butter* which lieth alongside of the *Isle of Ray*. In this isle is an exceeding steep high mountain capped with frozen ice that doth marvellously gleam and twinkle when the sun by day doth fall upon it, sending forth beams far and near of divers colours like to a great lantern. Also at night the moon gloateth upon the ice and it is like the opal for I did look upon it as I lay in my bunk, ashipboard. But to scale this mountain it were a thing impossible by reason of its steepness and the slipperiness of its perpetual ice. In the *Isle of Butter* is a great store of little pebbles that are round and smooth as marbles (that children be accustomed to play with), also in its waters lurketh a little fish called the butter-fish—it is so greasy in the broiling. . . . And hearing strange shrill cries, we lifted our wagging heads and espied a company of dwarfmen, with naked skins grey as the crocus, riding upon shaggy flat-footed beasts after the manner of our mules. But though we threw up our hands and besought them dumbly, our tongues being swollen beyond speech, they galloped away from us. And, when we looked, we counted only seven men left of us, with the boatswain. And I conjecture two men—namely, Benjamin and Robert Small, were taken in their sleep and devoured by these grey people; for such is their barbarous custom to eat men's poor flesh having dried it in the sun; and we asleep. But Heaven being pitiful to us that remained, we toiled on, the boatswain alone sitting down with courageous face to the west, unable longer to continue, his body being puffed out nigh double through chewing a root he had found. And he died there looking towards his own country and asking mercy on his sins. . . .'

What, after all, is the great globe itself but undiscovered or perhaps re-discovered country to every newcomer? What is life but a cryptogrammatical chart as yet uncompleted in the delineation of which Destiny or Providence helps us to guide the faltering pen? Who even can deny us the privy hope, if not conviction, that we walk and slumber, not, as it might appear, on a giddy ball chiefly consisting of metal in what is called Space—an exceedingly difficult pill for any self-respecting fancy to swallow; but on an endless sea-ridden plain whose furthermost bourne is called Death? Our jaded, sated greed for fact is largely a fallacy. A green meadow may be El Dorado and all the Indies to a simple, ardent and unexacting heart. The Well at the World's End *may* be found in one's backyard. Better be busy with the bucket while its waters are sweet. Thou art—what thou dost gaze upon. Thou dost gaze upon what thou art. To a tortured imagination the homely Thames may wander black as Acheron; to a happier, not Naaman's Jordan itself is a more miraculous stream. And if, possibly, one sometimes wearies of the old familiar places, of Greenwich time and terrestrial latitudes, how easy to take pencil and brush and idly map out the place where one *would* be. No need to be specific; no call to give it even a name. It would be quite unnecessary even to write a book about it. It would fetch not forty-four farthings in open auction. It would be only a poor thing, but it would be one's very own.